WHAT PREACHERS NEVER TELL YOU

ABOUT TITHES & OFFERINGS

The End of Clergy
Manipulation
& Extortion

Eric M. Hill

What Preachers Never Tell You About Tithes & Offerings:
The End of Clergy Manipulation & Extortion

Library of Congress Control Number: 2010905129

ISBN-10: 0-9673189-2-0
ISBN-13: 978-0-9673189-2-9

First Edition

Printed in the United States of America

Published by SunHill Publishers, P.O. Box 4921, Atlanta, GA 30302
Visit our website at www.SunHillPublishers.com or
www.PowerEvangelism.org.

Book Interior Design: Karrie Ross www.KarrieRoss.com
Book Cover Design: Asya Blue www.AsyaBlue.com

Acknowledgements

First, I must thank you Lord Jesus Christ for saving me and giving my life purpose. You've done so much for me that I am incapable of mentioning all that you've done. But I am capable of mentioning how you've blessed me with gifts of reading, writing, and understanding. Certainly you have blessed others with these gifts in greater measure and with more elegant expression. Nonetheless, although I am awed and humbled by the gifts of others, I am satisfied and happy with the measure you have given me.

Second, I must thank my other life-saver—my incredible friend, girlfriend, and wife, Sonny.

Third, thank you to those who have been fighting the stronghold of the financial tithe system long before I entered the fray: Dr. Russell Kelly, author of *Should the Church Teach Tithing*; Michael L. Webb & Mitchell T. Webb, authors of *Beyond Tithes & Offerings*; George Green, creator of the web site (and many other pro-Christ resources), www.NoMoreTithes.com. And to the many others who fight for Christian liberty, but are not named here: thank you, and God bless you!

Other Books by Eric Hill

Deliverance from Demons and Diseases:
Freedom from Incurable Diseases and Persistent Problems

Introduction

Apreacher heard that I was writing this book and commented, "Some things you oughtta just leave alone." I don't know why he said this, but I know that I can no more leave this subject alone than I can leave alone a child molester doing his evil deed. Some things demand outrage. Some things demand action.

What is so outrageous about modern church fundraising that it requires such confrontational words? Or an entire book? It is that raising funds through the threats and bribery of the modern financial tithe is a mainstream church practice. These threats and bribes pervert the message of the gospel, and make it more difficult for people to submit to Christ. What thinking person would believe the church's message of Jesus Christ while its behavior conflicts so violently with His life and words? Thinking people are repelled by such blatant hypocrisy.

The church's other outrageous sin is that its insatiable craving for money cruelly crushes the poor, and grinds their faces into the dirt of poverty.

A doctrine that both blocks sinners from coming to Christ and that fights against the poor is one that must be exposed and destroyed. That's what I hope to do.

Table of Contents

- Final Thoughts on the Law of Human Need
- Are You in Need?

Manipulation:
Management with use of unfair, scheming,
or underhanded methods especially for ones' own advantage.

Extortion:
to obtain by threats.

Why We Must Destroy the System of Mandatory Tithes and Manipulated Offerings

The modern system of mandatory tithes and manipulated offerings is false and built upon tradition supported by lies and lies supported by tradition. It must be destroyed.

Debating tithes is like debating the subject of Santa Claus. What is his Christmas Eve route? Does he really know who's naughty or nice? How does he read all of those letters? How does one (and why would anyone) debate these issues?

Modern tithes, like Santa Claus, have no basis for an intelligent argument. It's nonsense to argue about religious fiction. This gives credence to a myth. Yet we preachers desperately argue the merits of our tithe myth because it is scandalously profitable, and because American Christianity is obscenely dependent on money.

A money mentality governs the American church. Many Christian ministry decisions are based more on cash flow than on love for Christ and people. Some will label these statements extreme. Others will see them as stating the obvious: A large part of the American church is greedy and exploitative.

We Do Not Condemn the Good with the Bad

We don't need an anti-tithe version of the Salem Witch Trials or of the Inquisitions. Jesus warned us not to hurt true Christians in unwise zeal for purity.[1] It is irresponsible to condemn all ministers who raise funds for ministry. But it is also irresponsible to remain silent about harmful fundraising schemes of most of the church's leaders. Therefore, I try to distinguish clearly between the innocent and guilty.

The visible church consists of true and false Christians, strong and weak Christians, intelligent and ignorant Christians. The accusation of church greed and exploitation, as well as clergy manipulation and extortion, must be considered within this context. The church is one body, but comprises hundreds of millions of parts, or members, who are at varying levels of individual commitment, spiritual growth, and health.

The left hand may be diseased, but the right hand may be healthy. Or the right shoulder may be damaged, but the rest of the body is fine. So I joyfully acknowledge that a few parts of the body have escaped organized and systemic greed, manipulation, and extortion.

Nonetheless, although the entire body is not diseased, the disease affects the entire body. The disastrous effects of church greed and materialism have made virtually every Christian leader and ministry look like thieves and hypocrites. The sad thing is that many Christian leaders and ministries are thieves and hypocrites and don't even know it.

We easily understand that a Judas will create clever ways to steal money. He may raise funds in the name of Christ for his own purposes. Or he may simply grab the money bag and run off to Mexico. It breaks our heart. It shocks us. But it doesn't permanently confuse us. We simply conclude that our former leader is a thief.

Some *Good* Preachers Are Stealing from Us

What we find more difficult to discern and process is that true Christian clergy with good hearts can and regularly do steal from us.

Different methods may be used, but the result is the same: God's money is wasted, misappropriated, or stolen.

When I say *stolen* I don't mean that good ministers purposefully commit theft or fraud. Relatively speaking, I don't believe many ministers do this. Actually, on Judgment Day we will probably find that a commendable percentage of clergy served God with integrity.

Nonetheless, we will also find that pervasive false financial doctrines devastated the collective integrity, effectiveness, and efficiency of the church, especially in America. We will see these doctrines as spiritual fraud. We will also find that these frauds were vigorously taught by many good preachers who earned our respect through their moral lives and apparent commitment to Christ and His church.

These *good* preachers may be wonderful people and genuine Christians, but they are so blinded by church tradition that they can't see the wickedness of their fundraising tactics. Their overdependence on money distorts their ability to discern right from wrong, at least where money in ministry is concerned. They never see that much of what they teach about Christian giving is based on traditions of men rather than commands of God. They also never see that the real reason they are incredibly interested in our giving habits is self-interest: They covet our money.

This is the intoxicating power of money in ministry. It is a spendable liquor that perverts judgment and turns wise men into fools. It even makes good men behave as bad men. Men who would choose death before committing an actual theft of church funds regularly steal God's glory by corrupting His image.

This corruption steals not only God's glory, but the church's inheritance and the world's salvation. Thus, these otherwise *good* men are guilty of the grossest spiritual thefts and frauds.

Cash Flow Has Taken the Place of the Holy Spirit

The American church is rife with financial false doctrines. The foundation of these doctrines is mandatory tithes, and not far behind are coerced and manipulated offerings. These doctrines of demons must be challenged.

You may question the wisdom of debating such effective ways of raising funds. What would happen to Christian ministries if mandatory tithes and manipulated offerings were exposed as heretical and ungodly? Would this not severely damage the work of God? Is this book's purpose the repossession of church properties? Do we want to see missionaries abandoned? Are we advocating bankrupting the church?

Certainly some in the church would admit that reform is needed in the area of soliciting offerings. But the tithe? The tithe is untouchable! It's the backbone of the ministry! We can't make it without the tithe! Everything we do depends on the mandatory tithe! *And that is exactly why we must challenge this sacred error.* It has replaced the Holy Spirit.

The church's work should not depend on the guaranteed cash flow of mandatory tithes. When it does, leaders are reduced to servants of cash flow instead of servants of Christ.

Two False Assumptions of Cash Flow

Cash flow is wonderful. I'd rather have it than not have it. But when ministry decisions are based on cash flow instead of the dictates of the Holy Spirit, we make ourselves slaves of cash rather than of Christ. The decision-making process becomes poisoned by false assumptions. Namely, that money ultimately determines what can or should be done for God. These assumptions produce two unwanted results: overdependence on money and direction by cash flow.

First, money does not ultimately determine what can be done for God. It is only one of many tools that may facilitate or accomplish a goal for Christ. Examine the Bible from Genesis to Revelation and you will find surprisingly little money being used to accomplish God's will. The use of money was incidental and not critical, and nowhere do we find our great God's hands tied for lack of money. On the contrary, we are given many examples of God performing His will through, to, or for His people whether they had money or were flat broke!

George Muller was a 19th century English preacher who gave the universal church a timeless and invaluable gift: a testimony of what can be accomplished by faith and prayer alone. Over his long life—1805 to 1898—he housed more than 10,000 orphans, distributed tens of thousands of Bibles, and was the sole support of hundreds of missionaries. Today organizations do similar things through fundraising, but he used nothing but faith and prayer.[2]

George Muller absolutely refused to advertise his needs, drop strategic hints, or go into debt. In fact, his primary goal was not to care for orphans, distribute literature, or support missionaries. It was to prove to the church that God is faithful and can be depended on to keep His Word. Two of his diary entries powerfully make this point:

> I want to be the servant of the Church in the particular point on which I had obtained mercy—in being able to take God at His Word and rely upon it.
>
> This seems to me best done by establishing an orphan house—something which could be seen by the natural eye. If I, a poor man, simply by prayer and faith obtained, without asking any individual, the finances for establishing and carrying on an orphan house, this might strengthen the faith of the children of God. It would also be testimony to the unconverted of the reality of the things of God.
>
> This is the primary reason for establishing the orphan house. I certainly desire to be used by God to help the poor children and train them in the ways of God. But the primary object of the work is that God would be magnified because the orphans under my care will be provided with all they need through prayer and faith. Everyone will see that God is faithful and hears prayer (p. 73).

Second, the availability or unavailability of cash flow should not determine our direction in ministry. Ministers and churches that do not walk closely to the Lord are more prone to trust in their funds than in the ability, timing, and methods of God. They are unskilled and undisciplined in the art of praying, waiting, and recognizing the voice and moving of the Holy Spirit. Therefore, they make decisions based on protecting and increasing present or anticipated cash flow. Yet cash flow for a project does not validate it or prove that God agrees with our plans.

The False Dilemma of Either-Or

Here is where my position will inevitably be challenged on the false dilemma of either-or. A false dilemma is when two options are erroneously presented as the only available. You can have either this or that, but not both, and never an entirely different option. The false dilemma in the church is that we must choose either the extreme of overdependence on money or the extreme of not enough money. However, there is a third option.

This is to radically change our ministry model. Presently our model is to subjectively, and sometimes arbitrarily, get a vision (of course, we'll say it came from God) and then raise money to bring it to past. We do this by telling God's people overtly or subtly that they must finance our ideas or be directly or indirectly cursed by God. Of course, every appeal for financial support isn't as brash and crude, but unfortunately, many are sickeningly close.

Others use the softer approach of appealing to their followers' greed and love of pleasures. This is done by carefully presenting scriptures out of context. The tactics used depend on the charisma of the manipulative leader and the sophistication of the manipulated Christians.

Some Christians tolerate and even embrace strong-arm fundraising tactics. They are predisposed to slavery. So you can abuse them in the name of the Lord and get away with it. For some reason, many of them are perversely satisfied by ministerial abuse.[3]

Others, who are naturally turned off by domination, will not tolerate such foolishness for one moment, so a more subtle approach is used.[4]

A New and Honest Way to Raise Money

Here is where we must fundamentally change how we do business. Instead of getting a grand idea and coercing or manipulating God's people to finance it, why not be honest? Why not present the idea as just that, an idea? Why not deal with our followers the way God deals with us? He tells us the truth and is patient, kind, and loving, and never does He put anything on us we can't bear.

Ministers, however, often see no problem with placing the burdens of their financial decisions on God's people. Would it not be a better testimony to the world, and a better demonstration of love and integrity in the church, if we humbly presented our ideas and allowed Christians to give based upon what they hear directly from the Holy Spirit?

I am sure this concept throws many ministers into a state of utter paranoid anxiety. The very idea that the untrained, unsophisticated masses should be allowed—*and God forbid, taught!*—to hear from God for themselves rather than through a burdensome, exploitative system of professional religious middlemen is heresy and anathema! And ministers' fears are well justified, for an incredible amount of God's money is routinely squandered on fleshly ambitions, runaway visions, obscene salaries, duplicated services, expensive real estate, and under-performing ministry.

These professional, religious middlemen know that an empowered church, or better yet a *Him*powered church, would put the brakes on much of what happens in the name of the Lord. Oh, there would still be funds raised for unneeded buildings, and salaries for people who should be working in what we mistakenly call "secular" jobs, and projects that never were approved by the Holy Spirit, but there would also be a revolution of accountability, integrity, and efficiency in the church.

This revolution would remove much of what religious middlemen use to empower themselves: Namely, guaranteed cash flow through the false doctrine of mandatory tithes and offerings. Absence of guaranteed cash flow creates an environment where professional ministers must use something other than threats of God's curses or bribes of His blessings to raise funds. Perhaps we could use the novel approach of deliberating the proposal, waiting on God, searching the Scriptures, examining the character and track record of the person seeking our money, and deciding accordingly.

But Will Christians Give without Threats and Bribes?

Someone will inevitably bring up the possibility and probability that some Christians will use this freedom to say no to actually say no. How do we handle this concern?

Will people use their freedom irresponsibly? Some always have and some always will. This will go on until the Lord returns, but God's answer to irresponsibility has never been to limit our ability to make bad decisions. God didn't hide the Tree of Knowledge of Good and Evil in the Garden of Eden to keep Adam and Eve from eating of it and suffering horrible eternal consequences. He placed them near it to prove their love. God did this knowing His creation would choose death instead of life. The Lord set this precedent and I believe it is safe to follow His example of freedom in our giving.

For some, this freedom will be a Tree of Life. They will use their newly found liberty to obey God. This will result in generous, sponta-neous, and planned giving to causes approved by God, though not necessarily approved by man. The money will often not pass through clergy hands, but the support of professional, religious middlemen is not the priority. Obedience to the Holy Spirit is the priority.

For others, this liberty will be a Tree of Knowledge of Good and Evil. They will use their newly found freedom to justify selfishness. Many legitimate opportunities to give will come their way. Some will come through professional, religious middlemen. Others will come through direct contact with a person in need. Yet there will always be a seemingly good reason to not give. And if this latter category of peo-ple does give, the amount will usually be far less than what it should be (*less* not according to the demands of man, but the demands of love). But this is a matter for God and not us. Our job is to humbly preach the gospel, and not to prematurely judge people for the amount of their financial gifts.

The freedom spoken of in this book is scary, but not new. It is as old as Adam and Eve in the Garden of Eden. Generally, professional, religious middlemen hate this freedom for several reasons. Here are a few of them:

It frees God's people to think for themselves. This breaks the unholy monopoly power that religious professionals exercise over Jesus' people.

It allows the Holy Spirit to directly instruct God's people when to give, how much to give, and to whom to give. This puts every fleshly financial project at risk of being stripped of undeserved cash flow.

It requires religious, professional middlemen to walk extremely close to the Lord. This means projects that don't come from God are no longer automatically supported by manipulated followers of Christ. Clergy would then have to spend considerably more time in prayer than in business meetings, conferences, Starbucks, or watching television. This is a terrifying thought for many fleshly preachers.

It places stringent qualifying criteria on financial appeals for buildings and salaries. This threatens the very foundation of superficial and misdirected Christianity. But financial accountability is not too much to ask of someone who demands our money.

It makes it harder for preachers to manipulate God's people into taking care of their ambitions and personal financial needs. This addresses one of the main stumbling blocks to salvation of intelligent people who see glaring contradictions in the life of Christ and the greed and materialism of His so-called followers.

It forces preachers to be patient in their ambitions. This takes away their ability to prematurely commit God's resources without at least being seriously scrutinized and questioned by the church.

A Revival of Financial Integrity in the Church Is Possible

I earnestly believe that *What Preachers Never Tell You About Tithes & Offerings* is the articulated groanings of the heart of God and of multitudes of people who know that something is dreadfully wrong with the financial practices of the church. This includes Christians and non-Christians. All are fed up with the financial sins of the church.

This effort is by no means a perfect treatise against such an old, entrenched, and formidable clergy money-maker. Every page testifies of my imperfection. Still, as He did to the walls of Jericho, God may yet mercifully roar upon these words and miraculously crumble the impregnable walls of financial clergy domination and manipulation.

I pray that God will use this book to spark a flame that will devour every trace of financial waste and abuse in the church. The Reformation was sparked by men with a flame in their heart and a pen in their hand. Words on paper have changed the world before. It can happen again.

CHAPTER 2

The Psychology of Clergy Financial Manipulation

re you tired of preachers harassing you about money? Are you tired of the trickery and manipulation they use to squeeze one more dollar out of your budget and into theirs? Are you tired of going to church to meet Jesus and instead being hijacked by a religious version of the IRS? We all are, including God.

In many churches and ministries it doesn't matter where the sermon starts, it ends with cash. Even the more responsible organizations appear obsessed with getting more of our money. Yet you may never hear them make an obviously threatening or presumptuous statement to get your money. The approach they take depends on the psychological category of the church.

Rich People and Giving

Churches that are primarily comprised of affluent people must be "handled" delicately. This category can rarely be talked into giving more money by promising them God's financial blessings. They're already well-off or even rich. What is a preacher's promise of prosperity worth to a cardiologist or businessperson who grosses hundreds of thousands a year in salary? Besides, these types of people are highly educated and extremely skeptical of outlandish spiritual promises made by preachers. (Of course, there will always be exceptions.) Their keen minds are disciplined in economics, politics, sociology, psychology, law, and other academic disciplines.

They've done enviably well without Christian witchcraft, and would be offended by questionable fundraising schemes. They respond better to solicitations presented in a business format. If they like the idea, they fund it. If they don't like it, they don't fund it. Either way, there's usually enough excess money available to fund whatever preachers desire (in the name of Christ, of course). So preachers don't have to deal with the dynamic of scarce resources.

The premier question in affluent churches is not, can the church afford what the preacher wants, but does the church desire what the preacher wants? This is critical because usually affluent churches have a system of checks and balances that prevents preachers from arbitrarily burdening them with ridiculously expensive projects. But there is a way around this.

Corporate America routinely builds wildly expensive and ornate headquarters buildings to announce to the world that they're successful. A pigeon building, so to speak, may have been more functional and definitely less expensive, but in most cases the peacock building is chosen for its ego effect on the audience. Rich church people often have this same tendency. The shrewd preacher may manipulate this tendency toward opulence by providing his audience spiritual reasons for purchasing even bigger peacocks—for God's glory, of course.

Poor People and Giving

The kingdom of God consists primarily of people who are considered losers by the world, if not for lack of worldly achievement, then for their primitive devotion to Christ. Oh, here and there, a rich, powerful, or celebrated person lives for the Lord. But in comparison to the loser crowd, the big shot crowd is exceedingly small.

I can't scientifically prove the percentage of big shots in the kingdom of God. But in light of statements made by Jesus Himself, and of my own observations of 30 years, I believe that no more than 1%-2% of God's true church is financially rich by American standards, politically powerful, or celebrated by the world.

The Bible is silent on these figures; it doesn't discuss actual numbers. But it emphatically and comprehensively supports my premise that almost all big shots are disqualified from eternal life because of pride and love of stuff. A fatal irony is that worldly success blinds their view of either the existence or need of eternal life.

The "losers," on the other hand, don't have the comfortable obstacle of worldly success to keep them from God. Their obstacle is not primarily the deceitfulness of riches, but the bitterness of poverty, and often envy. So whether one is rich or poor, powerful or weak, celebrated or scorned, we are all cell mates in the universal prison of sin.

Nonetheless, all bondage is not equal. A single rope may tie a person's destiny to Hell. But it is easier to cut a rope than a steel chain. Ropes bind the poor; steel chains bind the rich. It is because of this that the apostle Paul made the following statements to the Corinthian church:

> For ye see your calling, brethren, how that not many wise men after the flesh, not many mighty, not many noble are called:
>
> But God hath chosen the foolish things of the world to confound the wise; and God hath chosen the weak things of the world to confound the things which are mighty; and base things of the world, and things which are despised, hath God chosen, yea, and things which are not, to bring to nought things that are:
>
> That no flesh should glory in his presence.
>
> 1 Corinthians 1:26-29

These people are not closer to God than others because of their low status in society. Nor has their low position secured divine favor automatically denied the rich, powerful, and celebrated. What has worked on their behalf is the absence of earthly prosperity has

prepared their hearts for the promise of a better life. This is an incredibly attractive proposition for someone who has experienced the least
or worst that this earthly life has to offer.

So what do shrewd fundraisers do with the understanding that the
simple (the world may say *simpleton*) and denied crowd is eager for a
better life? They offer it to them for the price of ten percent of their
gross income for life, as well as other regular financial offerings.

Needy People and Giving

Audience need level is another factor in clergy fundraising. This is
most important when the appeal is made to poor (and even middle-
class) people. Rich people have needs, but not the kind of needs I'm
speaking of. The rich are concerned about finding good tax shelters.
The poor are concerned about finding good shelter.

This immediate "*make or break*" kind of need (utilities, food, health
care, transportation, etc.) makes the less-than-affluent person vulnerable to the manipulations of predator fundraisers. It's hard for
a needy—and perhaps gullible—Christian to ignore a preacher's plea
if he promises that God will bless him for giving. Furthermore, if the
Christian doesn't know how much God loves him, he will find it
exceedingly difficult to ignore the preacher's threat that God will curse
him for not giving the little money he has.

Greedy People and Giving

Another group of church people that is easily manipulated by predator fundraisers is the greedy. They are greedy not because they want
more, but because "more" is their god, not Jesus Christ. They
perversely "suppose that godliness is a means of gain" (1 Timothy 6:5).

This group is usually comprised of the less-than-affluent. They
may or may not be genuine Christians; it's not always easy to tell. One
trait of this group, however, is that its members want more of the

"good" life, and they see God as a way to get it. Another trait is they believe they can control God through using Scriptures, verbal confessions of faith, and giving. So when the preacher promises that God will bless them for giving, they eagerly give.

Sinful People and Giving

Most churches consist of many people who don't actually love or serve God. In some churches this is the majority of membership. They often are not easily identifiable. On the outside they look like true lovers of Christ. But inwardly they are eaten up with sin and have no intentions of ever living a righteous life. Their attendance and participation is usually limited to Sunday mornings. They go to church regularly for a variety of reasons.

Some do it out of tradition. Some do it because they're attracted to certain programs. Some do it to establish business contacts. Some do it to appease their conscience. Some do it to make themselves look better than they know they are.

Whatever their dubious reasons for church attendance. many definitely are not servants of Christ. This group, however, is often a lucrative source of income to the church. For many of them believe they can bribe their way into God's good graces. Shrewd fundraisers are happy to accept these bribes on behalf of God with no questions asked.

Common Christians and Giving

A trait of true followers of Christ is their generosity. They give because God first gave to them. Their gratitude to God for delivering them from eternal damnation overflows into spontaneous and planned acts of generosity and selflessness. It is natural for them to give; so they give. Unfortunately, this group's love of God is often the very tool that predator preachers use to get their money.

Their love of God often blinds them to their responsibility to *"test all things"* (1 Thess. 5:21) and to *"not give what is holy to the dogs; nor cast your pearls before swine, lest they trample them under their feet, and turn and tear you in pieces"* (Matt. 7:6).

Life is short. Resources are limited. They both eventually run out. We can't afford to waste either. Money given to preachers and ministries that can be characterized as "dogs" and "swine" is misdirected. They should not get one cent of financial support from God's people, tithes, offerings, or otherwise. Yet surprisingly, these types of ministries are regularly funded by true Christians. How can this be?

Often this is done out of ignorance. The Christian doesn't know any better. He doesn't know that the ministry he supports is extremely ineffective or inefficient with funds.

Supporting Ineffective and Inefficient Ministries

Ineffective use of funds occurs when ministries either don't do what they promise to do with the money, or they can't do what they promise. A preacher may promise that if you give him enough money, he'll win Las Vegas to Jesus and establish 50 Las Vegas churches in three years. The only problem is there is nothing in this preacher's past that suggests he can do this. He has never won a city to Jesus and he isn't known as a church planter. The critical question here is the probability of the promised results.

Inefficient use of funds occurs when more of God's resources are used for a project than is necessary. Speaking of inefficiency, there's a lot of talk going on in the church about excellence in ministry. The popular religious opinion of many fundraisers and church people is that if it's going to be done for Jesus, it ought to be done in "excellence." I admit that this is an apparently unassailable argument. What Christian wants to go on record as giving God less than best?

The problem, however, is not with aspiring to excellence. It's with the corrupt interpretation of "excellence." Ministries and preachers are notorious for wasting money. Does the "only the best for God" doctrine justify our needless, unwise, and prideful purchases? I'm convinced not. But I am convinced that Judgment Day will reveal that much of what we did in the name of "only the best for God" was done to satisfy our lust for materialism, comfort, and pride. The critical issue here is the wasting of our assets.

Both of these types of ministries, the ineffective and inefficient, can be classified in the fundraiser context as "dogs" and "swine" ministries. This does not mean they are necessarily evil. It may simply mean they have more zeal than ability, or more ideas than wisdom. In these cases, you must resolutely proceed with caution and many questions, as well as prayers.

Of course, there is always the dark possibility that a preacher's weaknesses go far beyond deficient skills. Frequently the problem is dishonesty, manipulation, irresponsibility, or abuse of our money.

The number of incompetent and evil ministries and preachers that should never receive a dime of support from Christians because of lack of ability or lack of integrity is high. Yet they are funded by a large proportion of the Christian community who give based on their own innocence rather than the worthiness of the request for funds. I'll use two scriptures to explain this unfortunate irony.

Too Pure to See the Truth

First, Titus 1:15: "To the pure all things are pure." This group of Christians sees the world through the lens of purity. Their own moral purity acts like a pair of sun shades on a sunny day. The "dog" and "swine' qualities of the ministry or preacher who asks for money may shine as bright as the noon sun. Yet their tinted lens of purity dims the brightness of the evidence of these negative qualities. In essence, this group projects its own purity onto others. So even if people are not pure, it sees them as pure. Obviously, this works in favor of undeserving requests for funds.

Too Loving to See the Truth

Second, 1 Corinthians 13:7: "[Love] bears all things, believes all things, hopes all things, endures all things." This group of Christians may or may not project its own good qualities onto others. What it can be counted on to do, however, is to tolerate evil in the name of good. They don't want to judge anyone harshly. So they abdicate their responsibility to use either common or spiritual sense. They don't want to be unmerciful. So they support men and ministries who are not supported by God. They don't want to rebel against the man of God. So they rebel against God by being more loyal to the man than to God.

This group does not know that its misguided quality of longsuffering is used by Satan to empower ministries that don't qualify for Holy Spirit assistance. Perhaps one of Satan's most effective means of protecting this unholy empowerment is by highlighting the good that many of these ministries do. What do we do with the fact that many bad ministries produce good fruit?

Bad Ministries, Good Fruit

The answer is found in Paul's response to the issue of doing evil to bring about good. In Romans 3:5 he asked, "But if our unrighteousness demonstrates the righteousness of God, what shall we say?" He answered this question in Romans 3:7 with a question that provided the answer: "For if the truth of God has increased through my lie to his glory, why am I also still judged as a sinner?" Catch the significance of Paul's answer. If we bring glory to God by telling a lie, I am still judged as a sinner.

How can we bring glory to God through a lie? Here's an easy way. Fabricate or exaggerate a testimony of deliverance, provision, or healing and broadcast it to the church. Christians will go wild with excitement at the greatness of God. Many will be encouraged to trust God and persevere in their own trials. Some may even come to Christ—and you'll still be judged as a liar.

Now apply this principle with a preacher who uses manipulation and extortion to extract funds from God's people, or one who abuses those funds. Do we overlook his evil because people are saved under his ministry? Do we refuse to judge his behavior by God's word simply because he has blessed us? Do we continue to support him because we like him? Just how long do we act as allies of evil through our silence?

This system of financial unaccountability makes it easy for unworthy ministries to raise tremendous amounts of money from good-hearted, but "hopeful-to-a-fault" Christians.

Such Christians also empower ministerial unaccountability by using the lame disclaimer, "That's between him and God." Often this statement is used by Christians to escape responsibility to give only to ministries worthy of financial support. They mistakenly believe that God will hold them guiltless for supporting an ineffective, inefficient, or worse, ungodly ministry. But on Judgment Day God will make us answer for every dollar given to support bad ministries.

What will be revealed on that dreadful day? Will not such supporters of bad ministries be exposed as unwitting partners in crime? Certainly there are some bad ministries that are so carefully disguised that no one could be blamed for supporting them. There are others, however, that are so obviously materialistic, worldly, and ungodly that there is absolutely no excuse for supporting them.

So why do so-called Christians support bad ministries and bad preachers? There may be several reasons. But I believe on Judgment Day we will find that many have supported obviously bad ministries and preachers because they also are bad. They are drawn to these enemies of the cross because of their own materialism, worldliness, and ungodliness.

CHAPTER 3

The Crisis of Crisis Giving

Emergency!

Help!

S.O.S.!

"This is a faith ministry and if you don't send cash now, we're going under!"

We have all heard these emergency requests for money coming from our televisions, radios, mailboxes, and to a lesser degree our churches. I suppose there are real emergencies that require prompt giving. But the frantic requests we usually receive aren't because of a tsunami, earthquake, or famine. On the contrary, our emergency solicitations are frequently to pay routine bills.

It is well-known in marketing that sex sells. Do you want to sell a car, some toothpaste, or a gallon of milk? Breasts, thighs, and a nice behind will work every time. Similarly, in the church it is well-known that crises sell. Some ministries are sustained, and some even thrive, on crisis giving. Christians should ask two questions when presented with a crisis request.

First, is the crisis real? Often preachers exaggerate to get us to give more and to give quicker. Take your hand off your wallet, step away from the ATM, and study the situation before giving. Who is making the request? Is the minister known for moderate living and sacrificial giving? Or is he known for his collection of homes, cars, and expensive suits?

Really now, if the situation is as bad as the preacher says it is, and if he believes in it half as much as he wants us to believe in it, shouldn't he set the example by parting with his stuff and giving sacrificially? How can we take the emergency request seriously when the preacher is not moved enough by his own words to sacrifice? The minister must sacrifice before asking others to do so. Anything less than this is hypocrisy. Now let's qualify the sacrifice.

King David once said, "Nor will I offer burnt offerings to the Lord my God with that which costs me nothing" (1 Samuel 24:24). A sacrifice is not really a sacrifice if it costs you nothing. Therefore, the preacher's sacrifice must proportionately cost him as much as it costs the poorest giver. But since he is a church leader, he should sacrifice far more than those whom he solicits. Leaders are judged more strictly than those whom they lead (James 3:1). They must set the example.

If the preacher gives a thousand dollars towards the so-called crisis and has a bunch of money left over, he really hasn't sacrificed. He has simply given a routine gift, a gift that may be subtly returned to him through the ministry in a hundred different ways. Christians should never feel obligated to give proportionately more towards the "crisis" than the person who asks them to give.

Second, why is there a crisis? Is this a natural or man-made crisis? A natural crisis is one of those serious human emergencies that intrude upon the normalcy of life's routine. For instance, if a single mom loses her job and has no means to support her family, this is a natural crisis. The church should sacrifice if necessary to provide financial support. A man-made crisis, however, is a purported grave situation that is more the result of the preacher than the situation. Let's review this list of preacher–induced possibilities:

The preacher's sense of perspective.
The preacher's sense of timing.
The preacher's sense of expenses.
The preacher's sense of aloneness.
The preacher's sense of privilege.

The Preacher's Sense of Perspective

A preacher's perspective can cause a financial crisis. Here in Atlanta, there are a few mega-churches with the perspective that Jesus can't come back until the church takes over the world. The perspective is generally referred to as "kingdom now" theology. This false doctrine is especially useful to worldly, materialistic, and spiritually blind preachers because it serves as the foundation upon which they justify their ungodly ambitions of greatness.

If Jesus can't return until the church takes over the world, then the church must take over the world. And what does this mean in practical terms? It means "kingdom now" people must infiltrate and rise to the top of every conceivable level of business and society. This must be done individually and corporately.

It is the corporate efforts of the church that may be presented as crises. Give, give, give, we must build this auditorium, this radio station, this television station, this mega-complex, this school, this college, this university. We absolutely must build this bank or credit union. Give, give, give, it takes money to build our own communities and simultaneously take over the world.

Unfortunately, gullible Christians who aren't students of church history don't know that we have already done what they are ignorantly trying to accomplish. We have a 1000-year-plus example of religious rule. It's called the Catholic Church. For more than a thousand years it directly or indirectly controlled every facet of Western society: the arts, the sciences, the military, and the government. What did this produce? Heaven on earth? The Second Coming of Christ? No. It caused what is commonly referred to as the Dark Ages. It brought about stifling civil oppression, horrific religious wars, and several church sponsored campaigns of terror against innocent civilians.

If history tells us anything, it tells us this: the last thing this world needs is to be controlled by the church. Requests for money to resurrect this disaster do not qualify as a crisis.

The Preacher's Sense of Timing

Preachers often cause crises by their sense of timing. They want what they want, and they want it now. They want their own building now. They want a bigger building now. They want a radio or television ministry now. They want to expand their radio and television ministry now. They want, they want, they want. The list could go on indefinitely. The point is preachers often create crises by impatiently and often insensitively demanding what they want now.

The Preacher's Sense of Expenses

Many preachers create crises by spending funds like they own their own money farm. The reasoning seems to be, "We can afford it; so let's go for it." What the preacher means by, "We can afford it," is he can raise the money. The project could be done at the lesser price of X. But the higher price of Y is chosen because the excess amount can be raised. There is no overwhelming reason why the higher priced project is chosen other than the preacher wants it this way. This request for funds absolutely does not qualify as a crisis.

The Preacher's Sense of Aloneness

Some preachers create crises because they see themselves as God's only true servants. In 1 Kings 19:1-18 the prophet Elijah told God that he was the only one in Israel who was still faithfully serving Him. God answered, "Yet I have reserved seven thousand in Israel, all whose knees have not bowed to Baal [the false god], and every mouth that has not kissed him."

What happens when a preacher sees himself as the only true servant of God? Inevitably he takes upon himself a burden too heavy for any one man to carry. His sense of self-importance grows beyond reality. Frequently, this burden and exaggerated ego costs a lot of money to manage.

Count the large number of Christian television programs on Sunday morning. Notice the striking similarity of content. Nonetheless, the preacher who sees himself as God's last faithful servant feels compelled to join the crowd and preach the "true" gospel. In too many cases, however, the preacher only duplicates the ministry of others. A request for funds to support such a ministry certainly doesn't rise to the level of a financial crisis.

The Preacher's Sense of Privilege

There is a group of preachers that has a tremendous sense of material privilege. Fortunately, its activities are usually limited to independent, non-denominational, and generally unaccountable ministries—those with weak or easily manipulated boards.

These preachers create financial crises by demanding to be treated as CEOs, sole proprietor business owners, or protestant popes. The church is there to enrich them and their inner circle, so they believe. This results in exorbitant salaries and hidden financial benefits that drain the church and puts it in permanent emergency fundraising mode.

It is easy to assume this is primarily the practice of mega-churches and other large ministries. Yet this also describes multitudes of smaller ministries. It is not unusual for a small church of 25, 50, 100, or 200 to pay its pastors salaries and benefits that far exceed the boundaries of integrity, or even common sense. Why, my wife's friend just shared that her pastor quit his "secular" job so he can work full-time for the 25-member church. One of my highly placed unpaid spies told me that this preacher is kicking butts in that little church to get his tithe money.

It is a shame and a sin that so much time, manipulation, and threats are used on Sunday morning raising money that is destined for some preacher's pocket or to build another unnecessary building. This also does not qualify as a true crisis.

True Crisis Giving

There are certainly good preachers and ministries that deserve our financial assistance in furthering the gospel. Some of them may present problems or opportunities that require urgent action. You may support such a cause in the name of Christ, or you may refuse to support it in the name of Christ. It is a matter of conscience, what each person feels the Lord is telling him or her.

There is, however, a category of giving that absolutely requires us to give. This category is human need. Human need is not the same as organizational need. Organizations are creations of people. People are creations of God. We are not obligated to support organizations. But we are obligated to support people.

On Judgment Day we will be judged on how we treated people, not organizations. A clear example of this is in Matthew 25:31-40:[5]

> When the Son of Man comes in His glory, and all the holy angels with Him, then He will sit on the throne of His glory.
>
> All the nations will be gathered before Him, and He will separate them one from another, as a shepherd divides his sheep from the goats. And He will set the sheep up on His right hand, but the goats on the left. Then the King will say to those on His right hand, 'Come, you blessed of My Father, inherit the kingdom prepared for you from the foundation of the world: for I was hungry and you gave Me food; I was thirsty and you gave Me drink; I was a stranger and you took Me in; I was naked and you clothed Me; I was sick and you visited Me; I was in prison and you came to Me.' Then the righteous will answer Him, saying, 'Lord, when did we see You hungry and feed You, or thirsty and give You drink? When did we see You a stranger and take You in, or naked and clothe You? Or when did we see You sick, or in prison, and come to You? And the King will answer and say to them, 'Assuredly, I say to you, inasmuch as you did it to one of the least of these My brethren, you did it to Me.'

Notice that we will not be commended or condemned for how we treated religious organizations. The issue on Judgment Day will be our conduct towards people. This is no small difference of opinion.

True crisis giving is when we see individuals in genuine need, and we materially meet those needs. In Jesus' example above, it is clear that God considers genuine need as the essentials of life, as well as general acts of compassion: food, water, clothes, shelter, visitation, etc. When we help people in need, we help Jesus. When we ignore people in need, we ignore Jesus. Therefore, the only options we have when we see a person in genuine need is to help. This is consistent with commands such as 1 John 3:17:

> But whoever has this world's goods, and sees his brother in need, and shuts up his heart from him, how does the love of God abide in him? My little children, let us not love in word or in tongue, but in deed and in truth.

When we give the way God instructed us to give, we further the kingdom of God in the most effective and efficient way. There are at least six ways this is done.

Six Benefits of Giving Directly to the Person in Need

First, the Christian who sees a human need and personally meets it powerfully demonstrates the reality of God's love to the recipient.

Second, the gift creates a Jesus-bond between the giver and the recipient. This bond strengthens or creates godly relationships. These relationships can lead to sinners coming to Christ, or Christians growing in the faith.

Third, there are many more Christians than there are churches. Individual Christians are virtually everywhere there are people in need. They interact with them daily. Christians are already strategically positioned by God to meet their needs in His name. Thus, needs can be met without administrative costs whenever they decide to help people.

Fourth, the giver directly participates in the redemption of humanity. This provides the giver the joy of hearing and obeying God, and of experiencing the spiritual ecstasy of witnessing what God can do through the least of us—something that is diminished when we settle for partnership with organizations instead of with the Holy Spirit.

Fifth, direct giving to the person in need assures that the money gets to the person. This is a critical point. The vast majority of money given to churches and other religious organizations is not directly spent on human need or preaching the gospel. It is spent on salaries, benefits, buildings, and administration.

Sixth, giving directly to the person in need, as God commanded, is common sense. It is foolish to respond to immediate human need all around us by giving money to a preacher and then hoping something is done about the need. Why not just give to the person? This would meet the need quicker, and satisfy the demands of common sense.

There are several reasons why we violate common sense to give to preachers and organizations instead of people. We'll discuss them later.

An Example of True Crisis Giving

A traveler was beaten, robbed, and left to die on the side of the road. Religious leaders saw the man and ignored the need. Perhaps they reasoned that they had already given to the church, or that they would later give to the church.

Later a stranger helped the man by directly taking care of his needs. He didn't send money to an organization and hope the money would somehow find its way back to the man. God condemned the actions of the religious leaders and commended the man who took care of the need (Luke 10:25-37).

Now had the stranger been broke, he would have been justified to send out emergency requests for funds. Immediate human need requires extreme action in the shortest period of time, even if it requires us to ask others to help us meet that need.

A good thing to remember, however, about emergency appeals for money is that immediate sacrificial giving is normally only proper when it is directly related to human need. In this case, it's best to send the money directly to the person in need without going through a religious middleman. If you find it impossible to do so without a third party, diligently examine its financial dealings. If its financial records are unavailable, or its financial practices are questionable, find a ministry that can be trusted and use it as an intermediary.

CHAPTER 4

How Much Does It Cost the American Church to Preach the Gospel?

One of the Lord's last and most critical commands was for us to "Go into all the world and preach the gospel to every creature" (Mark 16:15). This is not an option. If we are true Christians, we will obey His commands, including this one.

Christian leaders insist that the primary way we do this is by giving money to the church. This is so consistently hammered into our minds that we now believe preaching the gospel and giving to the church are the same. Yet they are totally different actions that often have little or no connection to one another.

Nonetheless, our leaders regularly press upon us the extreme urgency of giving to the church so the gospel can be preached. The implication is that if we don't give, the gospel will not be preached. But is this true? Is the preaching of the gospel limited to church bank accounts? If this is true, the church's history should numerically reflect the greatest evangelism and growth in times and places where the church was or is financially prosperous. But is this so?

The Cost of American Church Activities

The American church collects approximately $80 to $85 billion a year in tithes and offerings.[6] Yet church leaders complain that only 3%-5% of people who give to churches regularly tithe. Obviously, in their estimation, it costs more than $80 to $85 billion a year to "preach the gospel." Why else would these leaders complain of scarcity of funds?

There is even a good Christian ministry on the Internet (www.generousgiving.org) that is organized solely to get Christians to give more, which is a noble cause. Here is one of their complaints:

> If members of historically Christian churches in the United States had raised their giving to the Old Testament's minimum standard of giving (10 percent of income) in 2000, an additional $139 billion a year would become available for the work of Christ.[7]

It is interesting and revealing that this same organization posts the following under the heading, "The Squandering of Church Resources":

> In 2000, nearly 97 percent of the entire income of all Christian organizations was spent on, and primarily benefited, other Christians at home or abroad: $261 billion spent on ministering to Christians, $7.8 billion on already-evangelized non-Christians, and $0.81 billion on unevangelized non-Christians.[8]

Do you see the irony of complaining that Christians don't give enough, while simultaneously admitting that the money given is mismanaged? What would the church do with more money? It would mismanage it. Had Christians given that extra $139 billion, how much of it would have gone to the work of winning the lost? According to this web site's own figures, only 3 percent, or $4.17 billion.

This is an inefficiency rate of 97 percent. At this rate, Christians would have to give $4 trillion to the church for it to actually use $139 billion for unevangelized non-Christians. Another way of looking at this fraud, waste, and abuse of our funds is to picture someone spending $3,300 of your money for $100 worth of groceries. I don't know of any organizations other than the church and the government that can handle our money like this and stay in business.

Mismanagement of Funds

The actual amount of Christian giving may be debatable, but the institutional church's spending habits are not. Research and common observation consistently prove that the American church spends almost all of its money on itself. Only a few pennies of every dollar make it outside of America, where the need is greatest—areas that have not heard the gospel even once.

The church's mismanagement of funds makes it more appropriate to not ask for more money, but to properly use the money it does receive. Several things have prevented this.

First, there is virtually no financial accountability in the church. Even those organizations that are audited by reputable firms are audited only for legal compliance. As long as the church doesn't break any civil law, it can mismanage and waste our money any way it chooses.

Second, it is a well-known human observation that the more money we have, the more we spend. Only the most disciplined and wise among us do otherwise. Generally, when we have less, we spend more wisely. We exercise patience and restraint. Conversely, when we have abundance we tend to find a way to spend more than is neces- sary. We creatively redefine our desires as needs. And, of course, if we need something and we have the money, it's ours.

Third, the American church has been discipled by American culture. Both are shamefully self-absorbed and grossly materialistic. We expect a prosperous and militarily powerful country to behave this way. This is the world's norm. But it is not normal for the church to adopt the materialistic values of a society that is in moral rebellion against Christ.

$400 Hammers

Over 20 years ago the Pentagon was mercilessly criticized after the Grace Commission audit appointed by President Reagan discovered that it routinely paid astronomical prices for ordinarily low cost items. How about $436 for an ordinary hammer, or $640 for an ordinary toilet seat? Yet 20 years after this revelation, the Pentagon is as wasteful as ever (makes you want to open a hardware store next to the Pentagon).

For instance, according to the Government Accountability Office (GAO), the military routinely throws away, gives away, or sells at a significant loss billions of dollars worth of items and later repurchases the same items (GA0-05-277, 2005).

The Grace Commission audit, however, revealed what all of us already knew: the federal government is full of waste and abuse. It showed in elaborate detail that at least $424 billion were being wasted every three years. How could such a thing happen? There are, no doubt, several contributing factors. But there is one that stands above them all: cash flow.

The federal government can be this dismally mismanaged because of its guaranteed cash flow. Here's a direct quote taken from the 2004 Financial Report of the United States Government: "The Government's main source of revenue comes from its ability to demand payments from the public (e.g., taxes, duties, fines, and penalties)" (p. 11).

Reports, audits, complaints, and television specials about waste and abuse in government doesn't cause one U.S. senator or representative to lose one wink of sleep. They know that irrespective of their behavior, their power to raise funds is absolute. They can waste and abuse hundreds of billions of dollars a year and still demand more from us. And we will pay because the penalties for disobedience are severe.

The church has much in common with the federal government. It wields similar power over its subjects. It can collect $80 billion a year and yet demand more. If its subjects refuse, it brings all the weight of Almighty God down upon their consciences. Christians are given the absolute choices of "obeying God" and giving to the church, or "disobeying God" and not giving to the church. The Christian's relationship with God is thus reduced to if he or she complies with the church's insatiable demands for money.

We have heard that "power corrupts, and absolute power corrupts absolutely."[9] The federal government has not proven this statement false, and unfortunately, but not surprisingly, neither has the church. The church's absolute power to demand cash flow has corrupted it. It has made it fat, wasteful, arrogant, and stained with human ambition. Furthermore, it has made it cruelly insensitive to the poor, who suffer the most by the church's inflexible and greedy demand for money.

Integrity demands that the church admits to its own purchases of $400 dollar hammers. Two of these hammers are buildings and salaries.

$400 Hammers and Church Buildings

Ralph Moore, author of *Starting a New Church: The Church Planter's Guide to Success*, is a cutting-edge church planter. This excellent book is the result of real world experience, not theory. He lists dedicated church buildings as one of the main obstacles to evangelism (2002, p. 102). Specifically, he states that they "take time and focus away from evangelism and discipleship" (p. 103). Moore's concern is that pastors and churches are too eager to buy or build a structure for their religious services. He believes, as do I, that churches can rent facilities and use the saved energy and money for evangelism and discipleship.

Dedicated church buildings that we insist on owning are one of our $400 dollar hammers. No one knows exactly how much is spent on church buildings relative to what is collected in tithes and offerings. But if observation is worth anything, we must conclude that an obscene proportion is spent on buildings.

The obscenity is not just that we *waste* billions of dollars on facilities that are used a few hours a week.[10] It is that our behavior rises to the level of *abuse*. An agonizingly large amount of these funds is raised and spent because preachers have a shameful need to appear successful to the world and to their peers. A building satisfies this need. This behavior is not against any civil law, but it definitely is against God's law, and will be exposed as such on Judgment Day.

$400 Hammers and Church Salaries

Perhaps more obscene and dangerous to the church's mission, evangelism and discipleship, is the waste and abuse of church salaries. The waste is that a select few are paid to do what the entire church should be doing. The abuse is that Christians are routinely manipulated, threatened, and deceived into supporting this counterproductive system.

The purpose of church leaders, apostles, prophets, evangelists, pastors, and teachers, is "for the equipping of the saints for the work of ministry, for the edifying of the body of Christ" (Ephesians 4:12). But this is only possible when church leaders see themselves as servants and not masters of the Lord's people. This enlightened perspective, however, hangs precariously on the damaged hinge of Christian equality.

Unfortunately, over time the equality of believers was displaced by a horrible system that divided the church into superiors and subordinates. The supreme superiors are the pastors, the junior superiors are the so-called parachurch leaders, and the subordinates are the lowly Christians who are commanded to financially support this system. This sounds unkind, but it isn't meant to be. It's just a sad observation that holds up under honest scrutiny.

Pastors are the supreme superiors because they have convinced us they are God's primary representatives on the earth. We are told that when God desires to do something, He tells His pastors. They then relay the message to us. Basically, they are our Moses. Most pastors, however, would vehemently disagree, and I don't blame them. It's an indefensible position when spoken aloud. Yet the actions of many pastors prove my point.

The parachurch leaders are the junior superiors because pastors control access to most of God's money. Parachurch ministries get what's left over after the traditional church gets its cut. Pastors also control physical access to the church.[11] This further puts parachurch leaders in a subservient role to pastors. Physical access to the church means the difference in a thriving itinerant ministry or a lot of locked doors. Nonetheless, parachurch leaders are resourceful and often get around pastors by coming directly to us through the mail, mass communication, and meetings held off church property.

The point is this: It takes a lot of money in salaries and benefits to support this system of religious professionals. If this system were created by God, it would be no problem. But the system was created by preachers for preachers, yet at the expense of God's people, especially poor people. And to make matters worse, this system that makes heroes of a few and spectators of the rest yields a horrible return on investment.

Is it a good use of God's money to train Christians to come to a building once or twice a week for a couple of hours to passively watch and listen to religious professionals perform? Is it a good use of God's money to pay a professional to do what every Christian is commanded to do freely? How can we not criticize such a system?[12]

Visiting the sick, the widows, and the fatherless; feeding the poor, sheltering the homeless, and verbally sharing our faith; counseling the troubled, praying for people, and worshipping the Lord; these are all things that every Christian must do with or without payment.

The paid pastoral system of preeminence, which has marginalized every other Christian office and ministry, and has made spectators and second-class citizens of the average Christian, is a colossal manmade traffic jam. It has turned a 12-lane superhighway into a single lane of traffic. This system of paid professionals and subordinate spectators is another of our $400 hammers.

The Bureaucracy of the American Church Needlessly Increases the Cost of Its Work

The American church is run like a huge bureaucracy. Even the simplest commands of God are converted into complex systems of rules and man-made barriers of ineffectiveness and inefficiency. The former white-water rapids of the River of Life are now so polluted and thickened by fleshly programs that they meander like a river of syrup.

Often, what ought to be done spontaneously and freely by a vast army of Christians led by the Holy Spirit is now a regimented and expensive project dominated by pastors. The work of evangelism and discipleship will continue to be needlessly expensive until the system that makes popes of our preachers and zombies of everyone else is replaced with the leadership and freedom of the Holy Spirit.

CHAPTER 5

How Much Did It Cost Jesus to Preach the Gospel?

There is a great difference in the cost of first-century and modern American church activities. This difference is not merely that first-century culture and lifestyle were much simpler. For even then they could have exponentially increased the cost of church activities had they adopted our beliefs and practices. Fortunately, they remembered how Jesus evangelized and made disciples and followed His example. Oh, that we would do the same!

The Evangelism and Discipleship Methods of Jesus

We have significant conflicts with Christ and His model of evangelism and discipleship. For instance, Jesus didn't complicate things. Preaching the gospel for Him meant opening His mouth and explaining concepts of sin, righteousness, and judgment, with the intention of turning people to God. Preaching the gospel for us too often primarily means a special event: a Sunday morning sermon, a city-wide meeting, a radio or television program, or something similar. All of these things have common traits.

First, they are all done by religious professionals.

Second, they are all special-event oriented.

Third, they are all expensive.

We have four narratives of Christ's earthly life and ministry: Matthew, Mark, Luke, and John. Where do we see Jesus limiting the preaching of the gospel to professional clergy? We actually see the opposite (Mark 9:38-40). Where is one example of Jesus spending large sums of money to plan, organize, and execute a gospel meeting? We see none. Where do we find one example of Jesus teaching, hinting, or modeling a connection between preaching the gospel and needing money to do so? There isn't one example.

What shall we conclude from this? That formal training is bad? That we shouldn't plan, organize, and hold gospel meetings? Or that money doesn't facilitate the preaching of the gospel? These aren't the conclusions at all. Formal training can *sometimes* be useful. Planned gospel meetings are *often* useful. And money assists *some* presentations of the gospel.

The point we must see, however, is that our Lord's concept of preaching the gospel and making disciples is much simpler than our complicated and elaborate beliefs and practices of these commands. A brief observation of several facets of Jesus' life and ministry reveals an incredibly simple, powerful, and inexpensive way of evangelizing and making disciples:

- *Jesus kept His personal expenses extremely low* (Matthew 6:19-21; 8:20). He lived more modestly than the people to whom He ministered. Therefore, He was under little pressure to generate cash flow for His needs. His modesty validated His message even when His mouth was closed. This is in stark contrast to many preachers who must raise questionable amounts of money just to first cover their fine tastes in clothing, cars, homes, travel, restaurants, vacations, and other amenities.

- *Jesus preached a demanding gospel that made no provision for phony conversions* (Matthew 7:13-29; 10:32-39; 15:1-9). The Lord demanded all or nothing. With the exception of Judas Iscariot, His gospel did not attract hypocrites and lukewarm people.

When He did notice the presence of false converts, He deliberately scared them away by emphasizing the rigorous demands of true discipleship. The absence of phonies removed the pressure to find ways to keep them interested. It's expensive, frustrating, and time consuming to minister to phony Christians.

• *Jesus used but didn't rely on special-event activities to preach the gospel* (Mark 1:39). The Lord preached in synagogues (we would call them churches) whenever He could. Yet almost all of His preaching was done in the streets, in homes, on hillsides, or anywhere there was a person or group. He strategically used His everyday interactions with people to preach and teach the gospel. This cost Jesus nothing.

Jesus Evangelizes the Samaritan Woman

There is a fascinating record in John 4 of how Jesus evangelized the city of Samaria. A bit of background about the deep hostilities that existed between Samaritans and Jews will help you appreciate why this evangelistic event was so remarkable.

When King Solomon died, his son, Rehoboam, became king. Unfortunately, Israel's idolatry and Rehoboam's arrogance and major political blunders caused the 12-tribe nation to split into two different nations. The new two-tribe Southern Kingdom was called Judah, and the new 10-tribe Northern Kingdom was called Israel.

The city of Jerusalem was located in Judah. Therefore, the Jews' most holy place, its temple, was located in the Southern Kingdom. The king of Israel was afraid that the inhabitants of his new country would defect back to Rehoboam because of their strong religious, sentimental, and historical connection to Jerusalem and its temple. He, therefore, created a false religion to rival the Jerusalem temple worship. The plan worked and King Jeroboam's subjects totally embraced idolatrous false religion.

Inevitably this rebellion provoked God to raise up enemies against Israel. Two of these enemies were the powerful and competing nations of Assyria and Babylon. The successful invasions of these two nations into Israel resulted in mass deportations of Jews to other lands. A remnant, however, was left in Israel. Over time many foreign captives of the Assyrian empire relocated to the Northern Kingdom, or what was then referred to as Samaria. The remnant of Jews and the migration of foreigners intermarried and their offspring were called Samaritans.

The Jews who had been previously deported by Babylon and Assyria into foreign lands never accepted the Samaritans as Jews. As far as the Jews were concerned, the Samaritans were half-breed traitors who had no claim on the promises of Israel or of God. This contemptuous attitude of the Jews toward the Samaritans, whether right or wrong, was not entirely without merit.

The sin of the Samaritans was not only that they intermarried, but that they embraced the religions of the foreigners among them. The rift between the Jews and Samaritans was so great that when King Cyrus gave permission for the Jews to return to their land (538 B.C.) and rebuild Jerusalem, the Jews strictly forbade the Samaritans from helping[13]. They were ostracized and treated as enemies of Israel. Naturally, this further inflamed the situation and matters got even worse. The Samaritans tried to stop the rebuilding of Jerusalem and the temple by use of intimidation. When that didn't entirely work, they resorted to politics. Their political maneuverings caused a 7-year delay. Nonetheless, the Jews finally rebuilt the temple and the city's walls. But they never forgot how the Samaritans hindered their work. In the Jewish mind, the Samaritans were not only disqualified from the promises of God through their commingling with foreigners. They were actual enemies of Israel and of God.

The Samaritans' history of commingling with foreigners and embracing their gods was enough for Jews to justify their contempt of the so-called half-breeds. But when you consider that the Samaritans had defiantly frustrated the Jews' efforts to rebuild their temple and city, it is understandable that they should view them as traitors and enemies. Nevertheless, there were other reasons to despise the Samaritans.

First, the Samaritans had created a rival religious system and had even built a temple on their own mountain, Mount Gerizim. They did this in the name of the God of Abraham and Moses.

Second, they accepted the first five books of the Old Testament, but rejected the rest.

Third, according to Josephus, a highly regarded first-century historian, they formally, publicly, and politically repudiated all links to the Jews to escape persecution from Antiochus IV Epiphanes, ruler of the Seleucid Empire.[14]

This was the environment into which Jesus entered. How did He overcome centuries of religious, cultural, and political bigotry and hatred to turn the hearts of the Samaritans to God? Surely this evangelistic effort must have been preceded by huge outlays of cash for professional demographic studies, radio, television, and print advertisement.[15] And what about the cost of salaries for the professional preachers and administrative assistance? That surely must have cost a small fortune.

But what do you find when you read John 4? You see Jesus walking into hostile territory and starting a conversation with a woman. He maneuvered the conversation to her need of God, the Holy Spirit gave Him supernatural knowledge of her life, Jesus sensitively shared this information with her, and she turned to God. She became so excited about her encounter with Jesus that she told several of her neighbors. The neighbors came to hear Jesus and they became excited. They asked Jesus to stay with them for a while, and He remained among them for two days. We have the record of what happened:

> And many of the Samaritans believed in Him because of the word of the woman who testified, 'He told me all that I ever did.' So when the Samaritans had come to Him, they urged Him to stay with them; and He stayed there two days. And many more believed because of His own word. Then they said to the woman, 'Now we believe, not because of what you said, for we ourselves have heard Him and we know that this is indeed the Christ, the Savior of the world.'

John 4:39-42

This successful evangelistic effort is one of the most exciting in the entire New Testament. Centuries of religious, cultural, and political hatred and bigotry were overcome by a spontaneous two-day evangelistic outreach.

You want me to ask the question, don't you? Okay, I will. How much did this cost?

This spectacular evangelistic outreach cost absolutely nothing. Jesus and His disciples were going to eat whether they were in Samaria or not. And they lodged as guests for two days with the Samaritans. So eating and lodging were not outreach expenses.

The Samaritan model of evangelism is extremely simple, inexpensive, and effective. Wherever you are open your mouth and tell people about sin, righteousness, and judgment. Make it plain that they have sinned against God and that they are doomed without His mercy. Explain that the only escape from the judgment to come is to turn from their lifestyle of sin and to ask God for mercy. Emphasize that total submission to Jesus Christ as Savior and God is the only access to that mercy. And do this with a heart full of compassion and a delivery free of arrogance. You can do this for free. This is the model of evangelism we see throughout the New Testament.[16]

What Jesus Taught His Followers about Evangelizing and Making Disciples

Jesus told His disciples, "Follow Me, and I will make you fishers of men" (Matthew 4:19). Much of what He spoke and modeled was designed to teach the disciples how to evangelize and make disciples, including this.

His strategy for making the disciples "fishers of men" was to reproduce in them the dependence that He had on the Holy Spirit, which was total. Only as they closely followed the directions of the Holy Ghost would they fulfill their mission. To do otherwise, to trust in man-made methods or support systems, would only cause failure. Worse, it may even cause fleshly success. That is, the efforts of man without the Holy Spirit may produce a Tower of Babel of evangelism and discipleship. Like the tower spoken of in Genesis 11, its apparent success would be celebrated and accepted by man, but despised and rejected by God.[17]

The Lord's Evangelism Boot Camp

Jesus once took an extreme measure to train His disciples to trust more in the Holy Spirit than in themselves or in people. Here you will see several truths concerning the work of evangelism and making disciples, and dependence on the Holy Spirit:

> After these things the Lord appointed seventy others also, and sent them two by two before His face into every city and place where He Himself was about to go.
>
> Then He said to them, "The harvest truly is great, but the laborers are few; therefore pray the Lord of the harvest to send out laborers into His harvest.
>
> Go your way; behold I send you out as lambs among wolves.
>
> Carry neither money bag, knapsack, nor sandals; and greet no one along the road.
>
> But whatever house you enter, first say, 'Peace to this house.'
>
> And if a son of peace is there, your peace will rest on it; if not, it will return to you.
>
> And remain in the same house, eating and drinking such things as they give, for the laborer is worthy of his wages. Do not go from house to house.
>
> Whatever city you enter, and they receive you, eat such things as are set before you.
>
> And heal the sick [and cast out demons] there, and say to them, 'The kingdom of God has come near you.'"
>
> Luke 10:1-9

Later in His ministry, on the night He was betrayed, He asked His disciples if they lacked anything when He sent them out on this mission with nothing. They answered that they had lacked nothing.[18] The lessons we see here are numerous.

First, the Lord commented on how big was the job of evangelism, and the immediate need for more workers. Conspicuously absent was any mention of a need for money. The issue has never been, nor is it now, lack of funds. Jesus powerfully demonstrated this truth by sending out His disciples *without any money.*

Second, the disciples were commanded to lodge with those who were open to their message, and to eat whatever was set before them. The hospitality of strangers was to be their payment. This is in stark contrast to today's practice of preachers demanding financial payment for preaching a sermon.

Third, Jesus specifically prohibited the practice of going house to house. In the context of His discourse on wages, this was the equivalent of trying to get more payment. A poor family certainly could not offer as much as a rich family. So it would obviously be a temptation to leave that family and lodge with a more prosperous one. But Jesus wisely forbade this type of mercenary ministry practice.

Fourth, and finally, He told them to minister in the supernatural power of God. This would be accomplished through healing the sick and casting out demons. Obviously, this type of ministry would require intimacy with God and total dependence upon the Holy Spirit—two things the American church is famous for not having.

How would it affect our insatiable desire for ministry funds if we took these lessons to heart and

- recognized that our most pressing need is not money but workers?
- rejected covetousness in ministry?
- ministered in the power of God instead of the power of the flesh?

The immediate and widescale adoption of such perspectives and practices would radically transform the church from a *life-sucking* force to a *life-giving* force. The gospel would once again be good news (instead of bad news) to the poor. It would once again qualify as God's counterculture antidote to a materialistic and pleasure-worshipping society.

Taxes, and Fishes and Loaves: Provision for Personal and Ministry Needs

The professional preacher's never-ending request for money is based on two things: the preacher's perceived or actual personal needs and the preacher's perceived or actual ministry needs. There is usually a great gulf between the perceived and actual needs of a preacher. Two incidents occurred in the life of Jesus that perfectly illustrates this truth.

Taxes

One day tax collectors asked Peter if Jesus paid taxes. (The IRS has been around a long time.) Peter went to Jesus and received these instructions:

> Go to the sea, cast in a hook, and take the fish that comes up first. And when you have opened its mouth, you will find a piece of money; take that and give it to them for Me and you.

> Matthew 17:27

This was no manufactured or perceived need; it was real. The taxes had to be paid. The Lord's deliberate response was more for our benefit than His. He didn't pressure His followers for money. Instead He received instructions from God that met His and Peter's need without declaring an emergency, promising a blessing, or threatening a curse. Ironically, though, some preachers use this incident to do just that. The reasoning goes something like this: "*If money is to come, it's going to come through someone. It's not going to fall out of the sky! Jesus represented the ministry and Peter represented the laity. When Jesus needed money, He went to His followers for it.*"

There are a number of obvious problems with this reasoning. First, this was not an artificial need. It was real. Second, Jesus didn't assume that His financial need was Peter's responsibility. Third, Jesus didn't go to Peter for money. He gave Peter money. Fourth, there is no biblical hierarchy of ministers (as it is currently taught) and laity except in the minds of those who teach and accept such error. And, fifth, the money never touched Jesus' hands. The money never came under Jesus' direct control!

Fishes and Loaves

Our second example of need occurred when Jesus noticed that a great multitude that had followed Him three days into the wilderness to hear Him had run out of food. Two gospels record this incident.[19] So it's doubly worthy of our attention. We'll use Matthew 15:32-38:

> Now Jesus called His disciples to Himself and said, "I have compassion on the multitude, because they have now continued with Me three days and have nothing to eat. And I do not want to send them away hungry, lest they faint on the way." Then His disciples said to Him, "Where could we get enough bread in the wilderness to fill such a great multitude?" Jesus said to them. "How many loaves do you have?" And they said, "Seven, and a few little fish." So He commanded the multitude to sit down on the ground. And He took the seven loaves and the fish and gave thanks, broke them and gave them to His disciples; and the disciples gave to the multitude. So they all ate and were filled. And they took up seven large baskets full of the fragments that were left. Now those who ate were four thousand men, besides women and children.

This is a perceived ministry need of Jesus because it wasn't actually His personal need. It was someone else's need.

Jesus fasted often; so three days without food for Him was nothing. But it was a big deal to Him that the crowd was without food. So He *assumed* this need; he made it His own.

We frequently see this. Preachers approach us with stories of great assumed need of others. It may be an unreached village in India, starving children in Africa, or the erection of a building in America, that weighs heavily on the preacher's heart. The need may be debatable to others, but to the preacher the need is obvious and urgent. Therefore, all of the minister's persuasive powers are pressed upon us for immediate action to meet the...*assumed need*.

To identify the above as assumed needs is not meant to belittle them or similar needs as illegitimate. They may be legitimate, and the preacher's concern may genuinely be from the Holy Spirit. The points I want to make are these:

- Assumed needs are often real.
- Assumed needs are often undebatable.
- Assumed needs are often worthy of immediate positive action.
- Assumed needs are often worthy of debate.
- Assumed needs are often worthy of rejection.

The challenge is to react properly to assumed needs. We can learn much from how Jesus presented and handled His assumed need in Matthew 15.

Here's what I see.

First, Jesus' actions were prompted by love. His only concern was for the welfare of the people. This is unlike many appeals we get from preachers whose covetous and wasteful lifestyles make it hard to believe what they say.

Second, there was no one else who could meet this need. This is a critical point. Often we are strongly urged, manipulated, or threatened by preachers to give to meet an assumed need that could be better met by someone other than them.

This is a subjective judgment that must be made, but many are afraid to make. But since we are the ones who will stand before God to give an account of what we did with His money, it is obvious that we have the responsibility and authority to decide where to give, how much to give, and to whom to give.

Third, Jesus did not use the assumed need to enrich Himself or to pad the ministry's bank account. It is a sad truth that money is often raised purportedly to meet an assumed need only to be used for other purposes. In some cases this is probably illegal; in most cases it is at best unethical. How can it be right to raise money under false pretences? Or how can it be right to keep receiving funds for a need that has already been met? Is this not deception? Are we dealing with men and women of God or Wall Street con artists?

Fourth, Jesus met the need without appealing for funds. He went directly to His Father and the need was supernaturally met in abundance. The lesson was and still is that God is our source. Yet preachers use this passage all the time to raise funds. They do so by emphasizing that the people received a miracle of provision only after Jesus was given what little they had to offer.

What preachers don't mention is Jesus didn't take the bread and fish from the crowd and put it in His pantry (or bank account). He took their bread and fish for the sole purpose of publicly blessing it so He could *immediately* return it to them in abundance. This whole event of receiving and praying over the food, and returning it to the people can be measured in minutes.

What similarity is there in what Jesus did in the wilderness and what preachers do now? I see no similarity in Jesus spending a minute to pray over someone's scarce resources to bring them immediate abundance, and a preacher taking those meager resources for himself, whether it's for his own wallet, a church building, or a village in India.

We can conclude this section by noting that assumed needs can be legitimate, undebatable, and worthy of immediate action. This is clearly seen in Jesus' words that "they have continued with Me three days and have nothing to eat. And I do not want to send them away hungry." When the Lord says that He does not want to send them away hungry, He has made His will known. It is not open for debate. The only godly response to this is to feed the people.

The challenge for us is to discern what is the voice of God and what is the voice of man. Jesus is not here in the flesh directly telling us to meet this or that need. Instead His Spirit moves upon His body, the church, to do His will. He may communicate to us directly through His Spirit, or He may speak to us through someone else. In either case we must "test all things [and] hold fast what is good."[20] If the appeal for funds does not pass the test of godly scrutiny, it not only must be debated, it must be rejected.

CHAPTER 6

How Much Did It Cost the Early Church to Preach the Gospel?

I t is enlightening to observe in the New Testament how the early Christians obeyed the Lord's command to evangelize the world. It is even more enlightening to see how little money it cost them to do such a phenomenal job. I believe this low cost was due to timeless and universal factors that transcend cultures and centuries. What worked for them can work for us.

Go Into All the World and Preach the Gospel

To appreciate the financial cost of New Testament evangelism and discipleship efforts, it is critical that we understand the mindset of the early church. For here is one of the great and timeless factors that enabled it to achieve evangelistic success that is unknown in America: It had a divine sense of purpose.

After Jesus was crucified and raised from the dead, He appeared to His disciples and spoke these words:

> All authority has been given to Me in heaven and on earth. Go there-
> fore and make disciples of all the nations, baptizing them in the

name of the Father and of the Son and of the Holy Spirit, teaching them to observe all things that I have commanded you; and lo, I am with you always, even to the end of the age.

Matthew 28:18-20

Many Christians recognize these words as the Lord's "Great Commission" to evangelize the lost. This is even as surveys and observation prove this is one of the most neglected commands in the Bible. Some Christians don't even know it's there. And if sermon scarcity means anything, some preachers also share this ignorance.

The early church's mindset on this issue was radically different from our own. The Great Commission was not simply a phrase that was acknowledged and yet disobeyed. Nor was it a command hidden by ignorance. It was a command that totally captured and energized the early Christian community. The command so invaded their minds that it changed their worldview and regulated their actions. Life's agenda was made within the context of obeying the Almighty's command to evangelize the lost and to make disciples.

This level of obedience to God's command didn't just happen. It was the direct and natural result of the preaching, teaching, and examples of the apostles and other church leaders. Unlike many so-called American Christian converts, sinners weren't accepted as Christians simply because they "accepted" certain facts about Christ or said a cheap prayer. To be accepted as Christians, they had to be willing to forsake their sinful lifestyles and to obey the commands of God.

One of those commands was the Great Commission. Jesus had earnestly commanded the apostles to urgently seek the lost. The apostles, in turn, emphasized the task with their Lord's sense of urgency. It resulted in a clarified purpose that took precedence over every other agenda and activity except individual devotion to God.

This consuming urgency in the early Christian community to spread the gospel was one factor that made it so inexpensive for them to do so. Conversely, our acute lack of urgency is one reason why it costs us so much to do so little.

The link between urgent purpose and cost is that a lack of urgency among the community of believers limits the availability of resources for evangelism. Therefore, what should be done quickly by many is now done slowly by only a few. The net effect of this is increased costs to those few Christians who actually do try to win and disciple converts. The cost is in time, money, material, and hospitality.

The early church had the benefit of a divine sense of urgency that compelled them to aggressively evangelize. They also had the benefit of effective prayer and miraculous power.

Effective Prayer and Miraculous Power in the First-Century Church

A strong belief in the power of prayer is another reason it cost the early church dramatically less to evangelize and make disciples. We clearly see this faith in action in several places in the book of Acts.

The religious authorities once arrested the apostles for preaching. They were sternly interrogated and severely threatened to stop preaching in the name of Jesus. Once released, the apostles went back to the church and reported all that had occurred.

This resulted in an immediate prayer meeting that's worthy of discussion. But first a side note.

What do you think of when you hear the term "prayer meeting"? In most of our churches a prayer meeting (if church sponsored prayer meetings are conducted at all) evokes thoughts of half-sleeping, distracted, bored people meeting once a week to go through the motions of talking to God. There are exceptions, but conspicuously absent is the ingredient of fervent emotion.

This absence has nothing to do with ethnicity, race, culture, denomination, or time. Nor does it have anything to do with personal preference. It has everything to do with desperation. Desperate people pray desperate prayers, and desperate prayers are emotional. Our prayer meetings lack emotion because we're not desperate for God. And we won't be desperate for God until we run out of answers.

Back to our first-century church.

These Christians were desperate because of their enemies' threats, but they believed that Jesus meant it when He said, "And whatever things you ask in prayer, believing, you will receive."[21] Therefore, they did not respond to the threats by signing petitions, forming political parties, or—surprise—sending out emergency requests for funds to fight the liberals. In their case it was the conservatives.

These things are not necessarily bad, but they are limited. They can only work where the government allows them to work. Christians in China, Vietnam, North Korea, Indonesia, the Middle East, and other places can't resort to such natural measures without being violently persecuted and even murdered. Prayer is their *only* answer. And prayer was the early church's only answer.

When the government ordered them to stop preaching in the name of Jesus, they prayed and God answered with miracles (Acts 4:23-31). When Peter was asked to pray that a dead woman come back to life, he prayed and God answered with a miracle (Acts 9:36-43). When Peter was thrown into prison and put on death row, the church prayed and God answered with a miracle (Acts 12:1-17). When Paul and Silas were beaten and thrown into prison, they prayed and God answered with a miracle (Acts 16:16-26).

The point of recounting these answers to prayer is not to insinuate that every prayer is answered immediately or with miracles. Rather it is to show how the early church relied on the power of prayer. They had a culture of dependence upon God, and that dependence produced miracles.

What does this mean for us? We can learn from their example. God has no favorites. Whatever He has done for the early church, He can and will do for the present church—for free.

Three Thousand Men Saved in a Day

The second chapter of Acts records an event that makes my mouth water. It's an example of successful evangelism that required not a single tithe or offering. Peter preached and 3,000 people turned to Jesus Christ and were baptized in water. Perhaps even more fascinating is "they continued steadfastly in the apostles' doctrine and fellowship, in the breaking of bread, and in praying" (vs. 42). In other words, these people didn't just pray a prayer and continue in rebellion against God, as so many of our so-called converts do. Instead they fully integrated into and committed to the church and its radical countercultural beliefs and behavior.

We do not have to wonder in confused awe at how such a thing could happen. All we have to do is read Acts 1-2.

In Acts 1 Jesus told the disciples that they would receive supernatural power from the Holy Spirit once He came upon them (vs. 8). After this promise, He ascended to heaven as they watched (vs. 9). They returned to Jerusalem and prayed and worshipped without ceasing as they waited for the Holy Spirit (vs. 12-14).

In Acts 2:1-4, the Holy Spirit interrupted their prayer meeting:

And suddenly there came a sound from heaven, as of a rushing mighty wind, and it filled the whole house where they were sitting. Then there appeared to them divided tongues, as of fire, and one sat upon each of them. And they were all filled with the Holy Spirit and began to speak with other tongues, as the Spirit gave them utterance.

Later, in Acts 2:38-40, it says:

Peter said to them, 'Repent, and let every one of you be baptized in the name of Jesus Christ for the remission of sins; and you shall receive the gift of the Holy Spirit. For the promise is to you and to your children, and to all who are afar off, as many as the Lord our God will call.' And with many other words he testified and exhorted them, saying, 'Be saved from this perverse generation.

Let's take note of the things that led to the 3,000 being saved, as well as the financial cost.

First, the disciples encountered the living Christ.

Second, the disciples received specific directions from God.

Third, the disciples watched Christ ascend into heaven.

Fourth, the disciples obeyed Christ and went to Jerusalem to wait for the promise of the Holy Spirit.

Fifth, the disciples were unquestionably baptized in the Holy Spirit and spoke in tongues.

Sixth, the disciples preached a gospel that consisted of radical repentance, immediate water baptism, and compulsory baptism of the Holy Spirit.

The result of this was that "those who gladly received his [Peter's] word were baptized; and that day about three thousand souls were added to them" (Acts 2:41).

This evangelistic event was phenomenal. It exceeded the wildest expectations. But what did it cost? The church must have spent a lot of money to get these kinds of results, right? Well, let's see. How much did it cost to encounter Christ? Nothing. How much did it cost to receive specific directions from God? Nothing. How much did it cost to obey God and go to Jerusalem? Nothing. How much did it cost to have a prayer meeting? Nothing. How much did it cost to be baptized in the Holy Spirit? Nothing. How much did it cost to preach to the crowd on the day of Pentecost? Nothing.

How is it that the early church could win 3,000 people to the Lord without spending one dollar or *denarii*? Acts 1-2 teaches us that when we encounter Christ, hear His voice clearly, see His ascension into heaven, obey His voice, pray without ceasing, receive the Holy Spirit, and preach the true gospel, we will have extraordinary results, without spending unnecessary money. Consequently, this minimizes the need to manipulate or pressure people into giving.

The Church Grows Daily

The church's evangelistic success of converting 3,000 people was not a one-day wonder. This level of success occurred so frequently it became normal. Yet the church did not depend primarily on special events for its growth. Instead it relied on routine Christian activities. These activities put into motion natural and spiritual forces that led to this: "And the Lord added to the church daily those who were being saved" (Acts 2:47).

According to Acts 2:42-47, there were several things going on in the early Jerusalem church that facilitated its growth. As we stated before, the new converts "continued steadfastly in the apostles' doctrine and fellowship, in the breaking of bread, and in prayers" (vs. 42). This signifies a strong sense of community, devotion, and leadership. Irrespective of denominations, these are dynamics that today's church universally accepts as desirable.

But there are other dynamics mentioned in the Acts narrative that are both painfully absent from the church, and yet surprisingly not desired by it. For instance, "Then fear came upon every soul, and many wonders and signs were done through the apostles (vs. 43).

Integral to the church's growth was the routine display of the power of God through signs, miracles, wonders, and gifts of the Holy Spirit. These are the absent, neglected, and even despised manifestations of God that the early church had in abundance, but that we rarely experience.

God has rarely left Himself without a witness. So we have had intermittent displays of His power through various people and ministries. Unfortunately, these displays have been (and presently are) rare, weak, and polluted by flesh. Therefore, our church experiences and evangelistic efforts are without the benefit of a culture of miracles. We are forced to believe what we don't experience and to preach what we can't demonstrate. Our deficit of the miraculous makes the church significantly less desirable to the world. This exponentially increases the financial cost of winning people to Christ.

This was not so in the early church. Its small and large meetings, whether planned or spontaneous, were blessed with demonstrations of God's power and mercy through supernatural signs, miracles, healings, and deliverances from demons.[22]

The combination of intense community and supernatural power proved irresistibly attractive. In such an atmosphere, God found it relatively easy to add "to the church daily those who were being saved" (Acts 2:47). We must note that the attractiveness of the church was not because of money, but of routine Christian activities, such as love, faith, and prayer.

Here we see a perfect example of Christians acting as "workers together with Him [God]" (2 Corinthians 6:1). They did what Christians are commanded to do irrespective of country, culture, or time: fervently love one another and have faith in God. For God's part, He did what He always does when He sees a church doing this. He supernaturally blessed its efforts and increased its size.

Five Thousand Men Saved in a Day

How much money would it take us to win 5,000 people to the Lord? Peter and John did it without spending one dollar. In Acts 3:6-9, Peter and John were on their way to the temple to pray. On the way they passed by a crippled man who asked them for money. Peter's response and actions provide exciting possibilities for the church:

> Then Peter said, "Silver and gold I do not have, but what I do have I give you: In the name of Jesus Christ of Nazareth, rise up and walk."
>
> And he took him by the right hand and lifted him up, and immediately his feet and ankle bones received strength.
>
> So he, leaping up, stood and walked and entered the temple with them—walking, leaping, and praising God.
>
> And all the people saw him walking and praising God.

This miracle of healing caused 5,000 people to come to Christ.[23] The dynamics of this event are timeless and universal. It is possible to follow Peter's example and to experience similar results. Here are brief highlights of the event:

Peter was asked for money. Like so many preachers, the apostle was confronted with an immediate and genuine need that could apparently be satisfied with money.

Peter didn't have any money. Again, like so many preachers, he didn't have funds to meet the need.

Peter was keenly aware of his spiritual assets. Here is where Peter was unmistakably different from the typical preacher. He didn't limit himself to money. Instead he viewed his faith in Christ as a spiritual currency that could supernaturally meet needs, even needs that money could not help.

Peter reclassifies the need. As the late John Osteen, founder of Lakewood Church, said, "The man asked for alms and got legs." The beggar had asked for money and instead received a miracle of healing. This resulted from Peter's ability to reclassify an "apparent" need to a "true" need. The apparent need was money; the real need was healing. Presumably, the crippling condition is what caused the man to beg. When the condition was removed, the man's need to beg was removed.

Peter used his faith to meet the impossible need. All the faith in the world is meaningless if not used. In fact, if it isn't used, the Bible doesn't recognize it as faith.[24] Peter's faith had action, as all true faith does. He didn't just say, "God bless you," and continue walking. Instead he gave the man a command of faith and pulled him up to his feet.

An apostle performed this miracle, but there is no reason to limit to apostles the possibilities of dramatic answers to prayer. Furthermore, I know that some Christian sects are more comfortable with miracles than others. Yet the example reveals things that can benefit all Christians, irrespective of their backgrounds.

First, we should note that an indisputable miracle in a Christian context has the potential to generate evangelistic momentum and results that our best and most expensive efforts fail to do. But we must also note that a miracle by itself is only a miracle. Miracles don't turn people to God. Neither do they make faithful disciples. They simply demonstrate God's power and compassion. Either directly or indirectly, the miracle must be closely reinforced with a corresponding message of repentance. The message has eternal preeminence over the miracle. But the miracle often opens the door for the message.

Second, we're often faced with situations that apparently can be fixed with more money. Peter could have flipped the beggar a coin or two and met his need. But would the need have truly been met? When we write our checks to meet needs, are we really meeting needs? Or are we simplistically dealing with symptoms instead of causes? The beggar's symptom was his poverty; the cause of his poverty was his crippled feet. We have created a multi-billion dollar religious industry that majors in symptoms and minors in causes.

If we follow the example of Peter, we will learn to let the Holy Spirit influence our response to apparent needs. We shouldn't be too quick to flip beggars coins, so to speak. Money is often not the answer, even when it appears to be. There may be a better way to meet the need. Peter's method of obeying the Holy Spirit instead of obeying man both met the man's true need and increased the church by 5,000 in one day.

Third, the miracle of healing didn't just happen; it was *worked*. This distinguishes it from a miracle that is performed solely by God. Miracles can be performed by God alone or by God's use of a person. If the miracle had been performed by God alone, there would have been no involvement by Peter. This miracle, however, required the participation of a person, as did many in the book of Acts. Actually, some people are so often characteristically used by God to perform miracles that the Bible calls them workers of miracles.[25]

But we do not have to be specially called to a ministry of miracles to participate in the miraculous. This is based on the premise that answered prayer, whether spectacular or not, is a miracle. And we all can and should regularly experience answered prayer.

We finish this section by noting that the miracle of the crippled man happened because Peter worked with God to perform it. It is reasonable then for us to conclude that many miracles are not accomplished because we fail to work with God to bring them to pass. Who knows? Some of these unworked miracles are no doubt provisions of money, buildings, land, equipment, favor, and most important, wisdom. Every unworked miracle puts more unnecessary pressure on religious middlemen to put unnecessary pressure on us for more money.

More Examples of Inexpensive But Effective Evangelism

There are many more examples in the book of Acts of extremely effective evangelism that were financially inexpensive. What follows are shortened but helpful observations of these examples.[26]

The Number of the Disciples Multiplied Greatly in Jerusalem

Acts 6:7 says, "Then the word of God spread, and the number of the disciples multiplied greatly in Jerusalem, and a great many of the priests were obedient to the faith."

Jews are perhaps some of the hardest people in the world to reach for Christ. But here we're told that not only were common Jews converting to Christ in record numbers, but great numbers of priests had come to the Lord! How many hundreds of thousands of dollars did this special outreach to Jewish leaders cost? How much did the special literature cost? How much did the radio time cost? How much did it cost to set up the Jerusalem Television Broadcasting Network? By now you know the answer—not a single dollar.

Multitudes Come to Christ in Samaria

Acts 8:5-6 says, "Then Philip went down to the city of Samaria and preached Christ to them. And the multitudes with one accord heeded the things spoken by Philip, hearing and seeing the miracles which he did."

Here's an extremely successful evangelistic endeavor that won multitudes of Samaritans to Christ. It is especially enlightening that it was performed by one man without the benefit of planning or coordination. This seems like a guarantee for failure. So why did Philip succeed? The multitudes accepted his message because of the miracles he worked in their midst.

Okay, here's my favorite question again. How much did this cost? The only possible costs I see are for food and lodging. Philip would have eaten whether he was in Jerusalem or Samaria. So really we can discount the cost of food. And there is a good possibility that Philip was offered free lodging in the home of one of his new converts. But even if he paid for his lodging, that's a small amount to pay for winning a city to Jesus.

A sad observation is that most of the church no longer believes in the manifest power of God. So we rely on our natural assets to do what Philip did supernaturally. We would have tried to win Samaria through non-miracle means: education, money, and traditional church services. This dependence on the natural instead of the supernatural would have dramatically increased the amount of money spent on Samaritan evangelism.

Ironically, experience proves that more money spent does not mean more souls saved. So if experience means anything, we can reasonably conclude that our way of evangelism is (I believe needlessly) more complicated, more expensive, and yet less effective than the early church's method of evangelism.

Two Towns Won to the Lord

Our next example of early church evangelism is in Acts 9:35, "So all who dwelt at Lydda and Sharon saw him and turned to the Lord." Here two towns came to the Lord because Peter healed a paralyzed man. The credibility and immediacy of the miracle caused widespread publicity that cost no money.

Joppa is Evangelized

Acts 9:42 says, "And it became known throughout all Joppa, and many believed on the Lord." The "it" spoken of here was a miracle of Peter raising Dorcas, a faithful disciple, from the dead. News of the outstanding miracle spread and many people came to the Lord. How many, we are not told. But "many" sounds good to me.

A comparison of Peter's miracles of raising Dorcas from the dead, and of his miracle of healing the paralyzed man in the preceding town, reveal an important strategic truth. Raising someone from the dead is obviously a greater miracle than healing a paralyzed person. So why did the healing of the paralyzed man cause two towns to turn to Christ, but the greater miracle of raising the dead caused only "many" to come to Christ?

I believe the issue lies in credibility and publicity. The paralyzed man had been bedridden for eight years. But the dead woman had apparently been dead for only a day or so. Everyone knew about the paralyzed man; his condition had been observed for eight long years. This was not the prop of some unethical evangelist.

Conversely, the death of Dorcas could be debated. She had only been dead a short while. Few people knew of her death. And perhaps she had never died at all. Maybe this was a trick of the Christians to help grow their new religion!

Therefore, from this evangelistic incident we learn that the credibility of a miracle affects its ability to promote the gospel. A miracle that can be validated under the severest scrutiny may potentially win large numbers of people to the Lord. Lesser miracles that may be debated are more limited in their evangelistic use. Nonetheless, both types cost no money and should be aggressively worked by the church.

Closing Remarks on Evangelism in the Book of Acts

We could list many other examples of evangelism in the book of Acts, but they would simply restate what we have already noted. The church grew like a weed fertilized with Miracle Grow primarily because of its culture of purpose, prayer, and power. Its culture made it unnecessary to trust in man-made methods of evangelism. Their trust in and obedience to God rather than human ingenuity resulted in multitudes coming to Christ in a very short time at minimal or no financial cost.

My conclusion is that we have rejected the church culture of the first century and are suffering the consequences. If we return to the biblical pattern of evangelism—purpose, prayer, and power— we will share in the evangelistic success of the first century.[27] This success will cost us next to nothing in terms of dollars. But it will cost us a tremendous amount in prayer, fasting, faith, love, and a total and absolute abandonment of our habit of replacing God's wisdom for man's wisdom.

Conversely, if we continue to embrace our wisdom and ways above God's wisdom and ways, we will continue to need great sums of money to finance our spiritual weakness. The fleshly answer to this self-inflicted problem is unqualified cash flow, our baby, the financial tithe.

CHAPTER 7

The Creation and Rise of the Financial Tithe

R are is the tither who knows the history of the farce of the modern financial tithe. It is like the theory of evolution—a lie told by so many for so long in so many ways, we accept it as true. To question its truthfulness is to admit to idiocy. Similarly, to question the tithe's truthfulness is to admit to thievery. Yet both lies, evolution and tithing, require a suspension of common sense to believe, a determination to believe what can't possibly be true, like believing the world is flat in the age of satellites. But the financial tithe requires even more than does evolution for its existence. It requires ignorance of its history.

Where Did the Financial Tithe Come From?

As the Church expanded and various institutions arose, it became necessary to make laws which would insure the proper and permanent support of the clergy. The payment of tithes was adopted from the Old Law... The earliest positive legislation on the subject seems to be contained in the letter of the bishops assembled at Tours in 567 and the [canons] of the Council of Macon in 585.

The Catholic Encyclopedia

"...to make laws which would insure the proper and permanent support of the clergy." This single sentence pulls back the sheets and allows us a full disgusting view of the financial tithe's dark night of incestuous conception. Our silent wonderings and whispered misgivings are finally answered. We understand clearly now why there is such a shocking discrepancy in the beauty of the Father and the ugliness of the child.

God is not the Father.

The tithe is a bastard.[28]

It's the illegitimate offspring of a religious bureaucracy that impregnated itself and later claimed God as its child's Father.

This accusation stings not because it's irreverent, but because it's true. Biblical doctrine and history, as well as secular history, irrefutably deny divine creation of the financial tithe. The above information comes from the records of the organization that created the financial tithe—the Roman Catholic Church.

It is to the Catholic Church's credit that they admit to creating the financial tithe several hundred years after the birth of the Christian church to support its growing bureaucracy and army of professional preachers. They can afford to be this stunningly honest because their religion is foundationally based on the belief that Catholic Church decrees and tradition are equal to, and often superior to, the Bible.

Protestant churches, however, believe the Bible is the Word of God, and nothing supersedes it—or at least that is our official position.[29] It is critical, therefore, to the integrity of this position that we be convinced that the financial tithe is God's child, and not the product of a room full of shrewd bishops.[30] For the moment the truth is known, that the financial tithe was birthed by man and not God, our tithe preachers will be judged as frauds and manipulators, or perhaps less sinister, but no less dangerous, as sincere, but ignorant teachers of lies.

Evolution of the Tithe

It is one thing to create a financial tithe; it is quite another to justify and enforce it. A short representative survey of church practice and eminent leadership sentiment in the early church on tithing and giving will help you understand the development of this lie.

Justin Martyr

Justin Martyr (A.D. 100-165) was a Christian apologist and martyr who courageously challenged the Roman government in his writings for its persecution of Christians. One of his books, First Apology of Justin, Section 67, describes in detail a typical Christian meeting. Here's what he said about collecting money:

> And they who are well to do, and willing, give what each thinks fit; and what is collected is deposited with the president, who succours the orphans and widows and those who, through sickness or any other cause, are in want, and those who are in bonds and the strangers sojourning among us, and in a word takes care of all who are in need.

Notice that it is the "well to do" who willingly gave to the common treasury for those less fortunate. This was given according to "what each thinks fit." Conspicuously absent is a legalistic command to give a certain percentage of income.

Tertullian

Tertullian was the brilliant apologist and defender of the faith against the heresy of Gnosticism.[31] His writings (Apology, Section 39) give us a glimpse of third-century fundraising, and its purpose:

> Though we have our treasure-chest, it is not made up of purchase-money, as of a religion that has its price. On the monthly day, if he likes, each puts in a small donation; but only if it be his pleasure, and only if he be able: for there is no compulsion; all is voluntary. These gifts are, as it were, piety's deposit fund. For they are not taken thence and spent on feasts, and drinking-bouts, and eating-houses, but to support and bury poor people, to supply the wants of boys and girls destitute of means and parents, and of old persons confined now to the house; such, too, as

have suffered shipwreck; and if there happen to be any in the mines, or banished to the islands, or shut up in the prisons, for nothing but their fidelity to the cause of God's Church, they become the nurslings of their confession.

Here is an example of beautiful and simple Christianity before it morphed into an ugly religious organization that disproportionately sucks money into the bottomless pit of clergy salaries and administrative expenses. Christians voluntarily gave small donations each month into a general fund to help those in dire need. Quite dissimilar to our practice of legalistically pressuring people into giving, this church taught a person to give "only if it be his pleasure, and only if he be able: for there is no compulsion; all is voluntary."

Bishop Cyprian of Carthage

Bishop Cyprian (A.D. 200-258) represents those early church leaders who did not advocate the tithe, but who strongly believed the clergy should be involved in no worldly activities that would encroach on its ability to serve the church. Of course, this belief, noble as it was, was used in later years by others to create and demand a financial tithe. That's one reason why we're including it here.

In 249 A.D. he explained that "every one honoured by the divine priesthood, and ordained in the clerical service, ought to serve only the altar and sacrifices, and to have leisure for prayers and supplications." [32]

Cyprian's letter uses the Levites as an example for ministers who are able to devote their full attention to the ministry of the church, which he considered to be prayers and supplications:

> ...the Levitical tribe, which was left free for the temple and the altar, and for the divine ministries, received nothing from that portion of the division; [the allocation of the land of Canaan among the tribes of Israel once they crossed the Jordan river with Joshua] but while others cultivated the soil, that portion [the Levites] only cultivated the favour of God, and received the tithes from the eleven tribes, for their food and

maintenance, from the fruits which grew. All which was done by divine authority and arrangement, so that they who waited on divine services might in no respect be called away, nor be compelled to consider or to transact secular business. Which plan and rule is now maintained in respect of the clergy, that they who are promoted by clerical ordination in the Church of the Lord may be called off in no respect from the divine administration, nor be tied down by worldly anxieties and matters; but in the honour of the brethren who contribute, receiving as it were tenths of the fruits, they may not withdraw from the altars and sacrifices, but may serve day and night in heavenly and spiritual things.

A careful reading of Cyprian's short letter reveals that its subject is not the Old Testament tithe, the modern financial tithe, or even financial support of the clergy.[33] It is the ideal of church sponsored clergy taking care of the church without distractions. Cyprian mentions the model of the Levites solely for this purpose, and not to encourage a financial tithe.

It is important to correct this error because Cyprian's letter has been cited by many anti-tithers as his attempt to support the clergy with financial tithes. This mistake gives the appearance that there was a credible effort to introduce the new tithe system a hundred years before bishops began to do so.[34]

The sentence in Cyprian's letter from where this idea comes doesn't support this view:

> ...but in the honour of the brethren who contribute, receiving as it were tenths of the fruits, they may not withdraw from the altars and sacrifices, but may serve day and night in heavenly and spiritual things.

Cyprian states that the clergy was supported "by the brethren who contribute," and that this was "as it were tenths of the fruits." *As it were* is a simile, "a figure of speech in which two dissimilar things are compared by the use of *like* or *as*."[35] The bishop was stating simply that freewill contributions given to support the clergy and tithes given to support Levites were similar in this manner: the object was to provide modest financial assistance so they could fulfill their leadership duties without distraction.[36]

It is significant that such a fervent and focused leader (and future martyr) should rely on freewill contributions to fulfill his clergy obligations instead of demanding money through a new tithe system.[37] If it were possible for him, why is it not possible for us?

Slide Towards the Tithe

I suppose the slide towards a financial tithe system in the early church was inevitable, human nature being what it is. On one hand, a mandatory system of church taxation in the name of God would be far more reliable and profitable than freewill offerings. Good shepherds with good intentions would be guaranteed unqualified cash flow while they devoted themselves to caring for the church and preaching the gospel. Thus their personal needs and spiritual obligations and ambitions would be predictably supported. Similarly, bad shepherds would benefit by not having to work as hard to extract money from their followers. The tax system's built-in promises of blessings for tithers and curses for non-tithers would do the work for them. Thus good preachers and bad had strong money motives to create and vigorously push the financial tithe myth.

Not surprisingly the seeds of deceptive systems of fundraising were already growing even in the first-century church. The apostles constantly complained and warned of this danger. Paul said, "For we are not, as so many, peddling the word of God...." (2 Corinthians 2:17). And Peter added, "...there will be false teachers among you... by covetousness they will exploit you with deceptive words" (2 Peter 2:1, 3).

The apostles' first-century concern that money-minded preachers were using, and would continue to use, the Word of God to exploit Christians far exceeded their worst fears. In those days the danger was obscure traveling preachers who operated on the edges of Christianity. They'd come into town and dazzle the audience with oratory, deep and mysterious revelations, and tales of spiritual conquest. Inevitably, (as it is today) this performance would end with the preacher's hand in someone's pocket.

A few hundred years later, however, the danger of financial molestation had evolved from veiled assaults committed in the dark by scorned individual strangers to blatant attacks committed in the light by respected institutional friends. In other words, the church began to rape its own.

Gleaning from the research of David Croteau, Ph.D., creator of the blog, *Slave of the Word,* several bishops during the late fourth century argued for mandatory financial tithes: Hilary of Poitiers (366), Basil of Caesarea (370), Ambrose (374), Chrysostom (375), Jerome (385), and Augustine (400). As our earlier *Catholic Encyclopedia* reference mentions, these individual requests for financial tithes grew into a unified demand from the clergy at the Council of Tours in 567 and the Second Council of Macon in 585.[38]

The church by this time was no longer a despised minority religion violently persecuted by governors and emperors. In 313 A.D. Emperor Constantine of the Western Roman Empire, and Emperor Licinius of the Eastern Roman Empire, jointly issued the *Edict of Milan,* a decree of religious toleration. This took the church off the enemy of the state list and granted it civil rights. Its confiscated property was returned, and Christians were then free to participate in the mainstream of Roman society without fear.

In fact, Constantine, who became sole ruler of the Roman Empire in 324 until he died in 337, became a great champion and defender of the church. He financially supported the church, built it great buildings in which to worship, and passed civil laws that both removed its shame and favored its clergy. Naturally this attracted multitudes of new church members. In fact, the church grew in such numbers and popularity that in 380 Emperor Theodosius I declared Catholic Christianity the state religion.[39] Thus the church and the empire formally became one.

Holy Bureaucracy

For three hundred years prior to Theodosius I, the Christian church had been decaying from simplicity to complexity, from spiritual equality to political hierarchy, from a family of life to an organization of death. So its marriage to the empire was natural and inevitable. It was also natural and inevitable that complexity, hierarchy, and organization should produce an expensive bureaucracy.[40]

The Catholic Church, as it now declared itself, developed a religious system of bishops and priests to stand between the people and God. This requires lots of cash, especially when tastes are fine and hearts are greedy.[41]

The organization required buildings in which to conduct religious services. This requires lots of cash, especially when buildings are numerous and extravagant.

For nearly 1200 years, the Catholic Church's bureaucracy was supported by government grants and extorted tithes, a mixture of favor and fear. Grants were always dependent on the financial state of the empire. Fear, however, was constant. One had to pay tithes to the Catholic Church or else.

Or else *what?*

Two threats kept the cash coming.

First, *religious superstition*. The Catholic Church claimed power to deny heaven to anyone who refused to tithe. You're laughing, aren't you? You little heathen. How do you know God didn't give veto power to the Catholic Church? He could've stationed a bishop at the gates of heaven to check financial records one last time to prevent non-tithers from sneaking their selfish behinds into glory.[42] But who would believe such foolishness?

Remember that we're talking about a time when most Europeans couldn't read. And even if they could, it wouldn't have helped much. The printing press had not yet been invented.[43] Consequently, Bibles were written by hand and were extremely expensive and rare.

Second, *civil authority*. Bishops had been complaining for nearly two hundred years that Christians should pay tithes.[44] But their complaints had been primarily to their congregations and to one another. Responses to these grievances were mixed. Some Christians yielded and it appears most did not. That's why in the Council of Tours in 567 and the Second Council of Macon in 585 bishops were still complaining that Christians didn't tithe.

A couple of hundred years later, however, a new era of civil enforcement of tithes emerged. In *Monastic Tithes: From Their Origins to the Twelfth Century*, Giles Constable quotes a (c. 765 A.D.) letter from Frankish King Pepin the Short to Bishop Lull: "You shall so provide and ordain on our authority that everyone, willy-nilly, must pay his tithe."

Willy-nilly. I like that.

After the king's death, his son, King Charlemagne, followed the precedent by commanding in his 779 A.D. capitulary of Heristal that Christians in his kingdom must pay tithes.[45] Subsequent European rulers passed similar laws. As Christianity spread over Europe, and as the church grew politically stronger, it became almost impossible to resist its demand for tithes. Nonetheless, throughout history many individuals and groups rebelled against this extortion. But it was not until the Protestant Reformation that its continuance was seriously threatened.

The Reformation

The Reformation is the name given the 16th century international religious and political rebellion against the Catholic Church. Its official birthday is commonly recognized as October 31, 1517. On this day, Martin Luther, the father of the Reformation, nailed his Ninety-Five Theses to the door of a university building. Luther's theses accused the Catholic Church of widespread corruption. The reformer's eloquent words and tireless preaching against much of Catholicism inspired far-reaching social, political, and religious revolutions of mixed results. Luther and the Reformation brought progress and decline, liberty and bondage, life and death.

European nations had always been quite gifted in finding the slightest reasons to declare war on themselves or their neighbors. The Reformation was too good an opportunity to not use it as an excuse to hurt or kill somebody. Peasant rebellions, and civil and national wars, ravaged Europe for the next 150 years.[46] These bloody conflicts determined whether Catholicism would continue its historic stranglehold, or be replaced by the new religious kid on the block, *Protestantism*.

The Catholic Church lost many of its military and political battles. This led to many nations declaring religious declarations of independence from Catholicism, so to speak. Germany, Switzerland, the Netherlands, Denmark, Sweden, England, and other nations rejected the Catholic Church for one of the many new non-Catholic Christian denominations.[47] The pope's power to impose or manipulate the Catholic Church's will on others was forever compromised or stopped entirely.

From the Church of England to the American Tithe

King Henry VIII politically severed England from the Catholic Church in 1534 and declared himself "the only Supreme Head in Earth of the Church of England."[48] But this was done primarily because Pope Clement had refused to grant the adulterous king a divorce so he could dump his wife for a young babe. Consequently, substantive religious reform didn't occur until his son, King Edward, ruled. But once death ended the teenager's seven-year, pro-Protestant reign, the fanatically Catholic Queen Mary reimposed Catholicism in the kingdom. These reforms were similarly gutted and replaced by newer, permanent Protestant reforms when death claimed her wretched soul after a bloody six-year reign.

Nonetheless, the eventual demise of Catholicism in England and ascendancy of Protestantism did not end religious strife in the nation. Englanders weren't content to kick the pope's hat down the street. Now many of them turned their restless agitation to Protestant infighting.

The pressing argument was who was the true champion of anti-Catholic religion? Whose brand of Christian religion was free of Catholic influence? Was it the Anglicans? The Congregationalists? According to one sizeable and fanatically energized influential group, the so-called Puritans, King James I (1603-1625) and King Charles I (1625-1649) were compromisers of the Protestant faith.

Puritans denounced the government as a pawn of the pope and generally made the king's life miserable. As might be expected, he made their lives more miserable. This prompted many of them (and others) to leave England for America—a land where they could practice religion free of Catholic influence, and not be persecuted for doing so.

American Religion without Tithes

The Catholic tithe in Europe proved its resilience and survived the Reformation. But would it survive the trip across the Atlantic Ocean?

Surprisingly, anti-pope/anti-Catholic sentiment appears to have been deep enough to cast the tithe overboard on the journey. Yet even more surprisingly, at least to my 21st-century American mind, is that the settlers overwhelmingly established local government churches. But I guess this is understandable. They did have a heritage of 1400 years of government religion under the Catholic Church, and most recently the Church of England.

Religion historian and dean of the divinity school at Vanderbilt University, James Hudnut-Beumler, states that "As the Revolution began [1775], ten of the original thirteen states had some form of tax-supported religion."[49] He further states:

> During the nearly two centuries while religion was understood by early Euro-Americans as a public good deserving public support, a variety of means to finance religion evolved, much as a hodgepodge of user fees, licenses, and taxes is used to this day to pay for public goods...In the case of religion, there were poll and property taxes, which could be quite high....[50]

Bill of Rights Kicks Religion off Public Welfare

The First Amendment of the U.S. Constitution says, "Congress shall make no law respecting an establishment of religion...." This 1791 law slowly but irresistibly dried the financial stream that once flowed from local governments to church budgets. Preachers and churches, therefore, had to create new systems of fundraising.

Dr. James Hudnut-Beumler describes in well documented detail the evolution of new religious fundraising.[51] The process went from receiving taxes to renting pews to asking for offerings to demanding tithes.[52] So the church in America that left the Church of England because it looked too much like the Church of Rome became a Protestant version of the Church of Rome.

This amazing departure from truth and freedom, and return to lies and bondage, required religious cunning and creativity—it still does. But cunning and creativity are two things tithe preachers have in abundance. Yet this abundance birthed by financial necessity is no match for spiritual truth and common sense. Or is it?

The Firstfruits Scam

Some of the most ridiculous, blatant, and heartless money grabs of tithe preachers come in the form of the firstfruits scam. The basic premise of the scam is that in addition to the tithe, God requires us to give tithe preachers an offering called the firstfruits offering. Yeah, you read that right. Ten percent of our gross income for life is not enough. We also have to give—better yet, pay—a mandatory offering.

Well, you say, I'll just give a little something and get the preacher off of my back. Uhhh, it's not that easy. You see, this particular offering has a set of variable rules that you must follow. What kinds of rules? Well, here again, it's not that simple as listing the rules. The reason is the rules vary with the preacher you serve. Some say this; some say that.

Some require an annual firstfruit offering. Some require it when unbudgeted bills are due. Some require one to celebrate the pastor's birthday, or the pastor's wife's birthday, or the pastor's anniversary, or the pastor and his wife's wedding anniversary, or whatever else they can dream up.

How much is this offering? I don't know why you keep asking these trick questions. This varies, too. Some preachers use the term tithe and firstfruits interchangeably, and some say it's an additional offering. (If you're going to go for bondage, I suggest you follow a preacher who uses the term interchangeably. At least this way, you satisfy the demands of the tithe and firstfruit with the same ten percent of your income.)

What makes this a scam is the money grab is done in the name of obeying a mandate from Almighty God via His number one representative, the preacher. Obey the preacher's unique interpretation of the firstfruit requirement and God will bless you. Don't obey the preacher and God will curse you.

I have not chosen to deal directly with this scam in length in this book. It's unnecessary. Virtually everything I say about the tithe applies to the firstfruit scam. Others, however, have given more direct and comprehensive attention to it in their books.[53]

Nonetheless, there are three things I want to briefly bring to your attention regarding the firstfruit offering error. First, like the tithe, the firstfruit offering is not money. It's an edible item.[54] Second, the terms firstfruit offering and tithe are not interchangeable. They have different meanings that will only lead you into irreconcilable confusion if you try to consistently use one word in the place of the other.[55] Third, the firstfruit offering is representatively defined, but not quantitatively defined in the Bible.[56] Attempts to place numerical values on the firstfruit offering are fleshly assumptions.

CHAPTER 8

Answers to Pre-Law Arguments for Mandatory New Testament Tithes

T ithes and offerings are only understood and appreciated when discussed in their proper contexts. There are three periods of time that comprise the various contexts: pre-law, law, and post-law. Each of the three has its own definitions and criteria for tithes and offerings.

The Old Testament provides a view of voluntary and mandatory tithes and offerings. Moses introduced to the Jews a comprehensive system of giving to God that included mandatory and voluntary giving. That system is exclusively in the books of Exodus, Leviticus, Numbers, and Deuteronomy. These four books are known as the law of Moses.

Israel's economic foundation was built on the law. So tithes and offerings were as ingrained in their society as taxes are ingrained in ours. Actually, their system of tithes and offerings was similar to the American tax system. That will be discussed later. Right now let's look at tithes and offerings before the law.

The Offerings of Cain and Abel

The first Bible record we have of someone giving an offering to God is in Genesis 4:2-7:

> Now Abel was a keeper of sheep, but Cain was a tiller of the ground. And in the process of time it came to pass that Cain brought an offering of the fruit of the ground to the Lord. Abel also brought of the firstborn of his flock and of their fat. And the Lord respected Abel and his offering, but He did not respect Cain and his offering. And Cain was very angry, and his countenance fell. So the Lord said to Cain, "Why are you angry? And why has your countenance fallen? If you do well, will you not be accepted? And if you do not do well, sin lies at the door. And its desire is for you, but you should rule over it.

This incident records the offerings of Cain and Abel, the first and second sons of Adam and Eve. Both brothers offered something to God, but only one brother's offering was accepted. Much can be learned from this example.

First, there is no record that God demanded an offering of the brothers. It is true that the law has many mandatory offerings. But this incident occurred 2,500 years before the law and was not under its authority. Since the Bible is silent about any so-called rules of giving during that period, it is clearly wrong for preachers to arbitrarily fill in the blanks with their own desires.

Second, the brothers gave to God what they possessed. This is no trivial observation. Preachers normally state that Cain was rejected of God because he offered something that came from the ground; while Abel's offering was accepted because he offered a blood sacrifice. Here we must emphasize that God's timeless and boundaryless characteristic is that He only requires what we have, not what we don't have: *"For if there is first a willing mind, it is accepted according to what one has, and not according to what he does not have"* (1 Corinthians 8:12). This point is mentioned because "Cain was a tiller of the ground" and "Abel was a keeper of sheep."

We shouldn't read too much into what they gave. They gave their respective offerings because that is what they had. Cain didn't have any sheep and Abel didn't have any carrots. But neither was penalized for not offering the gift of the other. Similarly, Cain was not rejected because he was a farmer and not a shepherd. His problem was far more serious than having the wrong occupation.

Third, Cain's offering was rejected because he was rejected. *"But He did not respect Cain and his offering."* The offering is linked to the person. If the person is rejected, the offering is rejected.

This is a timeless concept that few preachers acknowledge and even fewer preach. But much of our tithes and offerings, though accepted by man, are rejected by God.[57] I say this because the foundation of mandatory tithes and offerings is fear, obligation, and greed. Of course, many people give to God for the right reasons. Yet I believe (and I hope that I'm wrong, but I think not) that the majority of tithers do so primarily because the preacher tells us either directly or indirectly that we better do it or else.

If we give in fear, the offering is extortion. If we give under compulsion, the offering is obligation. If we give to get, the offering is manipulation. What a sad day it will be at the Judgment when many will see their gifts judged deficient because they gave wrongly.

The Tithe of Abraham

Preachers often tell us that we are obligated to pay tithes to them because Abraham paid tithes. It is true that Abraham gave tithes, but it is false that his example establishes tithing as either an Old or New Testament rule. Actually, the example teaches more against mandatory tithing than for it. Let's look to the scriptures instead of to the opinions of those who benefit most from mandatory tithing—preachers.

When Abraham's nephew, Lot, was taken as a prisoner of war by an invading army, Abraham raised an army and rescued him. When Abraham returned from the battle, he was met by the kings of Sodom and Salem:

So he brought back all the goods, and also brought back his brother Lot and his goods, as well as the women and the people. And the king of Sodom went out to meet him at the Valley of Shaveh (that is, the King's Valley), after his return from the defeat of Chedorlaomer and the kings who were with him. Then Melchizedek king of Salem brought out bread and wine; he was the priest of God Most High. And he blessed him and said: "Blessed be Abram of God Most High, Possessor of heaven and earth; And blessed be God Most High, Who has delivered your enemies into your hand." And he [Abram] gave him a tithe of all.

Genesis 14:16-20

There is no way to get around the fact that Abraham paid a tithe. But let's see if his example is binding upon us. If you read the first 13 chapters of the Bible, you will notice that tithing isn't mentioned. In fact, Genesis 14 is the first time we see it. Furthermore, the law of Moses was not given for more than 400 years later. So mandatory tithes and offerings were several hundred years away. Nonetheless, advocates of mandatory tithes and offerings still illogically see this example of one man's gratitude as another man's obligation. Hopefully, the following review will successfully undermine their unfounded assumptions.

For the record, Abraham was not obligated to pay tithes. Yet some tithe preachers use Abraham's example to justify the modern tithe. The rationale is that since Abraham tithed before the law, tithing is a timeless practice that is binding on us. We will go into great detail later to debunk that meritless theory.

Next, it is nonsense to state that we must do whatever Abraham did. For instance, should we practice polygamy? Should we circumcise our sons on the eighth day so they can become heirs of God? Should we offer God animal sacrifices? Should we wander in the desert? Should we go to bed with our wife's servant?

Another point is that Abraham voluntarily gave a tithe only from the spoils of the war, not from his own personal property. Therefore, this example doesn't support the teaching that Abraham practiced tithing from his personal income. It merely records a single incident where Abraham expressed his gratitude to God by voluntarily giving a tithe. It is certainly always appropriate for us to honor God with our increase. But it is always inappropriate to dictate how another person honors God with his increase. In support of this, notice that King Melchizedek did not demand a tithe from Abraham. He simply received it.

Additionally, Abraham did not tithe to "open the windows of heaven."[58] God had made him rich long before he gave a tithe to Melchizedek.[59] So much for the bribe that if we tithe, God will bless us.

Last, Abraham had other opportunities to "tithe," but no record is given of him doing so. In Genesis 12:16, Pharoah gave him "sheep, oxen, male donkeys, male and female servants, female donkeys and camels." No record of a tithe.

In Genesis 18, the Lord and two angels appeared in physical form to Abraham and had dinner with him in his home. No record of a tithe.

In Genesis 20:14-16, King Abimelech gave Abraham much livestock, as well as a thousand pieces of silver. No record of a tithe.

Ordinarily it is not a good practice to try to prove a point by the absence of reported facts. The fact that a thing isn't mentioned doesn't mean it doesn't exist.[60] I have, however, highlighted the absence of recorded tithing incidents in Abraham's life to show there is a good possibility that the incident in Genesis 14 may be the only time he ever gave a tithe. Sure, someone could debate this conclusion, but upon what grounds?

The Tithe of Jacob

The last time we hear of a tithe prior to the law comes through Jacob:

> Then Jacob made a vow, saying, "If God will be with me, and keep me in this way that I am going, and give me bread to eat and clothing to put on, so that I come back to my father's house in peace,

then the Lord shall be my God. And this stone which I have set as a pillar shall be God's house, and of all that You give me I will surely give a tenth to You.

Genesis 28:20-22

Here is the other pre-law example that is commonly used to justify mandatory New Testament tithing. I believe the Jacob argument is even weaker than the Abraham argument. Jacob offered God a deal. The deal was that if God satisfied Jacob's rules, Jacob would serve Him and give God ten percent of whatever the Lord would give him.

There is nothing in this example that remotely hints at mandatory tithes in either the Old or New Testaments. Instead what we see is another example of the concept of a voluntary tithe. What tells us that Jacob was referring to a voluntary tithe? Two things.

First, up to that point, the Old Testament did not mandate or even teach tithes. It simply reported the one time that Abraham voluntarily did it.

Second, Jacob presented it as a voluntary act. Of the three things that he offered God for jumping through his hoops, the final two were clearly voluntary:

1. "Then the Lord shall be my God."
2. "And this stone which I have set as a pillar shall be God's house."
3. "And of all that You give me I will surely give a tenth to You."

How can anyone in good conscience use Jacob's pre-law promise of a voluntary tithe as justification to require post-law mandatory tithes of Christians? Why not also require us each to find a rock and declare that God's house? After all, that also was part of Jacob's vow to God. The misuse of this passage of scripture is unmistakable. Yet it is allowed to go on because it is wildly profitable for preachers to continue the myth of mandatory pre-law tithes.

Where Abraham and Jacob Got the Idea to Tithe

With the confidence of an attorney who knows our answer will bury us, tithe preachers often ask us where Abraham and Jacob got the idea to tithe. The expected answer is that it came from God; the actual answer is that it came from Gentile society.

Tithing was a well established Gentile custom centuries before it was mentioned in the Bible or integrated into Jewish religious law. I can't improve upon what Dr. Russell Earl Kelly has written in *Should the Church Teach Tithing* about Gentile tithing. Here's what his research gives us:

> The *Encyclopedia of Religion* reads, "In the ancient Near East lie the origins of a sacred offering or payment of a tenth part of stated goods or property to the deity. Often given to the king or to the royal temple, the 'tenth' was usually approximate, not exact. The practice is known from Mesopotamia, Syria-Palestine, Greece, and as far to the west as the Phoenician city of Carthage."[61]
>
> The *Westminster Dictionary of the Bible* says, "A 10th part of one's income consecrated to God. The separation of a certain proportion of the products of one's industry or of the spoils of war as tribute to their gods was practiced by various nations of antiquity. The Lydians offered a tithe of their booty (Herod. I, 89). The Phoenicians and Carthaginians sent a tithe annually to the Tyrian Hercules. These tithes might be regular or occasional, voluntary or prescribed by law."[62]
>
> This general tithe is of pagan origin and precedes the Mosaic Law's tithe by many centuries. In Genesis 41:34 Joseph encouraged the Egyptians to double their tithe in order to cover the lean years. In Genesis 14 Abraham was obligated to pay a tithe from the spoils of war in obedience to the Arab war custom. In New Testament times the Roman Empire received the first tithe of ten percent of grains and twenty percent of fruit trees from its conquered subjects, including Judah.[63]

When Abraham offered a tithe to Melchizedek, who was both a king and priest, he was following the custom of the land. His action fulfilled the timeless instructions of Romans 13:7: "Render therefore to all their due: taxes to whom taxes are due, customs to whom customs, fear to whom fear, honor to whom honor."[64]

When Jacob offered to pay God a tithe if He fulfilled his expectations, he was merely following the example of his Gentile neighbors who honored their deities and kings with ten percent of their income.

CHAPTER 9

The Definition of Tithes During the Law of Moses

M andatory tithes, mandatory offerings, and some voluntary offerings became the law of the land for Israel under the leadership of Moses in approximately 1400 B.C. It is my earnest desire that as you learn of Israel's system of tithes and offerings, you will see that there is absolutely no similarity in our system of tithes and offerings and that of ancient Israel's. I also want you to see that we do not share with Israel common definitions of tithes and offerings. In fact, our version is totally man-made and has no authority over you except the authority you give it.

God gave Israel clear definitions and rules for tithes and offerings. New Testament Christians, however, are given ever-changing definitions and rules, depending on who does the teaching and what the preacher's financial need is at the time.

Early in my Christian walk I suffered through a two-hour sermon about why Christians supposedly really owe God about 30% of their income. Fortunately, it is rare to run across one of these thirty-percent rascals. The usual demand is normally only ten percent of our gross income, plus extremely frequent offerings. But where do preachers get their authority to demand *any* percentage of our income for their projects?

We know they didn't get it from the pre-law period. So did they get it from the period of the law? Let's explore the Bible and see whether we have been obeying the traditions of men or the commands of God.

The Definition of Tithes According to the Law

The law comprises the books of Exodus, Leviticus, Numbers, and Deuteronomy. These books provide the rules about tithing in the law period (c. 1400 B.C. – c. 33 A.D.) How does the law define the tithe?

Earlier I stated that the simple, but not technically accurate, definition is to give God a tenth. This is because the word *tithe* literally means *tenth*. However, the technically accurate definition is to give God a tenth *of what He demands*. This is no small contention. Jews could not satisfy God's requirement to tithe by submitting ten percent of whatever they desired any more than we can satisfy the IRS by giving whatever we desire. The law explicitly demanded Jews to give ten percent of particular items. These items are listed in the scriptures below:

"And all the tithe of the land, whether of the seed of the land or of the fruit of the tree, is the Lord's. It is holy to the Lord" (Lev.27:30)

Seed and fruit.

"And concerning the tithe of the herd or the flock, of whatever passes under the rod, the tenth one shall be holy to the Lord" (Lev. 27:32).

Herd and flock.

"You may not eat within your gates the tithe of your grain or your new wine or your oil…" (Deut. 12:17).

Grain, new wine, and oil.

"…The tithe of your grain and your new wine and your oil…" (Deut. 14:23).

Grain, new wine, and oil.

These scriptures do more than validate my contention that tithing under the law was an exact requirement that could not be changed by anyone. They also introduce a very embarrassing point for those who use the law to justify mandatory tithing for Christians. This point is that tithes were eaten! What does this do to the tithe preacher whose lifestyle and ministry depend on the continuation of the cash flow that is provided by mandatory tithes? It scares the holy oil out of him. He is forced to deny the scriptures outright or to find a creative way to explain this dilemma. Nearly all preachers choose the latter path. So let's explore this slippery road to Error Valley.

Preachers who acknowledge that law-era tithes were food items explain this by stating dogmatically that ancient Israel was an agricultural society that was based on bartering, not money. The obvious conclusion is that Jews did not pay tithes in money because money was either minimally used or nonexistent. But since we are a money society, they reason, we should pay tithes in money.

However, this explanation is totally wrong for three reasons: (1) Money was widely used in the Old Testament world, as well as in Israel, (2) Only shepherds, farmers, and Levites were required to tithe, and (3) Tithes were given as food because the eating of tithes represented spiritual truths.

The Existence and Use of Money in the Old Testament

As far back as Genesis 13:2 we are told that Abram, or Abraham, was "very rich in livestock, in silver, and in gold." Obviously he could use the livestock to trade in a barter economy. But what good would silver and gold do in a moneyless economy?

Matter of fact, we see two places where Abraham either received or spent money. In Genesis 20:16 King Abimelech gave him 1,000 pieces of silver. And in Genesis 23:12-18 we break into the middle of a monetary price negotiation for land that Abraham wanted to purchase:

> Then Abraham bowed himself down before the people of the land;
> and he spoke to Ephron in the hearing of the people of the land,

saying, "If you will give it, please hear me. I will give you money for the field; take it from me and I will bury my dead there." And Ephron answered Abraham, saying to him, "My lord, listen to me; the land is worth four hundred shekels of silver. What is that between you and me? So bury your dead." And Abraham listened to Ephron; and Abraham weighed out the silver for Ephron which he had named in the hearing of the sons of Heth, four hundred shekels of silver, currency of the merchants.

Notice a few things in this story. First, Abraham offered money for the field (vs. 13). Second, the field's owner gave it a monetary value (vs. 15). Third, silver was the currency, or money, of the merchants (vs. 16).

Michael L. Webb and Mitchell T. Webb, in their excellent book, *Beyond Tithes & Offerings*, list many examples of the use of money in the Old Testament (pp. 33-57). Here are just a few:

- Jacob purchased land for 100 pieces of silver (Genesis 33:19).
- Joseph was sold into slavery for 20 shekels of silver (Genesis 37:28).
- Joseph's brothers went to Egypt to buy food with silver (Genesis 42).
- King David purchased property with 50 shekels of silver (2 Samuel 24:24).
- Jeremiah purchased property for 17 shekels of silver (Jeremiah 32:9).

There are many other Old Testament scriptures that emphatically prove that Israel had a well-developed monetary system that was used by the general populace.[65] The gospels, the books of Matthew, Mark, Luke, and John, are placed in the New Testament. Yet almost all of the events recorded in these four narratives happened prior to the resurrection of Jesus Christ. For this reason, the pre-resurrection events of the gospels are actually Old Testament events. Therefore, I am using some examples from one gospel to further prove that Old Testament Israel had a fully developed money economy.

Look at the following scriptures:

> **Matthew 5:26.** Jesus refers to the payment of money for a civil judgment.
> **Matthew 10:9.** Jesus refers to gold, silver, and copper being kept in the disciples' "money belts."
> **Matthew 10:29.** Jesus refers to the selling price of two sparrows being "a copper coin."
> **Matthew 17:27.** Jesus refers to the use of money to pay the temple tax.
> **Matthew 18:24, 28.** Jesus refers to "talents" and "denarii," measures of money, to pay debts.
> **Matthew 20:2.** Jesus refers to the payment of a "denarius" a day as payment for a temporary employee.
> **Matthew 21:12.** Jesus kicks out of the temple "all those who bought and sold in the temple, and overturned the tables of the money changers and seats of those who sold doves."
> **Matthew 22:19.** Jesus refers to money being used as the Jews' means of paying Roman taxes.
> **Matthew 25:27.** Jesus refers to the practice of money being placed in banks to accrue interest.
> **Matthew 26:15.** Judas conspires to betray Jesus for thirty pieces of silver.

The use of only one of the four gospels proves overwhelmingly that Israel had a fully developed money economy. We could have added more examples with the other three gospels, but that is unnecessary. It is abundantly clear that anyone who says Israel didn't tithe with money because they were an agricultural society is either not informed or dishonest. The truth, again, is that Jews were forbidden to pay their tithes in money. They were required to use edible items.

CHAPTER 10

Who Paid Tithes Under the Law of Moses?

Only Shepherds, Farmers, and Levites Required to Tithe

One of the greatest rebuttals to New Testament mandatory tithing is that in the Old Testament only certain people were required or allowed to tithe. Tithers were those whose increase was in animals and produce. This limited the payment of tithes to shepherds and farmers. Additionally, the Levites were commanded to tithe on the tithes they received from those shepherds and farmers.[66] So there were only three categories of tithers.

This rebuttal of occupational tithing presents a serious problem to preachers of universal tithing. For one of their basic tithing doctrines is that everyone in Israel tithed. Their logic is that since everyone under the law tithed, we all have to tithe. But since tithing was limited by occupation, their logic must be rejected.

Tithe preachers could always answer that everyone in Israel was either a shepherd or a farmer, and therefore everyone tithed, but this also is false. There were several occupations in Israel. Some were fishermen (Matthew 4:18), stonecutters (1 Chronicles 22:15), hunters (Genesis 10:9), carpenters (Matthew 13:55), innkeepers (Luke 10:35), garment makers (Exodus 28:3), merchants (Matthew 13:45), bankers (Luke 19:28), tanners (Acts 9:43), day laborers (Matthew 20:2), tax collectors (Luke 5:27), and doctors (2 Chronicles 16:12), among other things. It wouldn't make sense to think that everyone in Israel was a shepherd or farmer. If this were so, how would anything else get done?

Nonetheless, the tithe preacher has one last possible argument. He could state that those in occupations other than shepherding and farming converted their money into animals and produce and then offered them as tithes. This would get us back to everyone in Israel paying tithes, but this explanation doesn't work either.

First, this explanation directly contradicts the erroneous tithing rationale that Israel did not have a money economy.

Second, it does something that the tithe preacher does not want done. It converts money into animals and produce. Preachers don't want turtle-doves and grapes. That won't finance a new building or additional staff. They want paper with a dead president's face on it.

And, finally, purchased animals and produce had to be the increase of the one offering it as a tithe. It could not simply be a purchase of another person's increase. The only time a person could use money to purchase a tithe to offer later was if a tithe was being redeemed.

"Can I Have My Tithe Back?"—Redeeming Tithes

A redeemed tithe was a tithe that was sold by its owner for money. This was done because tithes had to be offered in specific locations. If it were impractical to carry or herd a tithe to a location because of distance or terrain, God allowed the person to sell the tithe. The tither would then go to the place where the tithe was to be offered, and there the new tithe was purchased and offered as the law directed:

> You shall surely tithe all the increase of your grain that the field produces year by year. And you shall eat before the Lord your God, in the place where He chooses to make His name abide, the tithe of your grain and your new wine and your oil, of the firstborn of your herds and your flocks, that you may learn to fear the Lord your God always. But if the journey is too long for you, so that you are not able to carry the tithe, or

if the place where the Lord your God chooses to put His name is too far from you, when the Lord your God has blessed you, then you shall exchange it for money, take the money in your hand, and go to the place which the Lord your God chooses. And you shall spend that money for whatever your heart desires: for oxen or sheep, for wine or similar drink, for whatever your heart desires; you shall eat there before the Lord your God, and you shall rejoice, you and your household.

Deuteronomy 14:22-26

This provision to sell the tithe for money in one place and purchase a substitute tithe in another place shows God's practical concern for the tither. Notice that God's priority was not the tithe, but the tither. He cared if the tither's journey was long and difficult. Also notice that the tithe was edible and was eaten by the tither. This is unlike today's illegitimate version of the tithe that is instead eaten by a religious system (buildings, salaries, perks, egotistical dreams, waste, etc.).

The other provision to purchase, or redeem, a tithe was if the tither for some reason wanted the tithe that had been given:

And all the tithe of the land, whether of the seed of the land or of the fruit of the tree, is the Lord's. It is holy to the Lord. If a man wants at all to redeem any of his tithes, he shall add one-fifth to it.

Leviticus 27:30-31

These scriptures are used by greedy, heartless preachers to extort even more money from God's people. They are interpreted to read, *"If a man is late with his tithe or fails to give it, he shall pay the original tithe, plus 20% interest."* Yet this interpretation comes from man's covetousness and not God's love. The passage says absolutely nothing about late or delinquent tithes. The issue is the cost of retrieving a tithe, not the penalty of not giving a tithe.

If we do not add or take away anything, we see that the tither could ask the Levite to return his tithe. This is another example of God's mercy.

Yet it is also an example of God's understanding of human nature. We devalue what comes to us too easily. The tither, therefore, was charged 20% of the tithe's value for this privilege. This assessment was low enough to make mercy accessible, but high enough to make flippancy expensive.

Payment of Tithes Limited to Inhabitants of Israel

God instituted a strict worship rule that limited the requirement to tithe to only those who physically lived in Israel. This explicit rule is mentioned often in what I call the "in the land" scriptures. For instance, Deuteronomy 12:1, 5-14 states:

> (1)These are the statutes and judgments which you shall be careful to observe in the land which the Lord God of your fathers is giving you to possess, all the days that you live on the earth.
>
> (5)But you shall seek the place where the Lord your God chooses, out of all your tribes, to put His name for His dwelling place; and there you shall go.
>
> (6)There you shall take your burnt offerings, your sacrifices, your tithes, the heave offerings of your hand, your vowed offerings, your freewill offerings, and the firstborn of your herds and flocks.
>
> (7)And there you shall eat before the Lord your God, and you shall rejoice in all to which you have put your hand, you and your households, in which the Lord your God has blessed you.
>
> (8)You shall not at all do as we are doing here today—every man doing whatever is right in his own eyes—
>
> (9)For as yet you have not come to the rest and the inheritance which the Lord your God is giving you.
>
> (10)But when you cross over the Jordan and dwell in the land which the Lord your God is giving you to inherit, and He gives you rest from all your enemies round about, so that you dwell in safety,
>
> (11)Then there will be the place where the Lord your God chooses to make His name abide, There you shall bring all that I command you: your burnt offerings, your sacrifices, your tithes, the heave offerings of your hand, and all your choice offerings which you vow to the Lord.

(12)And you shall rejoice before the Lord your God, you and your sons and your daughters, your male and female servants, and the Levite who is within your gates, since he has no portion nor inheritance with you.

(13)Take heed to yourself that you do not offer your burnt offerings in every place that you see;

(14)But in the place which the Lord chooses, in one of your tribes, there you shall offer your burnt offerings, and there you shall do all that I command you.

These instructions were given to the children of Israel before they entered Canaan. It is important to mention that Israel had not yet begun to tithe. During their 40-year wanderings in the wilderness, they only gave offerings. This was no oversight on God's part. Mandatory tithing had specific purposes that linked it to this new land of Canaan.

Purposes of Limiting the Tithe to Israel

One purpose of tithing in the new land of Israel was to show that God considered the land special above all the lands of the earth. The land was special because it was the primary tool He would use to demonstrate Himself to the Jews and to the world (v. 5, 11). In a sense, the promised land represented the promised Christ. Entry into the land spoke prophetically of entry into Christ. Tithes, therefore, gathered outside of the promised land and offered to God would be disqualified as unclean offerings. We can only approach God on His terms, not ours.

The second purpose is closely related to the first. God's special land would be inhabited by a peculiar people who would prophetically demonstrate to the world a society ruled by heaven's ideals. The specific ideal I refer to here is economic compassion. Economic compassion is God's answer to poverty.

Economic compassion was integral to the law of Moses. It was so intertwined with the law that when someone asked Jesus which was the greatest commandment of all, He answered:

You shall love the Lord with all your heart, and with all your soul, and with all your mind. This is the first and great commandment. And the second is like it: You shall love your neighbor as yourself. On these two commandments hang all the Law and the Prophets.

Matthew 22:37-40

The commandment to "love your neighbor as yourself" was worked out practically in the tithe. Poor people, widows, orphans, and foreigners were supported by tithes. More will be said about this later.

The last purpose was that it compelled systematic fellowship with God. Tithers did more than simply give God ten percent of their animal and produce increase. They presented the tithe to the Lord and rejoiced in His presence (Deuteronomy 12:7, 12).

This dynamic of using the tithe as an avenue to fellowship with God is foreign to us. Our man-made version of tithing tries to duplicate it, but has no more life or fragrance than a plastic flower. Every Sunday Christians give hundreds of millions of dollars to a religious bureaucracy that uses most of the money on buildings and salaries.

Nonetheless, the saints are encouraged to rejoice as they shovel their money into this bottomless money pit. Contrary to this, Old Testament Jews rejoiced when they gave their tithes because their system of tithing brought them into the presence of God. It also directly benefited them in a material way. This last point requires explanation.

The present day illegitimate system of tithing directly benefits preachers in immediate material ways, but it does not similarly benefit tithers. It benefits preachers by immediately giving salaries, benefits, and a way to finance their dreams. In contrast, tithers receive no immediate, personal material blessings.[67] Their blessings will come later, so say the preachers.

Old Testament Jews had a very different experience. They received an immediate material blessing when they tithed. What was this blessing? It was their tithe. They literally had a party and ate their tithes in the presence of the Lord.

This limited festive banquet with God was a prophetic preview of the unlimited fellowship with God that Christians would enjoy under the New Covenant. Therefore, it was not only permissible to eat the tithe, it was necessary to demonstrate partaking of Christ, who was represented in the tithe.

Tithers eating their tithes make absolutely no sense to the modern church. This is because the church sees the illegitimate tithe as property of the church manager, whether it is one man or a board. But fundamentally it makes no sense because our man-made version of tithes is based on money, and is designed primarily to provide preachers with unqualified cash flow.

Poor People Excluded from Paying Tithes

A great difference in the tithing system God created for the Jews and the system preachers have created for us is that God's system included mercy. Poor people did not pay tithes; they received tithes.

This is exceedingly difficult for legalists to accept because the law of Moses is not often thought of as an instrument of mercy. It is usually viewed simply as a set of unbending rules that were to be obeyed or else. This limited perspective distorts our understanding of God and makes it difficult to see that He is full of mercy. This distortion rolls over to our understanding of tithes.

Consequently, we have erred by illegally reviving the corpse of Jewish tithing that was nailed to the cross of Christ.[68] Furthermore, we've increased our error by using the corpse to create a new tithe system built on a deficient understanding of the corpse's anatomy. This double offense of robbing graves and building financial edifices with wrong blueprints supports a modern tithe system that suffocates the poor and grants them less mercy than even the law provided.

The Law of Tithing and the Tithing Holiday

For clarity, I repeat that tithes under the law were not money; they were animals and produce. Keep that in mind as we review how God used the tithe to demonstrate His love.

God's system of tithing was based upon a seven-year and fifty-year cycle. Tithes were paid the first six years of the seven-year cycle and not paid at all during the seventh and fiftieth years.

The Seventh-Year Holiday from Tithing

Have you ever heard about a year long holiday from tithing? I didn't think so. Let's turn on the lights:

> ²Speak to the children of Israel, and say to them: 'When you come into the land which I give you, then the land shall keep a Sabbath to the Lord.
>
> ³Six years you shall sow your field, and six years you shall prune your vineyard, and gather its fruit;
>
> ⁴But in the seventh year there shall be a Sabbath of solemn rest for the land, a Sabbath to the Lord. You shall neither sow your field nor prune your vineyard.
>
> ⁵What grows of its own accord of your harvest you shall not reap, nor gather the grapes of your untended vine, for it is a year of rest for the land.

⁶And the Sabbath produce of the land shall be food for you: for you, your male and female servants, your hired man, and the stranger who dwells with you,

⁷For your livestock and the beasts that are in your land—all its produce shall be for food.

Leviticus 25:2-7

Do you remember when I told you that the law was filled with God's mercy, even the command to tithe? Well, here's a good example. The Jews were commanded by God to not tithe at all during the seventh year of every seven-year cycle. Let that sink in: commanded to stop tithing.

Why would God command someone to stop tithing for an entire year? Out of His own mouth it was to "be a Sabbath of solemn rest for the land, a Sabbath to the Lord." The people were commanded to rest for a full year. Isn't that refreshing? Isn't that typical of God? Jesus said,

Come unto Me, all you who labor and are heavy laden, and I will give you rest. Take My yoke upon you and learn from Me, for I am gentle and lowly in heart, and you will find rest for your souls. For My yoke is easy and My burden is light.

Matthew 11:28

God loved His people so much that He built into the law a rest from tithing! This benefit helped all economic classes, but especially the lower ones.

How Would a Tithing Holiday Affect Us?

How refreshing do you think a one-year tithing holiday would be for the single mom of two children who annually grosses $24,000? Would an extra $200 a month help her? That extra $200 a month could answer any one of these millions of prayers that are desperately prayed every day by women:

- *Lord, how am I going to make it this month? My car is broken and I have no way to get to work. How am I going to get the water pump fixed?*
- *Lord, the day care is going up on their costs. Please help me.*
- *Father, please protect us. This neighborhood is so dangerous. If I had even a hundred dollars a month more, we could get out of here. And I just got a notice today that the car insurance is going up. What am I going to do?*

The tithing holiday would literally change the lives of millions of poor people. Many of them would no longer have to choose between providing for their family and giving their money to a religious organization. Perhaps some of them would even be able to afford community college or vocational technical college. This would help them escape the clutches of poverty. It would also help them see that God values them above money. This is something the present system of tithing does not do.

Middleclass people would also find relief. For many of them are left with precious little after they pay their ten percent tax to the church. It may seem a small matter that millions of the middleclass, whose bills are presently paid, are nonetheless one check away from eviction. This is not due to irresponsibility with money, but scarcity of money. The old Jewish tithing holiday would've given them a year to build a savings account.

How would this act of love affect the organized church? Easy to answer, but sad to acknowledge. We would collapse like the twin towers on *9-11*. Only the rubble would fall and the smoke would rise in ten thousand cities instead of one.

This is because with the exception of house churches (and other nontraditionally structured churches), the organized church is almost totally money oriented. The church would be like a *Fortune 500* company suddenly losing its cash flow. Panicked scurrying, frantic phone calls, and anxious meetings would finally subside as the dark curtain of organizational death is pulled to a close by the inflexible demands of commercial religion.

Some traditional churches are rich enough to live off of their bank accounts for a year, but very few. So you'd see most pastors getting non-church jobs and many congregations losing their property. Basically, we'd have to operate in an environment much like the one that existed for the first several hundred years of the church's history, or like the church that exists in Middle Eastern countries, China, Vietnam, Cuba, Indonesia, Russia, India, Pakistan, Mongolia, Haiti, and 30 other countries where it is an extreme hardship to be a Christian. We'd have to trust in God rather than material riches and human ingenuity. So don't hold your breath waiting for a tithing holiday. It's not coming.

Why No Tithing Holiday?

We can confidently say that the church will not declare a tithing holiday. Any organization as highly dependent on money as the church could never give up its guaranteed, unqualified flow of income. Yet this dependence on money won't prevent me from making an incriminating observation.

The observation is that today's version of tithing does not include a tithing holiday. This directly contradicts God's version of tithing in the Old Testament. How are preachers able to get away with this glaring contradiction? They tell us that we must pay tithes because the Jews did so under the law. But these same preachers conveniently omit God's tithing holiday. Is this a grand conspiracy, or is it simply grand mistake?

A conspiracy requires the conscious cooperation of tens of thousands of preachers. This obviously is not the case. That leaves the explanation of a grand mistake. The possibility of so many preachers making such a theological mistake on the same issue is hard to believe, yet entirely possible—and probable.

The business world speaks often of a dynamic that has been credited with destroying large, profitable companies. This dynamic is called *groupthink*. It's when a group of people buy into an idea because of peer pressure instead of the merits of the idea.

This has happened to Christianity. It was founded by Christ as the family of God and slowly regressed into the religious business enterprise of men. They changed the currency of the new religion from faith to money. To support this change, they created religious doctrines and civil laws to force obedience to the new money generating tithe system.

That an ancient government should do such a thing is no surprise. Governments, whether secular or religious, have always oppressed people. What is surprising is how such antichrist doctrines forced upon the masses thirteen centuries ago can still hold such absolute control over the modern church.

This is where *groupthink* comes in. Mandatory tithing was so wildly profitable to the early institutional Roman Church that it became unthinkable to question its validity. Every extorted dollar from the Christian community made the next dollar that much more expected and necessary. Money became the foundation of the church. Therefore, to question the tithe was to threaten the church's foundation. This is why for centuries anyone who did so was declared an enemy of God, excommunicated by the church, and some were even imprisoned or killed.

Today's modern tithe preacher doesn't dare question the validity of the tithe for much the same reason the clergy didn't question it several hundred years ago: it's profitable. But we can say the same thing of prostitution and selling drugs. Is God behind everything profitable?

It is alarmingly easy even for preachers to naively follow the crowd. Yet I find it difficult to accept that people who claim to speak for God don't see that their logic for mandatory tithing is against God's character and Word. Shouldn't leaders of the church understand something this elementary?

Another disturbing thought is that many tithe preachers are *willingly* ignorant of the fact that mandatory tithes are nonbinding on Christians. These preachers are too smart to not know that something is foundationally wrong with this doctrine. Yet there is nothing in their character that compels them to find out what that something is. It is more acceptable to them to ignore their conscience and to perpetrate a doctrine they suspect is wrong than to seek the truth.

They fear that if they seek too hard for truth, they may find it. And, of course, if they find it, they must obey it. What would that obedience require? Courage. They would have to preach a gospel that values people above money. They would have to expose the tithing doctrine as false and cruel. They would have to practice a gospel that demonstrates more dependence on the Holy Spirit than upon money. All of this would provoke fierce denunciation and persecution from professional preachers.

Unfortunately, many preachers don't have the courage to speak out against the church's sins. They're only comfortable condemning the world, even though God said that judgment must "begin at the house of God."[69] So I expect relatively few to defy the oppressive error of mandatory tithes.

Sadly, there is another group of preachers who intuitively, and maybe even academically, know that this doctrine is man-made. Yet they keep their mouths shut, or they teach a mixture of grace and law. They fear either offending man or losing income. Either way they are condemned of God and must answer for this cowardice and deception on Judgment Day.

For these reasons, the church will not declare a tithing holiday.

The Tithing Holiday and Supernatural Provision

God's tithing holiday demonstrated a few things.

One, it demonstrated God's love and practical care for His people. *The man-made version of tithing distorts God's love and makes the payment of money to religious organizations more important than practical care of people.*

Two, it showed that tithing was temporary and that the welfare of Israel was not dependent upon it. *The man-made version of tithing is permanent because the church is more dependent on money than on God.*

And, three, it revealed that God deliberately wanted to show that He could and would supernaturally bless His people in the absence of the tithing system. *The man-made version of tithing is inflexible and unmerciful, and therefore provides no way for God's blessing unless one tithes.*

This third reason deserves special attention. When God started the tithing holiday, he anticipated that Israel would have a question:

> And if you say, What shall we eat in the seventh year, since we shall not sow nor gather in our produce?" Then I will command My blessing on you in the sixth year, and it will bring forth produce enough for three years. And you shall sow in the eighth year, and eat old produce until the ninth year; until its produce comes in, you shall eat of the old harvest.
>
> Leviticus 25:20-22

God's answer is both exciting and refreshingly liberating. Israel had no need to worry that such an act of grace on God's part was practical. In effect, God told Israel that they did not have to worry about working in the seventh year. He would bless them so much in the sixth year that they would have enough for the sixth, seventh, and eighth years! What can we learn from this? Two extremely important lessons stand out.

First, the fact that God promised to bless Israel with a 300% increase for doing nothing except following His command to not tithe in the seventh year is proof that His blessings were not limited to them tithing.[70] Why did God do such a thing? He did it because He wanted them to understand grace. He wanted them to understand that grace could bless them whether they tithed or didn't tithe.

The issue wasn't tithing; it was obedience. The issue has never been tithing; it has always been obedience. God knew that man's tendency is to justify himself, to trust in his own righteousness. The tithing holiday destroyed self-righteousness. No one could say he had earned God's blessing by giving tithes. How could he say such a thing when he had received a 300% increase *for not tithing?*

Isn't it strange and contradictory that we are taught by tithe preachers that God either can't or won't bless us unless we give ten percent of our income to the church, yet we see such a clear example of God blessing people who didn't tithe?[71]

The second great lesson was that God wanted to institute a system that would require Israel to trust in His supernatural provision. Mandatory, systematic, and scheduled dependence upon God's supernatural provision required two things of Jews under the law that are also required of Christians under grace.

We begin by noting that Israel was ordered to stop tithing so they could learn that God was ultimately their Source. God's bountiful blessings during the 7- and 50-year Sabbath cycles could not be attributed to anything they had done; since the only thing they had done was obey God to stop paying tithes for that period! This recurring mandatory process constantly reminded Israel that the fate of the nation did not rely on tithes or any other religious act. Their prosperity and blessing depended solely upon God.

Finally, we observe that God's requirement to not pay tithes was to prevent Israel from falling into the trap of religious witchcraft. Religious witchcraft is the act of unlawfully using biblical scriptures and principles to control situations, people, and even God!

We regularly see this type of presumptuous behavior in Christians who think they can obligate and control God by paying monetary tithes to a religious organization. Scriptures such as Malachi 3:10, "And try [prove] Me now in this [tithing]," and Isaiah 45:11, "And concerning the work of My hands, you command Me," are foolishly interpreted in ways that exalt the power of man over the sovereignty of God.

The foolish (and perhaps false) Christian does not understand that any Scripture explained in a way that it gives man power over God is a doctrine of demons. So to treat the payment of a tithe as an obligation of God to do anything for you is pure foolishness. It is witchcraft.

There are multitudes of disappointed and bitter Christians who will readily testify that their faithful payment of monetary tithes to some religious bureaucracy resulted in nothing but mounting bills they could not pay, layoffs and firings from their jobs, repossession of items purchased on credit, sickness and disease, and a host of other tragic situations they thought were taken care of by their tithing.

In none of these situations did God come to the rescue just in time because He was obligated by someone's ten percent payment to a religious middleman. Personally, I believe that it is possible that many people do not receive a miracle from God because they believe God owes them one. "God resists the proud, but gives grace to the humble" (1 Peter 5:5). We would have significantly better results receiving from God by developing intimacy with Him and learning to hear and obey His voice than by trying to manipulate Him through financial payments.

Do you now see the genius of God's command to Israel to not pay tithes at certain times? The continued and increased blessings of God upon His non-tithing nation served as a rebuke to anyone who thought they were receiving blessings because He owed them. How could He owe them blessings for tithing? They weren't tithing!

The Most Abused Scriptures in the Bible: Malachi 3:8-11

M any Scriptures are twisted to promote the aims of false teachers, but none so consistently and vigorously as Malachi 3:8-11:

> 8Will a man rob God? Yet you have robbed Me! But you say, 'In what way have we robbed You?' In tithes and offerings.
>
> 9You are cursed with a curse, for you have robbed Me, even this whole nation.
>
> 10Bring all the tithes into the storehouse, that there may be food in My house. And try Me now in this, says the Lord of hosts, If I will not open for you the windows of heaven and pour out for you such blessing that there will not be room enough to receive it.
>
> 11And I will rebuke the devourer for your sakes, so that he will not destroy the fruit of your ground, nor shall the vine fail to bear fruit for you in the field, says the Lord of hosts.

The above four Old Testament Scriptures have been masterfully corrupted by Satan to pervert the gospel, to introduce a false Christ, and to curse those whom God has blessed. Furthermore, preachers use them to dominate the church through fear, and to manipulate it through greed.

This wickedness deadens the Christian's sensitivity to the Holy Spirit. Consequently, the Holy Spirit Who helps and leads us is greatly restricted from doing either. Actually, His compassionate and wise leadership is replaced by a grievous, impersonal tithe system that sucks the blood of the poor and pumps artificial life into religious bureaucracies.

Four Scriptures...Malachi 3:8-11, the backbone of a man-made dinosaur that tramples and eats the unwary. Its weight and power so intimidating that few dare challenge it. But for the sake of the poor we must attack this beast as little David attacked the giant of Goliath.[72] By God's help our stones will find their target, slay the monster, and free God's people to obey God rather than man.

The Doctrine of the Malachi Lie

The Malachi lie is the total mythical belief system that comes from the corruption of Malachi 3:8-11. This horrible structure is carried by four pillars of error.

First, Christians are obligated to pay tithes.

Second, all tithes are to be paid to the institutional church.

Third, Christians who pay tithes will be financially blessed.

Fourth, Christians who do not pay tithes will be financially cursed.

I contend that the concept of a financial tithe is totally the mastermind of men. I further contend that this creation of man grossly contradicts the Bible and the character of God. Consequently, none of the four pillars are legitimate.

We will review the book of Malachi and further prove the illegitimacy of the modern tithe. First, however, I want to take a sledgehammer to the last two pillars.

Will Tithers Be Financially Blessed and Non-Tithers Financially Cursed?

These are lies that many people want to believe. Yet I'll question them anyway. Someone may be ready for truth.

Do you realize that if we follow these lies to their logical conclusions, we must believe all rich people tithe, since money supposedly comes as a result of tithing? Is this what you believe? Do you believe every rich entertainer pays tithes, or that their riches came because of paying tithes?

What about organized crime? Did it get its money because it pays tithes? Does it prosper because God "rebukes the devourer," law enforcement, for it? Is this what you believe?

What about prosperous sinners and atheists? Are they all tithers? Is that where their financial "blessings" come from?

In the face of such overwhelming common sense evidence, it is amazing that otherwise intelligent people are so easily convinced that we must tithe to get money, especially since most people get their money without tithing. Oh, the mysteries of the human mind.

Now let's consider poor people? If we believe tithing brings financial blessing, we also must believe poverty is a sign of not tithing. Yet multitudes of poor people tithe. Why the discrepancy?

This discrepancy exists for many reasons.

One, the modern tithe is a total creation of man and has absolutely nothing to do with God giving or withholding financial blessings.

Two, poor people tithe their way into deeper poverty by giving too much money to preachers.

Three, formal education is positively linked to financial success.[73] On average, the more education people have, the more money they earn. So it should be no surprise that poor tithers fit the national profile of having little education. Thus it makes more sense to attribute their poverty to lack of education instead of not tithing.

Four, the government greatly determines the availability and limits of financial prosperity of its citizens. Saudi Arabia, China, Vietnam, or any of 50 or so countries make it extremely difficult, if not impossible, for Christians to prosper. The government and populace view them as undesirables and often as enemies of the state. In countries where Christians suffer government sponsored persecution, pursuit of the American version of prosperity (stuff, stuff, and more stuff) is not only unrealistic, it's foolish.

Prosperity in China or Iran for a Christian is not being imprisoned, tortured, or murdered by the government or an antichrist mob. It's a courageous pastor not having his wife or daughters raped by government agents for his service to Christ.

And for the tens of millions of Christians who live under these harsh conditions, will we blame their trials and poverty on a failure to pay tithes? Will payment of tithes change their government's hatred of Christians? Will it calm the fury of murderous mobs that savagely beat and kill Christians for their faith?

Five, families and even neighborhoods serve as contributors or barriers to prosperity.[74] A child born to an affluent family of educated parents has a significantly higher probability of achieving financial success than does a child born to uneducated crack addicts in the ghetto. Success breeds success; failure breeds failure. In each case, forces work for or against the person's success whether tithes are paid or not.

Ghetto churches are filled with people without cars. Many of these people faithfully give preachers money that God intended them to use to purchase their own cars. The preacher drives off in a nice car paid for by their tithes, and the poor tithers are left in the cold rain at the bus stop wondering when their own blessings will arrive. "Soon," the preacher tells them. "Soon."

Six, paying tithes for many poor people is like playing the lottery. Instead of buying a handful of lottery tickets in the faint hope of hitting it big with the state, they give the preacher their money and hope to hit it big with God. They go on year after year faithfully sacrificing and giving money to the preacher. Silently they wonder why they seem to get further and further behind financially even though they tithe. They wonder if they will ever get their jackpot, their breakthrough.

Then they hear a testimony of someone who hit it big.[75] It resurrects misguided hopes. Like the lottery fool who uses bill money to purchase more tickets to increase her odds of winning the big one, the tither follows suit. She tries to increase her odds of getting her "breakthrough" by sending the preacher even more money. Thus the cycle of poverty is reinforced.

What Does Malachi Really Teach?

When you hear preachers quote Malachi, you may think the book was written to criticize and correct common Jews for not paying tithes and giving offerings. The truth is Malachi was written to rebuke Jerusalem's priests for many sins.[76] Among them were stealing tithes and offerings.

A Survey of the Priests' Sins That Related to Tithes and Offerings

This survey will conclusively show the depraved condition of the priests of Malachi. It will also show to whom Malachi was written.

The Priests Were Guilty of Offering Unacceptable Sacrifices

> [6]A son honors his father, and a servant his master. If then I am the Father, where is my honor? And if I am a Master, where is My reverence? says the Lord of hosts to you priests who despise My name. Yet you say, 'In what way have we despised Your name?'
>
> [7]You offer defiled food on My altar, but say, 'In what way have we defiled You?' By saying, 'The table of the Lord is contemptible.'
>
> [8]And when you offer the blind as a sacrifice, is it not evil? And when you offer the lame and sick, is it not evil? Offer it then to your governor! Would he be pleased with you? Would he accept you favorably? says the Lord of hosts.
>
> Malachi 1:6-8

Who and what does God criticize? God names three sins of the Jerusalem priesthood. First, they despised His name. Second, they offered defiled food on the altar. Third, they spoke evil of the Lord. There are a couple of things about these accusations we must consider.

One, the Lord accuses the priests; He doesn't accuse the average Jew. God specifically named the priests, and He specifically named their unique duty of presenting offerings to the Lord. The reference to their duty of offering "food on My altar" is significant. For no one but the priests were authorized to do so. Even the Levites were prohibited from direct altar ministry.[77] We know definitely, therefore, that the culprits spoken of here are priests.

Two, the Lord speaks of defiled offerings, *not missing offerings*. The offense was not stingy Jews, but priests who violated the law by giving defective animals to the Lord. This was deliberate fraud. Under some circumstances defective animals could be offered to the priests.[78] Yet there were some animals that were never to be offered as a burnt offering to the Lord. The priests offered these animals anyway. Why?

They did it because of their contempt for God, and I believe their lust for money. The priests apparently kept the good animals for themselves and offered to God "...the blind...the lame and sick" (Malachi 1:8). The remaining healthy livestock could be sold for more money than a bunch of intensive care animals.

The Priests Were Guilty of Stealing

"And you bring the stolen [animals], the lame, and the sick; thus you bring an offering! Should I accept this at your hand?" says the Lord.

Malachi 1:13; NKJV

This accusation is exceptionally significant because it connects directly with God's later command to "Bring all the tithes into the storehouse, that there may be food in My house" (Malachi 3:10). We saw earlier that Israel had already given their tithes and offerings.[79] The tithes were now missing because the priests were thieves.[80]

The Priests Were Guilty of Departing from God and Causing Many to Stumble at the Law

"But you have departed from the way; you have caused many to stumble at the law. You have corrupted the covenant of Levi."

Malachi 2:8

The rebellion of the priests was so widespread that it fully corrupted the Levitical priesthood. This perverted much more than Israel's system of tithes and offerings. It corrupted the representation of God and made it more difficult for some people to serve the Lord.

The Priests Were Guilty of Not Bringing All of the Tithes and Offerings into the Storehouse

[8]"Will a man rob God? Yet you have robbed Me! But you say, 'In what way have we robbed You?' In tithes and offerings.

[9]You are cursed with a curse, for you have robbed Me, even this whole nation.

[10]Bring all the tithes into the storehouse, that there may be food in My house...."

Malachi 3:8-10

Preachers of the modern tithe want us to believe these Scriptures obligate us to give them our money or else. Yet they have absolutely nothing to do with Christian giving, money tithes, or the institutional church. Money tithes are a creation of a backslidden church. For these reasons, no Christian should fear for one moment the weekly Malachi threats hurled at us by preachers.

The above Scriptures instead continue God's accusations against Israel's corrupt priesthood that was stealing tithes and offerings and also offering unacceptable sacrifices. Yet like the cult member who tries to use a Bible Scripture to prove Jesus Christ is not God, tithe preachers have found one verse (actually *a phrase*) to prove they have a right to our money.

Malachi 3:9 says, "You are cursed with a curse, for you have robbed Me [Get ready; here it comes.], even *this whole nation*."

There it is; these last three words. This is the little phrase that desperate preachers cling to in the hopes of convincing us that God's accusations were against the common Jew and not exclusively the priests. They want us to believe that "this whole nation" refers to common Jews and not exclusively to the priesthood.[81] But to do this we would have to ignore both the content of Malachi and the direct references to the priesthood:

> ...to you priests who despise My name....
>
> 1:6

> And now, O priests, this commandment is for you...I will send a curse upon you....
>
> 2:1-2

> For the lips of a priest should keep [produce] knowledge...But you have departed from the way; you have caused many to stumble at the law. You have corrupted the covenant of Levi...you have not kept My ways, but have shown partiality in the law.
>
> 2:7-9

The rest of the second chapter and the remainder of the third chapter of Malachi are long accusations of God against the priests. Why would God directly and indirectly accuse the priesthood from Malachi 1:6 through Malachi 3:8 and suddenly shift responsibility in Malachi 3:9 from the priests to the people? The answer is He didn't make the shift; preachers did. They did it for the obvious reason of raising cash.

Bring All the Tithes into the Storehouse—of Someone's Bank Account

The Old Testament obligation for certain Jews to tithe their produce and flocks no longer exists. It was nailed to the cross of Christ, along with every other requirement of the law of Moses. "For Christ is the end of the law for righteousness to everyone who believes" (Romans 10:4).

We are Gentiles under grace, not Jews under law. So a discussion of whether or not the church is the storehouse, and what percentage of the tithe belongs to the church, is as necessary as discussing is the earth still flat. The earth has never been flat; so why discuss if it is *still* flat? Likewise, the church was never authorized by Christ to impose and collect tithes; so why discuss percentages and ownership of imaginary tithes and locations of imaginary storehouses?

Unfortunately, we must discuss these myths because preachers have consistently preached with great energy that the modern tithe system is a descendant and reflection of the old tithe system. We are told that we must take all of our tithes to the church just as the Jews took all of their tithes to the storehouse. *The Bible's rebuttal of this is that even under the law all of the tithes did not go to the priesthood or the temple.* They were divided among the tither, the poor, the Levite, and the priest.

A Portion of the Tithe Shared with the Tither

The tithing system of the Old Testament obligated tithers to eat a portion or all of their tithes and offerings. Deuteronomy 12 is clear about this rule and privilege:

> [17]You may not eat within your gates the tithe of your grain or your new wine or your oil, of the firstborn of your herd or your flock, of any of your offerings which you vow, of your freewill offerings, or of the heave offering of your hand.

[18]But you must eat them before the Lord your God in the place which the Lord your God chooses, you and your son and your daughter, your male servant and your female servant, and the Levite who is within your gates; and you shall rejoice before the Lord your God in all to which you put your hands.

This command of God for Old Testament tithers to eat their tithes and offerings directly contradicts our man-made version of tithing. Our version curses tithers who eat their tithes. Of course, since we have changed the true, edible tithe into a false, financial tithe, our version of eating the tithe means spending any of it on ourselves.

God's command for Old Testament tithers to eat the tithe is discussed more fully in the chapter, *Who Paid Tithes Under the Law of Moses?* The point here is to show that all of the tithes were never given to the priests or the so-called storehouse.

Also notice that priests did not determine what portion of tithes were eaten by tithers. God had said to tithers, "...you may eat as much as your heart desires" (Deuteronomy 12:21). This is a freedom that the typical tithe preacher despises.

A Portion of the Tithe Shared with the Poor and the Levite

Israel's tithe system was based on a seven-year cycle. Deuteronomy 14 shows that every three years the entire tithe went to the poor and the Levite:

[28]At the end of every third year you shall bring out the tithe of your produce of that year and store it up within your gates.

[29]And the Levite, because he has no portion nor inheritance with you, and the stranger and the fatherless and the widow who are within your gates, may come and eat and be satisfied, that the Lord your God may bless you in all the work of your hand which you do.

Some preachers contend that these tithes were additional tithes imposed upon tithers. This may be true. Yet even if it is, it would not change the fact that these tithes belonged to the Levites and the poor. Levites were included with the poor because they received no physical inheritance when Israel entered the promised land of Canaan.[82]

Significantly, the tithes were not given to the priests to be distributed to the Levites and poor. Instead, each town designated a place within its borders to store the third- and sixth-year tithes. Those in need went directly to the town storehouse to get what they needed. This way, poor people's immediate needs were not at the mercy of a religious bureaucracy. They weren't required to cross the street to get next door.

Furthermore, the Levite and the poor had equal access to the storehouse. This is quite different from today's version of tithing that gives storehouse access (the church's bank account) only to the preacher or the church board. Under our version, the poor are not granted direct access to the storehouse. The best they can hope for is to gain indirect access by asking the pastor for a handout. If they are judged worthy, a handout is given. If they are judged unworthy, it is withheld.

Shamefully, the thing that often qualifies or disqualifies a needy person for help is devotion and obedience to the pastor and his vision. This scandalous practice of using God's money to help only those who help the pastor is only possible because we have unwisely adopted the Old Testament concept of a physical storehouse. To make bad matters worse, we have created a type of protestant pope, the almighty pastor, who we have foolishly authorized to arbitrarily control the goods in the storehouse.[83]

We overlook the facts that Old Testament local storehouses were created solely for the poor and were directly accessible to the poor. Consequently, donations to the poor from the storehouse were not a favor, but an obligation. Therefore, no priest had a right to demand any portion of the storehouse's contents for salaries, buildings, or anything other than care for the poor. Nor did he have a right to create additional qualifying rules for the poor to get what was theirs by commandment of God.

A Portion of the Tithe Shared with the Priest

Today's tithe pastor erroneously teaches that the church is obligated to pay him tithes just as ancient Israel was obligated to pay tithes to the priests. They energetically remind us that Malachi commanded, "Bring all the tithes into the storehouse."

Tithe preachers interpret this command to say there was one mandatory place Jews took their tithes. They tell us that without exception priests had exclusive authority over the tithes.

As the error goes, since modern preachers—actually pastors, according to them—are spiritual descendants of the Levitical priesthood, they, too, have exclusive control over the tithes. Entering deeper into this doctrinal darkness, we conclude that all tithes must be paid to the church. Otherwise, God's special representatives, the pastor-Levite, would not be supported and Christianity would cease to exist. Yet we have found that this entire belief system is totally false.

First, there was no one mandatory place where all tithes were paid. I remind you that the third- and sixth-year tithes for the poor were kept in local community storehouses and belonged to the poor. These were not synagogues, nor types of churches. They were exactly what the Bible describes: warehouses of food for the poor.

Second, priests did not have exclusive authority over all tithes. Levites, like poor non-Levites, could partake of the third- and sixth-year tithe storehouse, but only because of their poverty (is your preacher in poverty?). The preacher had no more claim on the storehouse than the widow, orphan, or foreigner. *So the precedent of priests not getting all of the tithes is firmly established by the law.*

Therefore, threats from preachers for us to give them the entire tithe or be cursed by God are not even supported by the law of Moses! Can you believe these people?

Two Classes of Priests in the Levitical Priesthood

Tithe preachers are quick to claim the tithe based on their delusion that they are special New Testament priests of God who descended from the Levitical priesthood. For this reason, we will again define the two parts of the priesthood. Maybe then we'll be able to make sense of this absurd claim.

All priests and Levites were descendants of Levi, one of the 12 sons of Jacob; therefore, they were all Levites. Furthermore, all Levites were either special or general priests. The distinction in the two is that one group of priests were descendents of Aaron (the brother of Moses), a son of Levi, and the others were not.

The priests from the lineage of Aaron were the special priests, the highest order of spiritual ministers under the law. They had the closest religious ceremonial access to God, with direct access to and ministry of the holy altar.

Levites who were not descendants of Aaron were the general priests. They had certain religious, political, and practical duties, but could not approach the altar. Actually, they were considered assistants to the priests of Aaron. Yet they also had privileges that were not given to the priests.

In essence, the priesthood consisted of the special priesthood of Aaron and the general priesthood of every Levite who was not a descendant of Aaron. One priesthood, two functions.

Now that we have defined the two classes of priests, we need to consider the tithe preachers' claim that we must pay them tithes just as ancient Israel paid tithes to the priesthood. So let's examine the process of how Israel paid tithes to the priesthood.

The Special Priests of Aaron Received Only One Percent of Israel's General Tithe

We have already seen that the third- and sixth-year tithes, the tithes of the poor, went entirely to Israel's poor. Both classes of priests were included in this distribution because, unlike the rest of Israel, they received no inheritance of land when they exited the wilderness and entered the land of Canaan. But that still leaves tithes from the first, second, fourth, and fifth years of the seven-year tithing cycle. How much of those tithes did the priests get?

The answer to this depends on whether we are speaking of the special or general priests. It is exceedingly important to understand that the priests spoken of in Malachi are the special priests, the descendants of Aaron. Remember, the priests spoken of in Malachi (1) offered sacrifices *on the altar* (Malachi 1:7), (2) kindled fire *on the altar,* (Malachi 1:10), and (3) cried *on the altar,* (Malachi 2:13).

Altar ministry was forbidden to everyone except the priests of Aaron. Had any priest outside of the line of Aaron done such a thing, he would have faced the death penalty. Speaking to Aaron, the Lord said in Numbers 18:2-3:

> ²Also bring with you your brethren of the tribe of Levi, the tribe of your father, that they may be joined with you and serve you while you and your sons are with you before the tabernacle of witness.
>
> ³They shall attend to your needs and all the needs of the tabernacle; but they shall not come near the articles of the sanctuary and the altar, lest they die—they and you also.

It's critical to identify which class of priests is spoken of in Malachi because tithe preachers see themselves as a type of priest of Aaron, that class of ministers closest to God. It is also because they use Malachi to assert that 100% of the modern tithe must be paid to them because 100% of the ancient tithe was paid to the priests spoken of in Malachi. Yet this can't be true because ancient tithes were divided between the special and general priests, and only a small portion of tithes ever made it to the altar priests or the temple.

The general priests received all tithes except what was eaten by the tither, and those collected for the poor in the third and sixth years. The priests of Aaron, however, received only a tithe of the tithes given to the general priests. This is ten percent of ten percent—one percent of Israel's tithes!

Furthermore, Israel did not pay tithes directly to the priests of Aaron. They paid them to general priests. The Levites took their portion and gave ten percent to the priests of Aaron.[84] This is the portion that was kept in the temple in Jerusalem. Now let's put all this in perspective.

When Malachi says, "Bring all the tithes into the storehouse," he was not talking about the third- and sixth-year tithes. These tithes were kept in local communities and were for the poor. He was not talking about tithes collected during the seventh year. For the seventh year was a tithing holiday. He was not talking about 90 percent of tithes that were given to the general priests. This was their portion for the service they performed for Israel.

The only portion of the tithe left was the portion due the priests of Aaron from the general priests. This was only ten percent of the general priests' tithes, or a total of one percent of Israel's tithes. So the command to bring *all* the tithes into the storehouse referred to only the one percent that was designated for the priests of Aaron.

Tithes Were Not Used to Support the Temple

Tithe preachers believe that Christianity can't exist without their modified and spiritually illegal tithe system. To this end, they point to Malachi 3:10: "Bring all the tithes into the storehouse, that there may be food in My house...."

In this Scripture, tithe preachers change *food* to *money* and *My house* to *church*. This allows them to tell us that Malachi 3:10 commands us to take money to church so there will be money in church. This practice of changing Scriptures they don't agree with is similar to what cults do with Scriptures that establish the deity of Jesus. "*Oh, John 1:1 calls Jesus God? No, that doesn't fit with what I want to do. Let's see...I'll just change 'God' to 'a god.'*"

Whenever you hear preachers interpret Malachi 3:10 this way, you are listening to the spirit of error.[85] It is a demon whose primary purpose is to confuse people about the Person or doctrine of Christ. This is the same demon that operates in religions that deny the supremacy of Christ. You ought to give as little credence to the preacher who twists the Bible to get your money as you do the preacher who twists the Bible to convince you Jesus is not God.

Let's take what we have learned so far and simply interpret Malachi without adding or subtracting from the Word of God. Malachi 3:10 means exactly what is stated. Tithes, which we know were food items, were taken to the temple for two reasons: (1) to support the priests who did the work of representing the people to God, and (2) to burn on the altar as sacrifices and offerings to God. Tithes were not used to take care of the physical temple.

How can tithe preachers squeeze money for the maintenance of buildings out of carrots, grain, and lambs that were offered solely to support priests and the worship of God? They rely on our ignorance of the Old Testament tithing system, our adoration or fear of man, our unfamiliarity with the biblical Jesus, and often our greed.

Voluntary Offerings Were Used for the Temple

Today's tithe preachers tell us we must tithe to the church so that it will have money to pay its bills. There's nothing wrong with asking for money to pay the church's bills. The organization may be worthy of support. If it is worthy, support it. If it is not, don't support it.[86] But there is something wrong with calling this process tithing.

The problem is even if the preacher does not deliberately bribe or beat people into giving by teaching tithing, using the word *tithe* is harmfully misleading. It is subtle manipulation. The word refers to either the obsolete Jewish religious law or the modern man-made fundraising scheme. Both of these have no claims on Christians and should not be used to raise money.

Therefore, a preacher may say he doesn't bribe or beat his people into giving. But when he uses the word *tithe*, he directly appeals to the common false knowledge of the subject of tithing. For whether or not he directly teaches the false tithing doctrine, the preacher knows this lie is entrenched in the church and people are influenced by it to give. So the preacher may not be guilty of actually breaking into the warehouse. But he certainly is guilty of knowingly accepting stolen goods.

The question inevitably is now asked, "But if we tell people they don't have to tithe, what will happen to the church?"

First, this question sadly admits that preachers believe Christians will not give unless they are bribed or threatened. If this is true, what kind of Christians have we created? Or perhaps the question should be, what kind of Christians have pastors created? This is a fair question. Pastors have more influence over Christians than anyone in the body of Christ. Personally, I believe pastors have more influence over Christians than even the Holy Spirit (and this has been disastrous for the church and world). So if Christians do not give generously to their churches, it could be that their pastors have given them no compelling, godly reason to do so.

Second, this question automatically assumes that Christianity's present system of the institutional church should be financially supported. The concept and practice of spiritual kings (pastors) ruling over obedient subjects (church members) is being exposed for the tragedy it is. Could it be that part of our reluctance to sacrifice our hard-earned money to the institutional church is that we sense something fundamentally wrong with this system? Could it be that we are growing cynical of the emptiness of corporate and commercial Christianity? Could it be that our reluctance to support today's version of the church is proof that we are finally hearing and obeying the Holy Spirit? I am just asking.

Our original question of what will happen to the church without mandatory tithes can be answered by looking at how the Old Testament temple was built and maintained.

The temple spoken of in Malachi is actually the rebuilt temple that was originally built by King Solomon and later destroyed by King Nebuchadnezzar.[87] The rebuilding of this temple is spoken of in great detail in the books of Ezra and Nehemiah. Conspicuously absent from both books is any mention of tithes being used for the building or maintenance of the temple. What we do find is that the building was financed with government grants and freewill offerings:[88]

> Also we made ordinances for ourselves, to exact from ourselves yearly one-third of a shekel for the service of the house of our God:
>
> For the showbread, for the regular grain offering, for the regular burnt offering of the Sabbaths, the New Moons, and the set feasts;

for the holy things, for the sin offerings to make atonement for Israel, and all the work of the house of our God.

Nehemiah 10:32-33

Notice that it was the Jews' ideas both to give freewill offerings and to pay an annual temple tax to take care of their temple. This was done because of their desire to worship God in a physical structure. If followers of Moses could act so selflessly and devotedly to the things of God, even to the point of imposing an annual tax on themselves, why do we not believe followers of Christ would do likewise?

The truth is, there are institutional churches and other Christian organizations that thrive financially without resorting to Old Testament threats and bribes. These organizations are prospering financially because they teach their supporters to give within the context of Christian freedom and responsibility. So instead of scaring or bribing a few people to surrender ten percent of their income to an IRS-style church command, they provide an atmosphere where people feel comfortable and blessed giving what they can or desire.

Synagogue Fundraising vs. Church Fundraising

Take a little Internet trip and pull up "synagogue." Notice how synagogues raise funds. One of the saddest yet insightful things you'll see is that the Jewish synagogue is run with more integrity and compassion than the Christian church. This is a troubling, but true accusation.

Christian churches, the grace and love people, demand ten percent of a believer's gross income as a God-given right. This demand is inflexible and unmerciful. It doesn't make a difference if you are a single mother of three with zero net worth and earn $36,000 annually and have no car. The Christian church uses Malachi 3 to demand that you pay it $3,600 as its right. You are then left with approximately $26,000 to $27,000 after taxes to support yourself and three children. What is the church's response to your family's financial dilemma?

It is to tell you to keep giving. You are told that sooner or later the Lord's blessings will appear.

And if you choose instead to not give as much so you may adequately take care of your family? These love and grace people will try to shame you into giving the full amount. If this doesn't work, they'll tell you you're cursed of God.

Jewish synagogues, the law people, take an entirely different approach to raising money. They use secret revolutionary concepts that could literally overnight make the Christian church the most attractive spiritual entity in the world if it used them. What are these amazing concepts? They're incredibly deep. So don't be discouraged if you have to ponder these concepts before grasping their incredible complexity.

First, synagogue fundraising is *honest*. The synagogue doesn't use Malachi or any part of the Bible to pretend that Almighty God has ordered Jews to give any particular amount of money to it. It simply determines what it needs and (1) asks for donations, (2) sells memberships, and (3) sells services.

Second, synagogue fundraising is *compassionate*. Check the requirements for synagogue membership. You'll see there is no single financial amount required of each member. Instead, membership fees are based upon age, marital status, student status, or financial ability. One can even get a discount for family membership.

Isn't this thing turned upside-down. Shouldn't it be the other way around? Why are the followers of Christ using the law of Moses to raise money and the followers of Moses are using the law of Christ to raise money?

And let me make an observation before anyone criticizes the Jews for selling synagogue memberships. Churches that teach tithing also sell memberships. The difference, however, is synagogues do so openly in integrity and tithe churches do so secretly in hypocrisy.

Tithe Churches Sell Memberships

There are very few tithe churches that will openly and directly sell formal memberships. The method of selling memberships in Christian churches is de facto. De facto is a Latin expression that means "in fact" or "in practice."

The tithe church preaches that God loves people with a love that transcends understanding, and that He is ever ready to save us to the uttermost. It preaches that we must love our neighbors as ourselves, and that we must even love our enemies. Jesus Christ is held up as our supreme example of this selfless and forgiving love. Nonetheless, a strange and mystifying thing happens when we tell the church that we're having second thoughts about this tithing thing.

It first tries to help us understand why Christians under grace should live like Jews under law. If that doesn't work, it tells us that tithing is a principle and not a law; nonetheless, we must keep it as if it were a law. When we tell them this is a *de facto* way of saying tithing is a law, they shake their exasperated heads and send us to a Crown Ministries class. Their exasperation turns to irritation when we tell them Crown Ministries' stewardship curriculum is a mixture of good and evil. When we tell them there is no right way to teach the wrong doctrine of tithing, regardless of the good budgeting and debt reduction advice that's mixed with it, we cross the line. This is where we are placed on *The List*.

The List may or may not be actually written down, but it does exist. This is the list that says this person does not support this ministry, probably does not love Christ, and should not be allowed a place of influence in the institutional church. This person also now is cut off from church resources and may even be asked to leave the church.[89] This is especially true if the person is on paid or unpaid staff.

The staff is highly vulnerable to blackmail. Some churches force the paid workers to allow automatic deductions from their checks to keep their jobs. And even the unpaid staff is bullied into giving. As my wife says, "Volunteer workers in a tithe church have to pay ten percent of their gross income to qualify to work for free!" It is not a good thing to have your name on *The List*.

Now how does a person get off *The List*?

Simply...pay...up.

The moment a person repents of his grievous sin of walking in Christian liberty and promises to obey today's twisted version of tithing, he is forgiven and again enjoys full fellowship in the church. My friend, this is just another way of selling church memberships. In fact, some of our bolder churches tell you upfront that you must agree to tithe to become members. And some of the more wicked churches even demand to examine the tax documents of prospective and current members to become or remain members in good standing. This is the blatant selling of church memberships.

Let's pray that the honesty and compassion of the Jewish synagogues become customary in our Christian churches. Would it not be refreshing to attend a local church where the leadership actually values you more than your money? You are not without hope. The Holy Spirit is raising individuals and churches that are rebelling against clergy extortion and manipulation.

Understanding the Original Sabbath Helps Us Understand the Original Tithe

Keeping the Sabbath was one of the most important religious laws in ancient Israel. Its inclusion in the Ten Commandments proves this:

> Remember the Sabbath day, to keep it holy. Six days you shall labor and do all your work, but the seventh day is the Sabbath of the Lord your God. In it you shall do no work: you, nor your son, nor your daughter, nor your male servant, nor your female servant, nor your cattle, nor your stranger who is within your gates. For in six days the Lord made the heavens and the earth, the sea, and all that is in them, and rested the seventh day. Therefore the Lord blessed the Sabbath day and hallowed it."

Exodus 20:8-11

The Sabbath was so important that anyone who violated it was executed: "Work shall be done for six days, but the seventh is the Sabbath of rest, holy to the Lord. Whoever does any work on the Sabbath day, he shall surely be put to death" (Exodus 31:15).

Unfortunately, some guy didn't take this law to heart and paid the consequences for breaking the Sabbath:

Now while the children of Israel were in the wilderness, they found a man gathering sticks on the Sabbath day. And those who found him gathering sticks brought him to Moses and Aaron, and to all the congregation. They put him under guard, because it had not been explained what should be done to him. Then the Lord said to Moses, 'The man must surely be put to death; all the congregation shall stone him with stones outside the camp.' So as the Lord commanded Moses, all the congregation brought him outside the camp and stoned him with stones, and he died.

Numbers 15:32-36

Deliberately break the Sabbath and you die. This is the context in which we find Jesus constantly confronting the Pharisees. Jesus routinely went out of his way to violate the Sabbath. Why would He do such a disrespectful and notoriously dangerous thing?

Man Was Not Made for the Sabbath

Now it happened that He went through the grain fields on the Sabbath; and as they went His disciples began to pluck the heads of grain. And the Pharisees said to Him, 'Look, why do they do what is not lawful on the Sabbath?' But He said to them, 'Have you never read what David did when he was in need and hungry, he and those with him: how he went into the house of God in the days of Abiathar the high priest, and ate the showbread, which is not lawful to eat except for the priests, and also gave some to those who were with him?' And He said to them, 'The Sabbath was made for man, and not man for the Sabbath.

Mark 2:23-28

The above incident reveals that man's understanding and God's understanding of the Sabbath were totally contradictory (just as His understanding and our understanding of tithing is totally contradictory). The religious leaders viewed the Sabbath as an inflexible rule of God that must be obeyed without regard to human circumstances (the same heartless reasoning used in modern tithes). If strict obedience to the Sabbath caused a person to be hurt or deprived, so be it.

Jesus, however, held a radically different understanding of the Sabbath. He believed it was created to bless man. Therefore, He considered interpretations and applications of the Sabbath that hurt people as pollutions of man and not commands of God. He referred to this as, "Teaching as doctrines, the commandments of men" (Matthew 15:9).

But how do we reconcile the stoning of the guy in Numbers 15 with Jesus' declaration that man was not created for the Sabbath? At first glance this appears to be a classic case of strict interpretation of the Sabbath at the expense of man. For when the man was found working on the Sabbath, he was brought to Moses, Aaron, and the whole congregation of Israel, who subsequently were instructed by God: "*The man must surely be put to death; all the congregation shall stone him with stones outside the camp.*"

Israel obeyed God's command to punish the Sabbath breaker, *but without any understanding of the Sabbath.* They thought they were punishing a man for gathering sticks on a Saturday. They thought the man had violated a day that was independently holy. The truth is they were punishing a man for not trusting God, and for allowing his lack of trust to lead him into defiant rebellion. This is clearly understood if you read Numbers 15:22-31, which directly precede the story of the Sabbath breaker. However, the man had also unwittingly violated the very blood of Christ. We will develop this point later in *The Second Great Sabbath Concept.*

The Creation and Explanation of the Original Sabbath

The explanation of the relationship between the original Sabbath and the biblical tithe (not the man-made tithe) will help us understand why the modern tithing system is obsolete, totally man-made, and spiritually illegal.

Our first reference to a divinely mandated day of rest is given in the account of the Creation:

> And on the seventh day God ended His work which He had done, and He rested on the seventh day from all His work which He had done. Then God blessed the seventh day and sanctified it, because in it He rested from all His work which God had created and made.

> Genesis 2:2-3

This short record doesn't reveal many details about God's initial day of rest. Nonetheless, that which is revealed is critical for our understanding of Christ's sharp disagreement with the Pharisees over the Sabbath.

The First Great Sabbath Concept

The first great concept is that the day of rest was not special until God declared it special. This is significant because the Jews later made the mistake of attributing an unhealthy significance to the seventh day. It is also significant because anything that is made special by God's declaration can be made common by God's declaration. Thus any issue's special status depends on the overall purpose, strategy, and timing of God.[90]

For this reason, a particular food or action may be acceptable today but unacceptable tomorrow.[91] The requirement for the Jewish tithe is in this category. It was once mandatory for Jews, but has long ago served its purpose and has been declared obsolete. It makes as much sense for a New Testament Christian to observe the modern day tithing system as it does to observe a modern day system of paying for sins through the blood of bulls and goats. But money has a way of distorting judgment; so we do it anyway.

The Second Great Sabbath Concept

The second great concept is that the day of rest was special because it represented God's rest. God doesn't rest in the sense that He needs to recuperate from His activity. So here it would be a mistake to traditionally define rest. In this context, rest means a state of completion.

The prophetic definition of the Sabbath is that Jesus is our Sabbath, our Rest. When we trust in Him for our salvation, we cease from our own labors. So, in essence, every Old Testament command to keep a Sabbath was a sign that pointed to obeying and trusting in Christ. This is why the Sabbath breaker in Numbers 15 was executed. His rebellion against the Sabbath was interpreted by God as rejection of God's Rest, Christ. Certainly, he could not have known the deep prophetic meaning of the Sabbath. However, the Sabbath breaker didn't need to understand this mystery to obey the command. He was without excuse.

From where did we get this interpretation that the Sabbath represented Christ? Actually, many of the Old Testament's greatest events represent Christ, as does the entire law:

- The Tree of Life in the Garden of Eden represented Christ. Adam and Eve would have lived forever had they eaten of the Tree of Life.[92] Speaking symbolically, Jesus said, "Whoever eats My flesh and drinks My blood has eternal life" (John 6:54).
- The blood of the Passover lamb that saved Israel from the death angel, who judged Egypt and killed the firstborn of every Egyptian family, represented Christ.[93] "For indeed Christ, our Passover, was sacrificed for us" (1 Corinthians 5:7).
- The cloud Israel followed in the wilderness, their passage through the Red Sea, their supernatural provision of food and water, were all acts and representations of Christ. "Moreover, brethren, I do not want you to be unaware that all our fathers were under the cloud, all passed through the sea, all were baptized into Moses in the cloud and in the sea, all ate the same spiritual food, and all drank the same spiritual drink. For they

drank of that spiritual Rock that followed them, and that Rock was Christ" (1 Corinthians 10:1-4).

Those are but a few of many examples of Christ hidden in the events of the Old Testament. The law has its own examples of rituals and rules representing Christ. But we will use one clear New Testament verse to conclude this point: "So let no one judge you in food or in drink, or regarding a festival or a new moon or Sabbaths, which are a shadow of things to come, but the substance is of Christ" (Colossians 3:16-17).

Paul gave these instructions to the Colossian Christians to keep them from being deceived by (1) Jews who did not believe Jesus was the Christ, or by (2) Jews who believed He was the Christ, but also believed one had to keep the law to be saved.[94]

The apostle's instructions clearly were intended to free Christians from any misplaced obligation to keep the law. He specifically named the core issues of the law: special diets, festivals, new moons, and Sabbaths. Obviously if Christians are free of the foundational issues of the law, we are free of all of its issues. This includes tithes and offerings.

The Third Great Sabbath Concept

The third great concept revealed in the original Sabbath is that a Sabbath is only holy if it is linked to God. God blessed the seventh day because on it He rested. The moment that God is removed from the Sabbath, the Sabbath loses its identification with God, and therefore is no longer special. In the following account in Matthew, Jesus discussed the logic of something being made special solely by its identification with God.

Religious Rituals Made Special through Identification with God

The concept of something that is not special being made special by its identification with God is developed in Matthew 23:16-22:

¹⁶Woe to you, blind guides, who say, 'Whoever swears by the temple, it is nothing; but whoever swears by the gold of the temple, he is obliged to perform it.'

¹⁷Fools and blind! For which is greater, the gold or the temple that sanctifies the gold?

¹⁸And, 'Whoever swears by the altar, it is nothing; but whoever swears by the gift that is on it, he is obliged to perform it.'

¹⁹Fools and blind! For which is greater, the gift or the altar that sanctifies the gift?

²⁰Therefore he who swears by the altar, swears by it and by all things on it.

²¹He who swears by the temple, swears by it and by Him who dwells in it.

²²And he who swears by heaven, swears by the throne of God and by Him who sits on it.

The contention here between Jesus and Israel's preachers was centered in the making of vows. Religious leaders believed that if someone made a vow and swore by the sacrifice on the altar or the gold in the temple, then the person was inflexibly obligated to pay the vow. Yet if the vow was made by an oath on nothing but the altar or the temple, the person may be relieved of the obligation.

The Lord publicly attacked their position as absurd and called them blind fools. He explained that the sacrifice on the altar and the gold in the temple were nothing without the altar and the temple. *It was the altar and the temple that made the sacrifices and gold worth anything at all in God's sight.* And it was God that made the altar and temple special.

If you take away the presence of God from the altar and temple, you're left with nothing but a dead religion. You're left with nothing but activities required and done in the name of God without any involvement of God. This is a sad but accurate description of most of the world's religions.

Even speaking of heaven, Jesus explained that the one thing that makes heaven special, or sanctified, is that it is His home. "And he who swears by heaven, swears by the throne of God and by Him who sits on it" (Matthew 23:22). Remove God from heaven and it is no longer special.

The point we are laboring to highlight is that when Jesus said the temple sanctifies the gold in the temple, the altar sanctifies the sacrifice on the altar, and the throne of God sanctifies heaven, He explicitly and implicitly told us that religious rituals and places are only special because of Him. The moment He is removed from any of these they are no longer special. We will refer back to this truth as we explore the link between Sabbath observance and modern tithing.

The Fourth Great Sabbath Concept

The final original Sabbath concept is that God did not require any special observance of this day in the Garden of Eden. It is not a stretch to use such reasoning. Jesus, Himself, pointed back to the Garden of Eden when He refuted the Pharisees on the subject of divorce.[95] And Paul used the Creation narrative to provide in-depth doctrine about original sin, justification by faith, and physical resurrection.[96] Certainly, if the Lord and the apostle Paul used the Creation narrative to explain such critical doctrines, it is permissible for us to do likewise.

The fact that the original Sabbath required no observance of special rules until after the Fall and after the giving of the law through Moses reveals a critical point. Approximately 1,400 years passed from the creation of the original Sabbath to the first mandatory Sabbath ritual.[97] During this period, prior to the Sabbath regulations of the law, many people were declared righteous by God.

We know of Abel, Enoch, Noah, Abraham, Isaac, Jacob, Joseph, and the multitude of others who must have served God during those 1,400 years prior to the Sabbath regulations. These people were right-eous in the eyes of God *without keeping external Sabbath rules.* This proves conclusively that external Sabbath regulations are limited to specific time periods specified by God. It also proves that the spirit of the Sabbath can be satisfied without keeping external laws. *This can be said of every Old Testament law.*

Original Sabbath Concepts and the Biblical Tithe

For ease of reference, here, again, are the four original Sabbath concepts:

- The Sabbath was not special until God declared it special.
- The Sabbath was special because it represented God's rest.
- The Sabbath was holy because it was linked to God.
- The Sabbath required no ritual observation until the giving of the law through Moses.

These four Sabbath concepts are critically important because they provide a context for perhaps the greatest of Israel's ritual laws. Violation of a Sabbath could lead to the death penalty. In contrast, there was no death penalty for failure to pay tithes (although modern preachers would have us believe otherwise!). Generally speaking, the law with the greatest penalty is considered more serious. Using this logic, the Sabbath was a greater law than the tithe.[98]

The following chapter explores the Sabbath confrontations between Jesus and the Pharisees. We shall see that the constraints God placed upon the greater law of the Sabbath pertain also to the lesser law of the tithe.

CHAPTER 14

Man Was Not Made for the Sabbath— Or the Tithe

The collective and consistent actions of the church reflect on the character of Christ. When the church demands ten percent of its members' income under threat of God's curse, it gives the appearance that God cares more about money than people. When it demands payment from people regardless of their financial status, it blasphemes Christ and preaches a false gospel. Yet many gullible people fall for this misrepresentation.

Many more, however, recognize the church's fundraising tactics as little more than a religious scam. In both cases the Lord is misrepresented and His appeal is damaged.

Fortunately, this is not the Middle Ages when access to the Scriptures was limited to church bureaucrats or the highly educated. We can read the Bible for ourselves and see whether Jesus values money above people. Not surprisingly, the Bible's portrayal of Christ directly contradicts the church's representation of Him as valuing money above people.

The Law of Human Need

There are several examples in the Scriptures that graphically and consistently establish what I define as *The Law of Human Need*. As we'll see in this chapter and the next, Jesus repeatedly appealed to this law when He confronted the religious legalists. This law simply demonstrates that God places the immediate welfare of people above external obedience to religious rules. Stated more simply: God values people above man-made rules. This includes the rule of paying tithes. The challenge is to determine what rule is God and what rule is man.

What makes this task so exceedingly difficult is humanity's naturally perverse and prideful tendency to create God in our own image. This results in a false god that looks more like the god of our imaginations than the God of the Bible.

Furthermore, we are exceedingly ready to believe lies spoken by preachers. In the context of mandatory Christian tithes, the lie is so old and interwoven with Scriptures, conjecture, tradition, and superstition that few Christians are free of its deception and torment.

Nonetheless, the following examples conclusively prove that God places human need above ritual requirement. People are infinitely more important to God than externally satisfying misunderstood and misapplied religious laws. I hope you will see that Jesus rejected the Pharisees' interpretation and application of the Sabbath for many of the same reasons He rejects our interpretation and application of the modern man-made system of mandatory financial tithes.

The Pharisees Attack Jesus Because His Disciples Plucked and Ate Grain on the Sabbath

[1]At that time Jesus went through the grainfields on the Sabbath. And His disciples were hungry, and began to pluck heads of grain and to eat.

[2]And when the Pharisees saw it, they said to Him, "Look, Your disciples are doing what is not lawful to do on the Sabbath!"

[3]But He said to them, "Have you not read what David did when he was hungry, he and those who were with him:

[4]How he entered the house of God and ate the showbread which was not lawful for him to eat, nor for those who were with him, but only for the priest?

[5]Or have you not read in the law that on the Sabbath the priests in the temple profane the Sabbath and are blameless?

[6]Yet I say to you that in this place there is One greater than the temple.

[7]But if you had known what this mean, 'I desire mercy and not sacrifice,' you would not have condemned the guiltless.

[8]For the Son of Man is Lord even of the Sabbath.

Matthew 12:1-8

There is enough in this confrontation of Jesus and religion to forever free you from the bondage of false Christianity.[99] It perfectly illustrates the differences in serving Christ and serving preachers.

The confrontation consists of three parts: (1) the disciples are hungry and therefore pluck and eat grain on the Sabbath; (2) the Pharisees condemn Jesus and His disciples for violating the Sabbath by plucking and eating, and (3) the Lord refutes the Pharisees with two Old Testament examples and two statements. A review of each part of this confrontation will help us understand that God values people above religious rules.

The Disciples Pluck and Eat Grain on the Sabbath

A point that must be noticed and celebrated is that the disciples were in the very presence of God, the Creator of the Sabbath, and yet felt comfortable plucking grain on the Sabbath. There was something so soothing and caring about His nature that they intuitively knew it would be okay to satisfy their hunger by plucking grain on the Sabbath—even though preachers would condemn them for doing so.

Somehow they believed that in Jesus' eyes, the Sabbath command—'*Remember the Sabbath day, to keep it holy. Six days you shall labor and do all your work, but the seventh day is the Sabbath of the Lord your God. In it you shall do no work..."* (Exodus 20:8-10)—did not mean they couldn't do a little work to satisfy their hunger.

The Pharisees Accuse Jesus and His Disciples

God's enemies, the preachers, however, saw things differently than the disciples. The offense was blatant. The disciples were guilty of committing the capital offense of breaking the Sabbath. And the Pharisees wasted no time in hurling their accusation at the Lord, "Look, Your disciples are doing what is not lawful to do on the Sabbath!"

Their accusation revealed an elementary, but insightful truth: Disciples of Jesus follow Jesus. This means they will often be out of step with legalistic people. Their Christ-centered beliefs and behaviors are condemned as rebellion against God. But really they aren't rebellious against God. They're rebellious against spiritually illegal, man-centered authority. For this reason, Jesus warned, "They will put you out of the synagogues; yes, the time is coming that whoever kills you will think that he offers God service. And these things they will do to you because they have not known the Father nor Me" (John 16:2-3).[100]

Finally, the Pharisees' accusation revealed their belief that the Sabbath was more important than people. Satisfying physical hunger was unimportant. Jesus' disciples should have eaten at home or brought food for the journey. It was no one's fault but their own that they had no food. Their picking grain on the Sabbath showed not only poor planning, but contempt for the law of God. If Jesus were truly a prophet of God, He would know that keeping the Sabbath was more important than satisfying hunger.

Jesus Refutes the Preachers

The Lord's four-part rebuttal of the preachers' heartless interpretation and application of His Word identifies and explains the utter blindness of people who value religious laws above people. You will notice striking similarities in the beliefs and behaviors of the Pharisees concerning the Sabbath and our preachers' beliefs and behaviors concerning modern tithes.

The Example of King David and the Sacred Showbread

> But He said to them, "Have you not read what David did when he was hungry, he and those who were with him:
>
> How he entered the house of God and ate the showbread which was not lawful for him to eat, nor for those who were with him, but only for the priests?"
>
> Matthew 12:3-4

Jesus answered His legalistic critics by pointing to an apparent ritual violation by one of Israel's most beloved heroes, David.

The story comes from 1 Samuel 21:1-6. While fleeing from the insanely envious King Saul, David and his men escaped to the city of Nob and asked the priest, Ahimelech, for food. The priest told the obviously famished men that the only bread available was the holy bread that was for use in the house of God. Now this was a dilemma. It was unlawful for anyone but the priests to eat the bread.[101] Yet standing before the priest were hungry people in need of food. The only choices available were to stick by the letter of the law and deny food to the hungry or violate the law by feeding the hungry. Fortunately, Ahimelech obeyed the spirit of the law and satisfied human need instead of ritual law.

Jesus used this example to rebuke the Pharisees' legalism because the actions of David and Ahimelech powerfully illustrated that their understanding of God and the law was different from that of the Pharisees. There is no doubt that given the same situation, the Pharisees would have watched David and his men starve to death rather than give them the showbread from the temple.

Linking the Example of David and Ahimelech to the Modern Tithe

For reasons stated elsewhere in this book, the modern tithe is considered by many churches to be the most holy and inflexible law of God. Christians are routinely commanded to tithe irrespective of their financial condition. Their immediate well-being is not as important as satisfying the tithe law. Of course, my position is that the modern tithe is a total lie that was created to support commercial Christianity, religious materialism, and clergy elitism. But for the sake of discussion, I will momentarily pretend there is such a thing as a biblical New Testament tithe.

The example of David and Ahimelech reveals that if ritual law conflicts with the immediate well-being of a person, the person is more important. David did not hesitate to request the holy bread even though it was ritually unlawful for him and his men to eat it. And Ahimelech, though he hesitated to place human hunger above ritual law, did finally give David the bread.

Similarly, we should place human need above giving a religious organization a tithe. What is more important? Trying to satisfy the insatiable financial hunger of a religious organization or meeting immediate human need, even if the need is our own?

Twenty or so years ago I attended a small Word of Faith church that had about 15 to 20 adult members.[102] I later left that group and began to attend a much larger church assembly of several hundred members. Then I heard that one of my friends from the previous church was quitting her job and going to another state to attend Bible college. Unfortunately, even though this woman had been faithful in every way to her church, it provided no financial support to her. Shamefully, I must say that it was as though she didn't exist; out of sight, out of mind. Now had this been a large church, I could see how this may occur. But in a church of 15 to 20 adults? I was incensed.

How could a church accept the tithes and offerings of a single mother for years and forget about her when she took such a step of faith to attend Bible college? I decided to direct my "tithes" to her. Every two weeks I sent her a check. She told me once she graduated that my financial support had been critical to her success in Bible college.

I am confident that I was right to help her instead of increasing the bank account of the church I was attending. Certainly, the church would have found something to do with the money. There's always another staff member to hire, a pastor's salary to increase, or a building to construct. But I accurately judged that the greater need was to help this single mother attend Bible college.

About a year ago I told this story to one of my pastor friends. The response was, "Did you feel comfortable doing that?" The clear unspcken implication was that my "tithe" was really the church's money and I had no right to give it to anyone other than the church. If I wanted to give money to the single mother who had been forgotten by the church she had supported financially for years, I should have given her an offering and given the tithe to the church. This way the law of the tithe would not have been broken.

My friend is an incredible minister who fervently loves God, has a heart for evangelism, and a wonderful gift of hospitality. Furthermore, this minister boldly preaches against many of the sins of the exalted clergy. Yet sadly my friend hasn't yet come into the full knowledge that the individual is more important than the law of the tithe.

The Example of the Priests Who Regularly Broke the Sabbath

Or have you not read in the law that on the Sabbath the priests in the temple profane the Sabbath, and are blameless?

Matthew 12:5

In this example Jesus pointed to a violation of the Sabbath that occurred so regularly that no one treated it as a violation. Actually, I doubt that anyone ever thought about it until Jesus brought it up. The violation was the work performed by priests on the Sabbath.

Each Sabbath the priests worked all day long in the service of representing God to the people and the people to God. This included listening to confessions from the congregation, inspecting and sacrificing animals, and performing other ritual duties.[103]

It is significant that no one viewed this work as a Sabbath violation. Jesus would not let His critics forget this. He publicly made them acknowledge that the priests routinely violated the Sabbath as part of their duties and were blameless. This brilliant strategy left the legalistic preachers speechless. Everyone knew that the Sabbath prohibited work of any kind under penalty of death. Yet everyone also knew that God had commanded the priests to work on the Sabbath. If the

Pharisees really wanted to inflexibly enforce the letter of the Sabbath law, they had to kill the priests of the Lord and outlaw their ministry.

The Lord was trying to show His critics the absurdity of applying a strict interpretation of the Sabbath law to every situation. He had built an obvious exemption to the Sabbath law directly into the priesthood and they didn't see it. Common sense should have told them that if there was one exemption, there could be others. Spiritual sense should have told them the exemption existed because the priests were working to support the Sabbath; they were trying to bring rest to Israel. The obvious conclusion here is that actions done on the Sabbath to fulfill the purpose of the Sabbath are exempt. *This would justify any action judged by God as bringing rest to His people.*

The problem with legalism is it steals both common and spiritual sense. It paralyzes the brain and spirit. Legalistic preachers see the rule, but not the purpose of the rule. Therefore, their goal is not the attainment of the purpose, but the performance of the rule. To the legalist, the sign to the destination becomes the destination, and the original destination becomes irrelevant. So the Sabbath, which was a tool to provide rest, became more important than the rest it was supposed to provide.

Linking the Example of the Sabbath-breaking Priests to the Modern Tithe

If Jesus felt it was ridiculous to inflexibly require strict adherence to Israel's greatest Old Testament ritual law, it is equally ridiculous to require such adherence to a lesser ritual law. We know it was a lesser law because the tithe demanded no death penalty for its violators. Neither was it listed as one of the Ten Commandments.

Nonetheless, we tell Christians that they must pay tithes under every circumstance, without exception. This heartless mandate is more burdensome and inflexible on Christians under grace than was the Sabbath law on Old Testament saints. How is it that a ritual requirement as serious as the Sabbath could have a built-in exemption and the New Testament tithe has none?

The answer is that the Sabbath law was created by God. Since God is wise and loving, it is natural that even His most serious ritual law reflected wisdom and mercy. On the other hand, the modern tithe was created solely by man to raise money. Since the American church almost totally depends more on money than the Holy Spirit, it can't afford exemptions to its tithe law. There are salaries to pay, buildings to build, and expensive programs to finance. Neither greed, nor ambition, nor creditors can afford to have mercy or common sense. Everything is based upon the cold, inflexible logic of financial realities. *Oh, the perils of running a church like a commercial business!*

The Example of "I Desire Mercy and Not Sacrifice"

But if you had known what this means, 'I desire mercy and not sacrifice,' you would not have condemned the guiltless.

Matthew 12:7

This statement of Christ is one of the deepest in the entire Bible. To the mind of the legalistic Pharisee, it was also one of the most outrageous. The quote comes from Hosea 6:6, "For I desire mercy and not sacrifice, and the knowledge of God more than burnt offerings." These few words reduced the greatness of the revelation of God to one revolutionary thought: God values mercy above sacrifice!

It is easy to consider such a thought and say, *That's nice.* But we can't afford to trivialize such an explosive eternal principle. Especially when the Lord's indictment against the legalistic preachers was summed as one thing: *They did not understand that God delights more in mercy than sacrifice.* Now let's make sure we understand this trait of God.

Let's begin at Jesus' statement, *"But if you had known what this means, 'I desire mercy and not sacrifice,' you would not have condemned the guiltless."* The spiritual blindness and hardness of heart of the Pharisees resulted directly from lack of not understanding God's values and priorities. This deficient understanding caused them to condemn as guilty those who were innocent in God's eyes. Had they understood His values and priorities, they would have understood that God was more interested in feeding the hungry than satisfying their misunderstanding of a ritual law.

Perhaps the greatest stumbling block for the Pharisees was the clear implication that Jesus' statement didn't just apply to if His disciples could pluck grain on the Sabbath. It went much deeper and was more dangerous than that. It undermined their understanding of the entire law by stating that mercy was greater than the law. If this were true, their understanding of God was false, and so was the authority by which they spoke.

Linking the Example of the Unmerciful Preachers to the Modern Tithe

Today's preachers are as rigid in their rules about the modern tithe as the Pharisees were in their rules about the Sabbath. Most, however, would be deeply offended to be compared with Pharisees. They know that Pharisees were bitter enemies of Jesus. But the comparison is justified. They value the tithe above people; the Pharisees valued ritual law above people. This is a dangerous similarity that absolutely must be addressed.

Tithe preachers would never publicly admit they value money above people. But their actions reveal the secret that they care more about our money than about us. Here's the shameful and easily recognized proof: *They require us to give them our money or be cursed by God and them.*

It would be funny were it not so tragic that tithe preachers tell us that God loves us so much that He sent His Son to die for our sins, but also tell us He will curse us unless we give them ten percent or more of our income. These curses may include anything: crimes, accidents, diseases. They also include such routine things as broken car transmissions, busted water heaters, and unemployment. The message of the cross of Christ is thus reduced from infinite, unfathomable love to hard cash.

Furthermore, you will see how serious your pastor is about your money should you ever stop giving it. It is the rare tithe church government that will love you if you don't give them at least ten percent of your income. In fact, pastors often treat non-tithers like heathen. They are ridiculed from the pulpit and accused of not being true servants of God.

Churches even discriminate against non-tithers by refusing to fully accept them into the local fellowship of believers. Don't get me wrong. Their less-than-ten percent offering will be accepted, but it isn't enough to purchase full membership. Full membership includes the following:

- Approval of and public praise from the pastor.
- Eligibility to apply for a paid or unpaid position at the church.
- Eligibility to receive pastoral counseling.
- Eligibility to receive emergency financial assistance.

How does God feel about the church's practice of discriminating against non-tithers?

> [32]But if you love those who love you, what credit is that to you? For even sinners love those who love them.
>
> [33]And if you do good to those who do good to you, what credit is that to you? For even sinners do the same.
>
> [34]And if you lend to those from whom you hope to receive back, what credit is that to you? For even sinners lend to sinners to receive as much back.
>
> [35]But love your enemies, do good, and lend, hoping for nothing in return; and your reward will be great, and you will be sons of the Most High. For He is kind to the unthankful and evil.
>
> [36]Therefore be merciful, just as your Father also is merciful.

> Luke 6:32-36

When the church creates and enforces policies that bless tithers and exclude non-tithers, it behaves as corruptly as the world. It exhibits no more morality and compassion than the most self-serving politician or greedy merchant. The *I'll-bless-you-if-you-bless-me* behavior of the tithe establishment demands a spiritual blood test to determine its true father. How can the church be the child of God when it lives in the opposite nature of Him? What's the relationship between a God who gives up heaven to save His enemies from hell and a religious organization that loves only those who purchase its favor for ten percent of their income?

A defender of the tithe system may say that I am wrong, that they do bless people who could never repay them. They may point to various domestic mercy ministries or overseas missions projects. Isn't this proof that they love those who give them nothing in return? This is a thoughtful rebuttal that deserves a thoughtful response.

The tithe church has more than one face and does not always wear the same one for every occasion. It shows a stern face to its members to keep tithers in line and non-tithers feeling guilty.[104] It shows a kind face to outsiders to project an image of true Christianity and to attract potential future tithers. In effect, it uses a hammer for maintenance and honey for expansion.

These two faces of the tithe church are eerily similar to the 1886 novel, *Strange Case of Dr. Jekyll and Mr. Hyde*, written by Robert Louis Stevenson. The story tells of a scientist named Dr. Jekyll who creates a potion that turns him into the murderous Mr. Hyde. He alternates between the two personalities whenever he consumes the potion.

The typical tithe church alternates between its two conflicting personalities. Its Dr. Jekyll personality genuinely cares for the things of God. It may even be fervent in its efforts to win the lost and serve its community. When in its Dr. Jekyll mode it exhibits the loving and giving nature of Jesus Christ. Its Mr. Hyde personality, however, is a ruthless murderer. He destroys in the dark those whom Dr. Jekyll helped in the light. Like those in the original story of Dr. Jekyll and Mr. Hyde, we find it almost impossible to conceive that two such conflicting personalities can exist in the same body.

Earlier I stated that a defender of the tithe church may submit that they do actually love those who give them nothing in return. I admit this is sometimes true of nonmembers. But using my analogy of Dr. Jekyll and Mr. Hyde, the good done by Dr. Jekyll does not undo the evil done by Mr. Hyde. No matter how many people are selflessly helped by the tithe church, it is still guilty of discriminating against, and even destroying, those who refuse to submit to its spiritually illegal financial demands.

How the church can be so obsessed with other people's money that it is willing to condemn those whom Christ has justified is one of the great mysteries of our time. Yet the secrets of this mystery may be unlocked when we consider that Jesus said the Pharisees condemned "the guiltless" because they did not understand His words, *I desire mercy and not sacrifice.*

The simple answer to this great mystery is that tithe preachers are unmerciful, and they are unmerciful because they follow God from a great distance. The brilliant light of His mercy is strangely dim in their legalistic eyes. In fact, many of them are no longer able to distinguish between light and darkness. They are those of whom Christ said, "But if your eye [perception; understanding] is bad, your whole body will be full of darkness. If therefore the light that is in you is darkness, how great is that darkness!" (Matthew 6:23). He accents this statement with the stern warning, "Therefore take heed that the light which is in you is not darkness" (Luke 11:35).

To them, the end justifies the means. If many are hurt so some may be saved, so be it. If the electricity of the poor person is turned off so the religious middleman can have a larger financial offering, so be it! If the single mom can't afford a reliable car because the religious system demands ten percent of her money, so be it! If the uneducated can't pay tuition to get an education and break their cycle of poverty because the money is going to the church, so be it! If the medically uninsured are reduced to substandard or no medical care because the church demands the money the poor could use to pay for medical insurance, so be it! If the poor are intimidated into giving to the church what should be going into their own retirement account, so be it! If the fixed income person is *guilted* into giving a portion of his or her pitiful income to the never-satisfied financial appetite of the church, so be it! If the person living in an apartment is never able to purchase a home because the down payment money is mercilessly taken by the church, so be it! If people are encouraged into the bondage of credit card debt by giving to the church money they don't have, so be it! *That's the price of winning the world to Christ!*

The Example of "For the Son of Man is Lord Even of the Sabbath."

For the Son of Man is Lord even of the Sabbath.

Matthew 12:8

This was Jesus' final answer to the criticism of the Pharisees that He was allowing His disciples to break the Sabbath. It was an incredibly confrontational and brave thing to say. Confrontational because Jesus, a non-Levite,[105] and therefore a non-priest, was insinuating that He was greater than the priests who were allowed to routinely profane the Sabbath as part of their general job description. Brave because He was declaring that He was God by claiming to be Lord of the Sabbath (only God was greater than the Sabbath).

It should not be overlooked that Jesus rarely clearly revealed to anyone that He was God, and this was especially true of His enemies. Yet there was something about this incident that provided the perfect teaching opportunity.

The Lord's critics were condemning Him and His disciples for breaking the Sabbath, and all the while the Creator of the Sabbath was standing right in front of them, as the Accused. What does this reveal? Something scary, something terrifying. The preachers did not know God. Consequently, they could not recognize Him, were offended by Him, and condemned Him. That's the bad news. But there is good news, as well.

Jesus' statement of ownership, *"The Son of Man is Lord even of the Sabbath"* destroyed the accusation and authority of the merciless preachers. How could the owner of the Sabbath be "guilty" of breaking what is His? If He breaks what is His, who has authority to penalize Him, and on what basis? And if He allows His disciples to break what is His, what business is it of any preacher to disagree?

Furthermore, the Creator and Owner of the Sabbath would know more about its purposes and provisions than any critic. The preachers were in no position to either critique or condemn.

Finally, the Lord's statement was not merely a defense of His position; it was an attack on theirs. His declaration of being Lord of the Sabbath was actually an accusation of criminal trespassing against the heartless preachers. Who had authorized them to determine if His disciples were guilty of violating the Sabbath?

Linking the Example of the Lord's Ownership of the Sabbath to the Modern Tithe

Each Sunday millions of Christians around the world hear preachers tell them openly or subtly that they will be cursed if they do not give ten percent of their income to the church. They are told through some twisting of Scripture or faulty reasoning that this is God's law; although some cleverly use the word principle instead of law. But this is just pretty make-up on a deeply aged and grotesque face. Underneath it all is the same old, ugly, pig-faced lie: an inflexible, religious rule that is considered more important than people.

This lie affects people of varying economic levels differently. Those at the top aren't inconvenienced at all. Actually, for them this is a great deal. A ten percent demand still leaves the rich a lot to consume on themselves.

The large middle-class may experience varying degrees of economic belt-tightening depending upon whether they are upper, middle, or lower middle-class. Members of this multi-layered group may tighten their belts one or two notches or not at all.

But the poor don't have the luxury of tightening their belt one or two holes. Their borrowed belts are already so tight they can hardly breathe. Yet they are commanded by the church to tighten them even if they have to make a new hole in the belt. Some even greedily require the belt be given as an offering. This is criminal.

We see glimpses of this in the story of Jesus and the Sabbath preachers. Certainly, there were people in Israel who couldn't care less that the Pharisees disallowed the hungry to pluck grain on the Sabbath. These onlookers had food to eat; so this wicked twisting of the Sabbath didn't concern them. But what of the poor and hungry? To them this wasn't just some silly religious law that could be ignored or joked about in private. It was a law that deprived them of God's provision and added to their misery. It made their belts unbearably tight.

This is exactly what the modern tithe law does to the poor. The poor love the Lord with all their heart, so they give. In fact, they give much more proportionately than the middle class and rich.[106] Then they suffer the negative financial consequences of giving away money they should have used on themselves. Thus they unwittingly give themselves into deeper poverty.

Or they may wisely deflect the church's efforts to get their money, and instead pay their bills so they can experience at least a small measure of what the preacher experiences: paid rent and utilities, food, transportation, these sorts of things. Yet to do so will make them enemies of God.

Of course, to take care of one's personal obligations before giving away one's money to the church does not make one an enemy of God. But the church routinely treats and represents such behavior as rebellion against God. So it takes a strong and brave person to say no to an organization that supposedly has authority from Almighty God to demand ten percent of our money even if it hurts us.

Some are strong enough and brave enough, but most aren't. Life is hard enough for the poor. The last thing in the world they need is to get on the bad side of God. So they make the sacrifice and give the church what it demands. And those who are not brave or strong, but are forced to resist out of sheer financial necessity live under a cloud of condemnation and guilt. They pay their bills and are made to feel guilty for doing so. To the many preachers who treat God's people this way, He says, "But if you had known what this means, '*I desire mercy and not sacrifice,*' you would not have condemned the guiltless" (Matthew 12:7).

Tithe preachers condemn the innocent whenever they accuse non-tithers of rebellion against God for refusing to purchase blessings and protection. They act in the same spirit as the Pharisees who condemned God's people as Sabbath breakers even though the Creator and Owner of the Sabbath did not see them as violators of His Sabbath. In actuality, the only thing they had violated was the Pharisees' understanding of the Sabbath. Similarly, today's so-called tithe violators have violated nothing except the profitable traditions of men.

The Lord repeatedly went out of His way to provoke confrontations with the Pharisees over the Sabbath so we could graphically see the great difference in God's expectations and men's. In the case of the Sabbath, we see that preachers demanded much more than God ever required. This is also the case with the tithe. Preachers want more than God has ever required.

Nonetheless, all of this talk about the negative effects of man's unjust and purely manufactured tithe law profits us nothing if we are addicted to the lie of the tithe. Merely talking about our addiction won't deliver us from it. We must desire and determine to stop it. The remaining question for us is whether we will satisfy our Lord or our preacher? Will we serve the mercy of God or the tyranny of man? Will we realize and admit that like the Sabbath preachers who had no right to condemn the disciples, our tithe preacher has no right to condemn us?

"Stand fast therefore in the liberty by which Christ has made us free, and do not be entangled again with a yoke of bondage" (Galatians 5:1).[107]

CHAPTER 15

The Law of Human Need Is Superior to the Law of the Tithe

We have discussed in detail that we were created neither for the Sabbath nor the tithe. Here we will further explore the relationship between them both. This time, however, we will see how our Lord's use of a particular argument against legalistic obedience to the Sabbath works also against legalistic obedience to man's tithe. Here we will fully develop the superior concept of *The Law of Human Need.*

There are five representative stories of confrontation between Jesus and the Pharisees over working on the Sabbath. We discussed one in detail: the disciples eating grain on the Sabbath. The other four occurred when Jesus on the Sabbath (1) healed a man with a withered hand, (2) healed a crippled woman, (3) healed a paralyzed man, and (4) healed a blind man. We will review and comment on only one of these incidents, the man with the withered hand. But you may refer to the footnote and read about the other confrontations.[108]

In each incident you will see that preachers criticized Jesus for doing these things on the Sabbath. You'll also see that He responded to the blind, merciless legalism of His critics by citing what I call *The Law of Human Need.* This timeless law was superior to the law of the ancient Sabbath and is superior to the law of the present tithe. If we understand how Jesus used it against the legalism of His day, we can successfully use it against the legalism of our day. This may be in the area of modern tithes or any other religious requirement of man.

The Man with the Withered Hand

The words of the Lord are precious. If God says something once, it demands attention. When He says the same thing three times, we absolutely must study His words. There are three narratives in the Gospels of the healing of the man with the withered hand (Matthew 12:9-14, Mark 3:16, and Luke 6:6-11). To save space, I'll list only one. But you should read all of them to get the full significance of the Lord's message.

Matthew 12

⁹Now when He had departed from there, He went into their synagogue.

¹⁰And, behold, there was a man who had a withered hand. And they asked Him, saying, "Is it lawful to heal on the Sabbath?"—that they might accuse Him.

¹¹Then He said to them, "What man is there among you who has one sheep, and if it falls into a pit on the Sabbath, will not lay hold of it and lift it out?

¹²Of how much more value then is a man than a sheep? Therefore it is lawful to do good on the Sabbath."

¹³Then He said to the man, "Stretch out your hand." And he stretched it out, and it was restored as whole as the other.

¹⁴Then the Pharisees went out and plotted against Him, how they might destroy Him.

Matthew 12:9-14

The Complete Picture of the Confrontation

This was a dramatic and tense confrontation over the Sabbath. If you recall, the incident where Jesus and the disciples were condemned for plucking grain on the Sabbath occurred in a field. Apparently the only players in that drama were Jesus, the disciples, and the Pharisees who were possibly hiding in the bushes waiting for an opportunity to catch Jesus breaking the law.

The healing of the man with the withered hand, however, was much more deliberate and explosive. It was not done on the outskirts of town in the relative obscurity of the bushes, but at church in full view of the Lord's enemies.[109] Furthermore, it was a confrontation that was solely and deliberately initiated by the Lord. It was His idea from beginning to end.

To help us appreciate the full significance of this confrontation, and so that we may follow the three narratives with ease, their main points are listed below:

1. Jesus went into the church on the Sabbath and saw a man whose right hand was withered.
2. The Pharisees watched Him intently to see if He would break the Sabbath by healing the man.
3. Jesus knew that He was being watched by the Pharisees and He knew their thoughts.
4. Jesus told the man with the withered hand to stand up and then publicly challenged the Pharisees with provocative questions about their understanding of the Sabbath.
5. Jesus healed the man in defiance of the Pharisees even though He knew it could cost Him His life.
6. The Pharisees responded in rage and conspired to kill Jesus.

Jesus Challenges the Pharisees

Jesus had a habit of violating religious rules whenever they interfered with helping people. The Pharisees' usual response to this was to accuse Him of breaking God's law. Often they would even say He was empowered by demons to break God's law.[110]

There was no doubt in His mind that any apparent violation of the Sabbath would end in nothing less than another confrontation. Yet Jesus deliberately orchestrated a situation that put Him in direct opposition to the religious system of His day. He would use this incident to graphically communicate to us the eternal truth that people are more important than religious rules.

Jesus entered a building that was filled with powerful religious figures who hated His guts and who were looking for the slightest excuse to destroy Him. In this combustible[111] atmosphere, Jesus lit a match. He looked around the room and saw the hate-filled faces of the preachers. *They were mentally daring Him to heal anyone on the Sabbath.* He knew it and they knew that He knew it. Furthermore, everyone else knew it.

Everyone anxiously wondered if Jesus would fall for the trap. The Lord's eyes shifted from His critics to the man with the withered hand, and so did the Pharisees.' They could hardly believe what they saw. There was something about the way He had looked at them that said He was going to heal this man on the Sabbath in full view of everyone. It was too good to be true.

Jesus, sadly, could also hardly believe His eyes. He saw no mercy in the eyes of the Pharisees for the man. They couldn't care less that a worshipper of God had a crippled hand. Nor did they care that their manual labor oriented society made it extremely difficult for a physically disabled man to financially support himself. They cared only about using the occasion to condemn Him for breaking the Sabbath.

The drama was set.

The tension was high.

The audience waited for Jesus' next move.

"Arise, and stand here," Jesus said to the man, without breaking His gaze from the Pharisees.

The Pharisees involuntarily leaned forward in excited anticipation of Jesus' next move. He was about to condemn Himself. They were like children waiting for their generous but hated uncle to take his hands out of his pockets. The present they craved would be theirs in only a moment.

The Lord, however, set the stage for the healing with three questions and a closing statement that justified His anticipated actions and condemned those of the Pharisees.

When His critics asked, "Is it lawful to heal on the Sabbath," He answered:

1. Is it lawful on the Sabbath to do good or to do evil, to save life or to kill?
2. What man is there among you who has one sheep, and if it falls into a pit on the Sabbath, will not lay hold of it and lift it out?
3. Of how much more value then is a man than a sheep?
4. Therefore it is lawful to do good on the Sabbath.

"Stretch out your hand!" Jesus commanded. He stretched it out, and it was restored whole as the other.

This defiance of the law enraged the Pharisees. Seething, they slithered off to conspire how to destroy Jesus. Yet it wasn't merely His defiance of the law that put Jesus at the top of their hit list. It was the fact that He had not only broken the law, but had introduced a superior law that freed people from religious legalism.

The Superior Law of Human Need

The Lord's preemptive strike was brilliant.[112] He had been asked a question intended to trap Him: "Is it lawful to heal on the Sabbath?" The Pharisees had used the old debate trick of creating the rules for the discussion. They posed the question narrowly as healing versus the law of the Sabbath.

The deeply held national belief was that the holy law of the Sabbath was infinitely and unquestionably more important than the interest of any individual. It was blasphemy to even consider exalting a human need above the law of God. To do so would make the person more important than God. At least this was the accepted logic of the belief.

Jesus wisely reframed the question from *"Is it lawful to heal on the Sabbath?"* to *"Is it lawful on the Sabbath to do good or to do evil, to save life or to kill?"*

The subtle brilliance of this reframed question was that Jesus redefined and enlarged the question from healing to doing good or evil, and saving life or killing. It was to the Pharisees' advantage to limit the conversation to healing. Why? Because Jesus was the only one healing people. Therefore, He was the only one who could possibly violate the Sabbath on that account. Yet when He redefined the question to include doing good or evil, and saving life and killing, He made the Pharisees possible Sabbath breakers.

The second subtlety of Jesus' question was that He was indirectly accusing His legalistic critics of breaking the Sabbath by doing "evil" and "killing." In contrast to Jesus, who wanted to "do good" and "save life" by healing the man with the withered hand on the Sabbath, the preachers were doing "evil" and "killing" by valuing the Sabbath above a person. Preachers of the modern day tithe are equally guilty of this sin by valuing money above people.

The third part of the Lord's question contained not a hint of subtlety: *"What man is there among you who has one sheep, and if it falls into a pit on the Sabbath, will not lay hold of it and lift it out?"*

It was obviously a routine practice for the Pharisees to rescue their fallen animals from pits on the Sabbath. This was the common sense thing to do, but there was no room in their legalistic religion for common sense.[113] They were clearly guilty of violating their own Sabbath policies. Humiliated and speechless, the preachers could do nothing but stand there in enraged silence. But their paralysis was short-lived. Jesus now pulled the religious rug from under their feet by citing the law of human need: *"Of how much more value then is a man than a sheep?"*[114]

God's arrow hit the target dead center. *The Pharisees did not understand or appreciate God's value of people.*

It was permissible for Pharisees to help animals in their distress on the Sabbath. However, a person who helped a man in his distress on the Sabbath deserved the death penalty! This was utter nonsense and Jesus was having none of it. Had they forgotten that man had been created in the image of God? It was ridiculous that He should have to tell people who claimed to be followers of Abraham and Moses that they were more important than sheep. If they had enough common sense to know it was proper to have mercy on an animal on the Sabbath, why was it so difficult for them to have mercy on people on the Sabbath?

Jesus pressed the issue home: *"Therefore it is lawful to do good on the Sabbath."*

Understand the significance of these words. The Lord masterfully proved that the Pharisees granted themselves exemptions from keeping the law whenever their sheep needed help on the Sabbath. Now He took it a revolutionary step farther. He applied this same rule of need to people. Human need was more important than keeping the strict letter of the Sabbath. When human need and the traditional keeping of the Sabbath conflicted, the conflict was to be resolved in favor of the person.

Such an interpretation of the Sabbath, and consequently of the law, was contrary to everything Israel had been taught. Nonetheless, when Jesus violated the Sabbath, at least in the eyes of the Pharisees, and healed the man with the withered hand, the common people greatly rejoiced. But as is so often the case, the religious leaders became furious and conspired against Him.

Linking the Example of the Healing of the Man with the Withered Hand to the Modern Tithe

Repeatedly I have stated there is no such thing as a New Testament tithe. It is a total and absolute creation of man that is rejected by the compassion of Christ and the Word of God. Nonetheless, since so many people are under the delusional bondage of such a tithe, I will again temporarily speak of it as a biblical reality. This is so you may see that even if such a tithe did exist, it would be subject to the superior law of human need.

The Sabbath was an actual creation of Almighty God. There were varied restrictions and obligations He had attached to it. So serious was God about proper observance of the Sabbath that He imposed a death penalty on anyone who violated it. This was bad enough, but the Pharisees went even further.

They added their own rules and interpretations to the Sabbath law. Not surprisingly this lessened their religious burdens and increased those of others. This hypocritical tendency was exposed by Christ in Matthew 23:4, "For they bind heavy burdens, hard to bear, and lay them on men's shoulders; but they themselves will not move them with one of their fingers."

In fact, the ancient Sabbath had been so polluted by preachers with their rules and merciless interpretations that the Sabbath no longer represented God; it represented man. Now let's follow this reasoning as we discuss the modern tithe.

Unlike the ancient Sabbath, which was a mixture of God's law and man's law, the modern tithe is 100% man's law. It is not a mixture; it is a new creation. However, the brilliance of this error is that the new creation uses the language of the now deceased Old Testament tithe. Think of it as identity theft. The modern tithe has stolen the name, social security number, and birth date of the Old Testament tithe. It now brazenly pretends to be the original. Yet it only fools those who don't know and understand the original tithe or the Creator of the original tithe.[115]

But I did earlier state that I'd momentarily pretend there is such a thing as a New Testament tithe. So here's a question that actually represents millions of real situations.

What do you tell the person who has to choose between paying the church a tithe and paying a light, gas, phone, or insurance bill? What if it is food, rent, or bus tokens to get to work?

Sadly, millions are told by their preachers they must pay the tithe. A friend of mine told me his pastor teaches, "You pay your tithes for protection and give your offerings for increase." I responded that it sounded like he's dealing with the Mafia and not Christ. We both had a good laugh, but this is no laughing matter. It is about as funny as a father molesting his child. The father is supposed to love and protect his child, not exploit the child's vulnerabilities. Similarly, preachers are supposed to love the people under their care. Instead they commit wholesale financial rape of the innocent through spiritual seductions and intimidation.

Another friend of mine got into an argument with his wife because when faced with the choice of paying tithes and taking care of their baby's needs, surprisingly, the wife chose to give the money to the church. I wish I could say without lying that his wife is an extreme example, but I can not. She is more the norm than the exception among the deceived multitudes who serve a Christ who values their money above their well-being.

How would the real Christ handle a conflict between the payment of a tithe and the payment of a bill? There's no need to speculate. How did He handle the conflict between the Sabbath law and the need of the man with the withered hand? He healed the man and boldly explained that this was not an exception to the rule. It was the rule.

The reasoning He used to reintroduce this rule demands repeating. He healed the man (1) *because he needed to be healed*, and (2) *because God valued him above the Sabbath*. Has the Lord changed? We know that He has not.[116] How then must we apply these superior truths of human need and value to the modern tithe?

Preachers can begin by admitting they were wrong in valuing money above people. They can start trusting in Christ more than money. They can replace legalism with liberty. They can stop bullying the body of Christ with threats. They can stop seducing the body of Christ with promises.

Church members, on the other hand, can apply these truths by immediately rejecting the false doctrine of the modern tithe. They can cut off financial support to anyone who uses threats or bribery to get their money. They can take care of their financial needs and the needs of their neighbors *before* they give money to a religious organization.[117] They can forever settle in their minds that God has declared by doctrine and example that the "immediate" welfare of people takes priority over the payment of a financial tithe.[118] Last, they can stop valuing the voice of their preacher more than the voice of the Lord Jesus.

Final Thoughts on the Law of Human Need

The beauty of the law of human need is that it awakens and delivers us from the long nightmare of serving a God who values our money more than He values us. It restores the reputation of our infinitely compassionate God from that of our merciless banker to our merciful Savior. This law that we see so graphically displayed in the ministry of Jesus gives us the right to humbly but resolutely demand the same treatment from our preachers. It frees us from being mute and power-less lambs on our passive journey to the financial slaughterhouse of the church.

The law of human need in all of its liberating beauty is made even more beautiful by the foundation upon which it lays—human worth. My heart warms and my face involuntarily smiles when Jesus asks the question of His critics, *"Of how much more value then is a man than a sheep?"*

There you have it: human value. We were and are so highly val-ued by our great God that He gave His life to deliver us from eternal damnation. We know He did not have to do this. Yet for some unfath-omable reason, He did. Books and sermons have been written and preached about His love for us, but all of them are utterly incapable of capturing the immeasurable vastness of the ocean of His love. Why does its tide rush toward us so forcefully and irresistibly? What have we done to deserve such waves of compassion?

The blood of Christ flows from the cross of Calvary and washes us clean of our sins and changes us from enemies to friends of Almighty God. We are even made more than friends; we are actual sons and daughters of the Almighty.

Human value.

There is something about us that turns God on. There is something about us that God considers valuable. That something, whatever it is, is the ingredient that gives the law of human need its life. For when the Almighty sees the object of His great love in need, He rushes to our rescue to hug us to His chest and asks us, *"What's wrong? Here, let me help you."*

And if any religious rule of man stands in His way, He violates it with the law of human need, that beautiful law that says people in need are more important than religious rules.

Are You in Need?

Are you in need? Do you have pressing bills that must be paid? Are you wondering where in the world is God? Are you wondering what to do with the little money you have? Here are some suggestions.

First, you can do what the preachers tell you. You can sacrifice and give them what little you have. If the Lord wants you to do this (not because of them, but in spite of them), you will be blessed.

However, this does not mean you will necessarily get a miraculous answer to prayer. Actually, things can and probably will go from bad to worse. Giving to God is not a business transaction; it is a love transaction. Your sacrificial gift will in no way obligate God or some spiritual force to meet your need according to your expectations or schedule. Of course, you will certainly be rewarded by Almighty God on Judgment Day for your sacrificial gift. You may even receive some blessing from God before then because of that gift. The tricky part is you don't know what that blessing is or when it will show up.

Now if you still want to give the preacher your bill money, you can. But at least do so with your eyes wide open and with the full knowledge that you're on a walking safari. You should not be surprised if a lion of financial reality jumps out of the bushes and bites you in the behind.

Second, you can apply the law of human need to your situation. This will probably cause your preacher and maybe even your friends to condemn you. That's okay. The people whom Jesus helped through the law of human need were condemned also.[119] God would much rather you pay your bills than for you to satisfy the religious spirits that control your preacher and friends. If you give in to their pressure, you will suffer the consequences of a fool. Conversely, if you pay your bills, you will be immediately blessed by God. The blessing? Paid bills.

Now let me give you a word of caution. Some people may accuse you of having no faith, of failing to support the work of God, or of loving God less than you should for paying your bills instead of giving your money to the church. Do not be moved by any of these accusations. This is how the spirit of legalism reacts to liberty. It hates freedom and will do almost anything to bring you into bondage.

You must resist the urge to worship the opinions of people. To assist you, I'll close this chapter with brief rebuttals of each of the above accusations.

Does Paying Your Bills Before Giving Money to the Church Show You Have No Faith in God?

This accusation comes from the false doctrine of the modern tithe system. In that system, you are obligated by God to give ten percent of your income to the religious organization we call the church before you do anything else. This is done even if it gets your car repossessed. Supposedly this shows the preachers of this doctrine that you have faith. However, since the system is man-made and is denounced by God, their approval of this so-called faith means nothing to God.

Actually, the act of giving money to the church shows neither faith nor lack of faith. One can give money to the church and have faith in God or no faith in God. We assume that a person has faith in God when the person gives money to the church, but this is an assumption based on blindness. Only God knows if the giver has faith. We judge the outward appearance, but God judges the heart.[120]

Truthfully, paying your bills before giving away your money is God's wisdom. The Bible says, "But if anyone does not provide for his own, and especially for those of his household, he has denied the faith and is worse than an infidel [unbeliever]" (1 Timothy 6:8).

What kind of God would require people to give away their money to a religious bureaucracy before paying their personal bills? The world looks at this kind of behavior as the madness it is. It is foolish irresponsibility wrapped in a religious robe.

Do you really believe this kind of insane behavior will attract the world to Christ? What's attractive about a deity who has more in common with the IRS than Jesus Christ? Will your children be inspired to believe in the God who forces their parents to give away their school clothes money or their college education fund to the church? Is that the message you want to give your children? That God cares more about their money than their well-being?

Ask yourself how much sense it makes to give away $300 to the church organization and then later wonder why you have no money to replace your car's bald tires? I can answer that one. Your new tires are in the offering plate. You can't blame God for not meeting your need. He met your need when He originally gave you the $300 that you sincerely, but foolishly gave away.

I say again, the law of human need has set you free from the law of the modern tithe. Stop giving away your bill money.

Does Paying Your Bills Before Giving Money to the Church Show You Don't Support the Work of God?

Tithe pastors see themselves as God's chief executive officers and the rest of us as assets to be used to make their spiritual dreams come true. I know it sounds harsh, but anyone who has been around preachers for a long time knows this is true.

Pastors will rarely admit this in public, but they believe they have a special place with God above the rest of the body of Christ. And with this special place comes special privileges. Why do I say this? I say it for two reasons.

First, pastors believe the worldwide church is organized by God into a hierarchy. The Holy Trinity is at the top of the spiritual organizational chart, then comes the pastor, and beneath the pastor are the rest of us. When God wants to do something, He speaks to the pastor who speaks to the people. Or at least this is how the fiction goes.

Second, pastors claim exclusive ownership of the modern tithe. This is done primarily because they believe God rules the body of Christ through them. They are like protestant popes without the fancy hats (although some of our preachers have begun wearing fancy hats). God directs all of His activities through His number one confidants, the pastors. Obviously it costs money to perform the things God desires; so He gives the pastors sole right to collect and manage the tithe. This way they can pay themselves secret salaries and benefits, hire staff, purchase and maintain buildings, pay special guest speakers, go on trips, and what's left over they can use for other "ministry."

Now you must understand that your pastor will probably see your use of the law of human need as a threat to his perceived special place and privilege in the church. If people's immediate needs are given too much priority, what will happen to the work of the ministry? What will happen to his salary?

The sad thing is that few ministers see the immediate needs of the would-be giver as the work of the ministry. Such mundane things like single moms living in bad neighborhoods, families with inadequate health insurance, and elderly people with very low incomes are not nearly as glamorous as radio and television ministries or overseas missions.

So what do you do with this information? It's very simple. You understand that most pastors labor under a self-imposed false burden of super-importance. They see themselves as the spiritual employer and us as the spiritual employees. They give the orders; we obey the orders. This is the product of tradition and not the Holy Spirit.

You look this tradition humbly, but squarely in the eye and recognize that the law of human need may make your immediate need at least as important as any the preacher presents you.[121] It may be important for the church to pave the parking lot or build a fellowship hall or increase the pastor's salary. But it is also important for you to get your car fixed so that you aren't fired from your job when you have no transportation to get to work. I know, I know, this doesn't seem as spiritual as putting money in an official envelope and dropping it in a bucket, but it is.[122]

Does Paying Your Bills Before You Give Money to the Church Show You Have Little Love for God?

Actually, the Bible says, "But if anyone does not provide for his own, and especially for those of his household, he has denied the faith and is worse than an unbeliever" (1 Timothy 5:8).

Providing for one's own family is fundamental to true Christianity. Failure to do it reveals a character deficiency so severe it is classified as denying the faith. The denial of "faith" is not necessarily a conscious rejection of Christ as Lord and Savior, although it could include this.

But here the focus is on behavior that contradicts your words and loudly declares you are a hypocrite: "I love God, but neglect my family."

The Christian who sacrifices his family's well-being to support the institutional church may be popular with the preacher and his crew, but he is denounced by Almighty God as a hypocrite who is worse than an unbeliever. We can define this negligent behavior even farther. Such a person is worse than most animals. For even animals take care of their own.

Take care of your immediate family, first, before you run around trying to save the world. You will answer to Almighty God on Judgment Day, not your preacher.

CHAPTER 16

The Gospels Do Not Endorse Christian Tithing

The modern tithe is spoken of as though it's actually a New Testament doctrine and command. This is shocking; since the New Testament strongly condemns it. The enemies of Christian liberty will no doubt snicker in smug confidence at such indefensible blasphemy. Even some of my allies may think this statement goes a bit too far. But I assure you my position is easily defended.

The New Testament directly names tithing in only one chapter in one book: Hebrews 7 (we discuss this later). The only other places tithing is mentioned is Matthew 23:23 and Luke 11:42; 18:12. Tithe preachers prominently display Matthew and Luke as part of their New Testament justification to demand financial tithes. But their attempt falls far short of the mark.

Matthew, Mark, Luke, and John are physically located in what we call the New Testament. But we must understand that although the Bible is the inspired Word of God, the chronological placement of its books are not.

The placement of all of Matthew, Mark, Luke, and John in what we call the New Testament was done by man. Technically, however, the New Testament begins when Jesus rises from the dead. He rises from the dead in Matthew 28, Mark 16, Luke 24, and John 20. Therefore, everything in the gospels prior to these chapters is Old Testament. With this in mind, let's look at the tithe scriptures in Matthew and Luke.

Tithing in Matthew

Woe to you, scribes and Pharisees, hypocrites! For you pay tithe of mint and anise and cumin, and have neglected the weightier matters of the law: justice and mercy and faith. These you ought to have done, without leaving the others undone.

Matthew 23:23

This Old Testament scripture records one of the many times Jesus criticized the religious leaders for their hypocrisy. He noted their bewildering and contradictory mixture of extreme tithing and injustice, unmercifulness, and faithlessness.

Sadly, as it is to be expected, tithe preachers focus on what Jesus said about tithing and nothing about what He said about justice, mercy, and faith. It is true that Jesus commended and encouraged the Pharisees and scribes in their tithing. They were under the law of Moses, and this was its requirement. So we would expect Jesus to tell them to tithe.[123] But what else did He say in that same verse?

Jesus compared the temporary ordinance of tithing to the eternal principles and qualities of justice, mercy, and faith. His verdict was that justice, mercy, and faith were "weightier," or more important than tithing, and that Israel's religious leaders were wrong to emphasize the latter over the former. Our tithe preachers are similarly guilty of valuing (their version of) tithes above justice, mercy, and faith.

Justice

Today's tithe system and tithe preachers are unjust. They are unjust because they raise money by requiring Christians to obey a twisted version of an obsolete Old Testament tithe law. They are unjust because their tithe law violates God's law of fairness and equity.

The apostle Paul referred to the law of fairness and equity when he asked the Corinthian Christians to financially support the much poorer Jerusalem Christians:

[13]For I do not mean that others should be eased and you be burdened;

[14]but by an equality, that now at this time your abundance may supply their lack, that their abundance also may supply your lack—that there may be equality.

[15]As it is written, "He who gathered much had nothing left over, and he who gathered little had no lack."

2 Corinthians 8:13-15

The modern tithe system violates the law of fairness and equality because it requires much more of the poor than it does of the rich. It demands ten percent no matter how much we earn. But does this affect the poor, middle-class, and rich equally? Absolutely not. It drives the poor into greater poverty and misery, while the middle-class gives with varying degrees of comfort or discomfort, based upon where they are on the middle-class ladder and on the level of their debt. And the rich, well they effortlessly cut a check for ten percent and go back to living a life of ease and luxury, happy to be required to give so little of their money to the gospel.[124]

This system is one hundred percent unjust.

Mercy

Today's tithe system and tithe preachers are unmerciful. They are unmerciful because they routinely impose heartless economic cruelty upon the poor. They are unmerciful because they can look a family in the eyes who is overwhelmed with medical bills and demand ten percent of its income. They are unmerciful because they don't care about the negative effects of their economic demands upon God's people.[125]

Somehow these preachers are able to harden their hearts and convince themselves that God approves of their brutality against the church. What is to be said of this kind of preacher? Jesus prophetically said it all:

²They will put you out of the synagogues; yes, the time is coming that whoever kills you will think that he offers God service.

³And these things they will do to you because they have not known the Father nor Me.

John 16:2-3

Don't underestimate the tithe doctrine's murderous effect on the poor. It kills their safety, comfort, opportunity, and hope.

Faith

Today's tithe system and tithe preachers are faithless. They are faithless because the modern tithe system is not based on a relationship of hearing and obeying Christ. It is based on a preacher's ability to generate and sustain cash flow through bribes, threats, and manipulation of gullible Christians. This is not faith; it's faithlessness.

Tithing in Luke

But woe to you Pharisees! For you tithe mint and rue and all manner of herbs, and pass by justice and the love of God. These you ought to have done, without leaving the others undone.

Luke 11:42

This is Luke's narrative of the same incident reported by Matthew. So I'll only comment on a phrase that powerfully illustrates the wickedness of the modern tithe system.

Jesus said the ancient tithe preachers "passed by justice and the love of God." Use your imagination for a moment. When you drive a car to reach a destination, you pass by many things. You don't stop by them because they are not your destination.

Similarly, the ancient tithe preachers had a destination that was not justice or the love of God; so they passed by them. Today's tithe preachers make the same grievous mistake. Their destination is cash flow at all costs. If it means they must pass by justice and the love of God to build their kingdoms in the name of Christ, they will do so. If it means they must cause wrecks or even run over pedestrians as they pass by justice and the love of God to reach their destination of cash flow, they will do so.

Tithe preachers are like drunken ambulance drivers who turn on their sirens and flashing lights and irresponsibly run over anyone in their path. This is bad enough, but what makes the crime even more evil is the preachers feel no remorse for their actions. Through some dark mental process, they justify the broken, bloodied bodies of God's people simply as the cost of helping the hurting and saving the lost. It never dawns on them that it is demonic wisdom that justifies destroying the church to save the world.

More Tithing in Luke

Also He spoke this parable to some who trusted in themselves that they were righteous, and despised others:

"Two men went up to the temple to pray, one a Pharisee and the other a tax collector.

The Pharisee stood and prayed thus with himself, 'God, I thank you that I am not like other men—extortioners, unjust, adulterers, or even as this tax collector.

I fast twice a week; I give tithes of all that I possess.'

And the tax collector, standing afar off, would not so much as raise his eyes to heaven, but beat his breast, saying, 'God, be merciful to me a sinner!'

I tell you, this man went down to his house justified rather than the other; for everyone who exalts himself will be humbled, and he who humbles himself will be exalted."

Luke 18:9-14

This story reveals one of the great sins of the tithing system: It encourages self-righteousness. People who tithe pat themselves on the back for giving the institutional church ten percent of their income. They won't actually say, "Look at me; I'm great for giving God ten percent of my money." No, that's too obnoxious and obvious. The way to properly congratulate yourself is to give a public testimony of how you were blessed through tithing.[126] This way it appears that you are giving glory to God, but you are actually letting everyone know you are a tither. This will make you look like an obedient Christian who loves God and His church, and may even help you get a nice unpaid position on the church staff.

The public testimony effectively draws attention to yourself, but it is also a great ministry fundraiser. This is one reason why preachers love public testimonies of how God has supposedly blessed someone for tithing. It satisfies the tither's need to be noticed and the preacher's need to convince people to tithe.

In Jesus' story, notice that the preacher was quite proud of himself for being a tither. His tithing was part of his delusion that he pleased God and was better than those who didn't tithe. Many so-called tithers suffer from this same delusion. They believe their tithing is evidence of their spirituality. I believe it is a sign of their lack of spirituality. *How could a spiritually mature Christian be convinced to live under a perversion of part of the obsolete law of Moses and pat himself on the back for doing so?*

It is obvious that Jesus used this story to expose religious hypocrisy and self-righteousness. But He also used it to reveal righteousness apart from the law. The tax collector in the story was condemned by the tither, but he was accepted by God. *Condemned by man, yet accepted by God!*

The church is filled with people who are justified by God, but condemned by people who claim to speak for God. It is no wonder that Jesus said, "Assuredly, I say to you that tax collectors [thieves] and harlots [whores] enter the kingdom of God before you [self-righteous preachers]" (Matthew 21:31).

Summary of Tithing in the Gospels

The gospels mention tithing in three places, and two of those places refer to the same incident. So the gospels actually mention two incidents of tithing. Both of these examples speak negatively of the tithers. Furthermore, in both examples, Jesus explained that the preachers had erroneously placed tithing above the more important issues of justice, mercy, faith, and humility.

What tithe preacher teaches that these qualities are more important than the modern tithe? Personally, in nearly thirty years of serving Christ, I have never heard—or heard of—a tithe preacher who publicly ranks the modern tithe beneath these Christian virtues. This should come as no surprise. Justice, mercy, faith, and humility are enemies of the modern tithe system.

Do you now see how ridiculous it is for tithe preachers to use the Gospels to justify their demand for our money?

CHAPTER 17

The New Testament Condemns Christian Tithing

Te Gospels record that Jesus' greatest enemies were legalistic preachers. Similarly, the New Testament records that legalistic preachers were a grave threat to the new church He founded. Experience proves they are still a grave threat.[127] In anticipation of this timeless struggle, the Holy Spirit interwove Christian liberty throughout the entire New Testament.

This liberty stems from truths of the sufficiency of Christ and salvation through grace and faith. If either of these foundational truths is compromised, the way is opened for legalism (giving motivated by fear) to replace liberty (giving motivated by love). Or in other words, legalism (tithing) in the Christian church survives only when Christ is no longer sufficient, or when salvation is gained through works instead of grace and faith. For if Christ isn't sufficient, people attempt to gain salvation through some other means. So the sufficiency of Christ and salvation through grace and faith can not exist without each other. If you get rid of one, you get rid of the other.

The apostles were extremely keen to this truth. For this reason, they vigorously challenged and refuted even the slightest doctrine or behavior that undermined the sufficiency of Christ or salvation through grace and faith. The modern tithing system undermines both and therefore directly contradicts foundational messages of the New Testament. For this reason, it must be recognized as a tool of Satan and an enemy of the church.

The Modern Tithe Undermines the Sufficiency of Christ

The sufficiency of Christ means we find everything we need in Christ. It is not Christ and anything; it is Christ alone. He is the only Answer, the only Hope, the only Savior. We do not conclude this by bending a Scripture here or twisting one there. It is not a doctrine that must be constructed with isolated and scattered fragments of oddly fitting truths. The general theme of the entire New Testament tells us Jesus is our wisdom, righteousness, sanctification, and redemption.[128]

The sufficiency of Christ is an overwhelming and all-consuming truth that is so interwoven throughout each New Testament book that one does not have to seek it to find it. It is like the noonday sun on a cloudless day. If you do not see it, you are blind or your eyes are closed.

Nonetheless, this has not stopped tithe preachers from pushing their cash flow doctrine. What is the non-negotiable contradiction in the sufficiency of Christ and the modern tithe? The contradiction is that one can not believe Christ is all one needs to be accepted and blessed of God and simultaneously believe that *any* man-made requirement can prevent or cancel this provision. What guarantees acceptance and blessing from God? Is it Christ or tithes? Tithe preachers would have us believe they are one and the same. But this is nothing more than a version of a *Christ and X* doctrine. The *X* is whatever a person decides to add as a requirement to be accepted by God. And whatever is added to Christ is *anti-Christ*.

Now most tithe preachers will not clearly state (especially in public) that you must tithe to receive or maintain salvation (although some may dare preach such a horrible doctrine). Instead they preach a condemning message that strips the benefits of salvation from anyone who refuses their tithe system.[129] This is basically the same thing as telling people that having Christ is not enough to receive the blessings of God: A person must have Christ *and* pay tithes.

Therefore, man's tithing system is an additional requirement to win God's kindness, and for this it is an enemy of the sufficiency of

Christ. *Consequently, the New Testament condemns the man-made system of the modern tithe.*

The Modern Tithe Undermines Salvation through Grace and Faith

Salvation is deliverance from sin, guilt, and eternal damnation. But it is much more than being delivered from something; it includes being delivered into something. This something is the literal family and kingdom of God, with all its rights, benefits, and privileges.[130]

Certainly, the Bible's emphasis is upon our eternal blessings and future rewards. But this does not conflict with its bountiful promises of special, present blessings for Christians. Blessings such as supernatural provision, supernatural healing, supernatural wisdom, and supernatural deliverance. And the best blessing: supernatural fellowship with God. Yet God and His wonderful blessings are attainable only through grace and faith.

The church has simply and quite accurately defined grace as unearned favor. I like to think of it as mercy, too. Mercy goes beyond unearned favor. It is good to someone who not only has not earned kindness, but to someone who deserves far less, possibly even punishment. Faith, in the general biblical context, means to believe what God says and to act accordingly. Applied to salvation, faith means to trust solely in the Person and accomplishments of Christ for deliverance from sin and to receive access to God.

All of the New Testament teaches that salvation and its blessings come solely by grace through faith. Human efforts to earn God's kindness are condemned as self-righteousness. This is without regard to whether or not the efforts appear religious. Furthermore, all efforts to keep God's blessings from those who fail or refuse to try to earn God's kindness are condemned. This is where the modern tithe system and grace and faith collide.

These several Scriptures prove this point and represent the entire New Testament perspective of salvation through grace and faith:

¹What then shall we say that Abraham our father has found according to the flesh?

²For if Abraham was justified by works, he has something to boast about, but not before God.

³For what does the scripture say? 'Abraham believed God, and it was accounted to him for righteousness.'

⁴Now to him who works, the wages are not counted as grace but as debt.

⁵But to him who does not work but believes on Him who justifies the ungodly, his faith is accounted for righteousness.

Romans 4:1-5

¹Therefore, having been justified by faith, we have peace with God through our Lord Jesus Christ,

²Through whom also we have access by faith into this grace in which we stand, and rejoice in hope of the glory of God.

Romans 5:1-2

⁸For by grace you have been saved through faith, and that not of yourselves; it is the gift of God,

⁹Not of works, lest anyone should boast.

Ephesians 2:8-9

⁴But when the kindness and the love of God our Savior toward man appeared,

⁵not by works of righteousness which we have done, but according to His mercy He saved us, through the washing of regeneration and renewing of the Holy Spirit,

⁶whom He poured out on us abundantly through Jesus Christ our Savior,

⁷that having been justified by His grace we should become heirs according to the hope of eternal life.

Titus 3:4-7

Is this not obvious enough for anyone with open eyes to see? To the extent that you work to earn God's blessings, you undermine your faith.

Salvation through Grace and Faith and the Modern Tithe System Can't Both Be True

The basic teaching of the New Testament is that God is motivated by such fervent, unexplainable, and infinite love for His fallen creation that He gave Himself as the Sacrifice for our sins. In contrast, the basic teaching of the modern tithe doctrine is that Christians who give the pastor ten percent of their income are blessed by God and Christians who fail to make these payments are cursed by God.

These are irreconcilable portraits of the Lord. Which is He? The God who demonstrates infinite and sacrificial love for His enemies through the Cross? Or is He the God who sells His love for ten percent of our income? He can't be both.

Tithe preachers have waxed themselves into a corner by preaching two Christs and presenting Him as one Person. One blesses His enemies, and one curses His family. One loves us just because, and one loves us just because our check cleared the bank. One came to preach good news to the poor, and one came to make the poor even poorer. This is a tragic comedy with no laughs.

Tithe preachers have trekked mud on the floor of God's provision of salvation through grace and faith and have corrupted its shine. Their footprints evidence the difficulty of preaching a Christ who freely dies for the world and declares eternal life a gift received by faith, but who later demands ten percent of income as the gift's price. This is the classic bait and switch con game. The merchandise is advertised at one price on the shelf, but when we get to the register, the clerk charges a higher price.

This is what tithe preachers have done to the message of salvation through grace and faith. They advertise a Christ who provides salvation and its benefits for the price of faith in Him. But when we get to the counter, they tell us that this particular model is gone, but they do have one that will cost us ten percent of our gross income—for life.

Let's open our eyes and stop playing games with ourselves and with these people. The truth is they never had the original model, and the one they're now trying to sell us is fake. *Stop focusing on the label and check the product.* This Gucci bag was made in someone's garage.

Which Christ are you going to serve? The one constructed by preachers to raise money? The one who loves you today, but abandons you tomorrow for paying your bills with money you worked for, but money the preacher feels is his? The one who offers you the gift of eternal life through faith, but then demands ten percent of your income to keep it? Why not serve the Christ of the Bible? Why not lay down your heavy load of religion. Did not Christ say the following:

> [28]Come to Me, all you who labor and are heavy laden, and I will give you rest.
>
> [29]Take My yoke upon you and learn from Me, for I am gentle and lowly in heart, and you will find rest for your souls.
>
> [30]For My yoke is easy and My burden is light.

Matthew 11:28-30

Child of God, when you give of your income to help someone in Christ's name, to worship the Lord, or to help proclaim the gospel, do you experience this kind of rest? Or are you filled with anxiety, fear, or guilt because you were coerced or manipulated into giving?

You will only experience God's rest in giving when you understand and accept the fact that the modern tithe system is an enemy of your salvation; the salvation you received through grace and faith (not by paying tithes). The modern tithe system and salvation by grace through faith can not peacefully coexist. One trusts in money to win God's favor; one trusts in Christ to win God's favor. If one belief system is to live, the other must die. Which belief system do you choose? Righteousness and blessing through tithes, or righteousness and blessing through Christ?

I call heaven and earth as witnesses today against you, that I have set before you life and death, blessing and cursing; therefore choose life, that both you and your descendants may live.

Deuteronomy 30:19

The Apostles Condemned Legalism (and thus Christian Tithing) in the Early Church

The book of Acts provides history of New Testament life in the early church. Its narrative shows the good and bad, the strengths and weaknesses of the church. It also provides graphic pictures of the internal and external opposition it faced in the first 30 years of its existence. Without question, the most lethal and insidious opposition came from within the church community.

Prior to the missionary ministry of Paul, the church preached only to Jews. The sole exception was when Peter was practically arm-twisted by the Holy Spirit to preach to Gentiles in Caesarea.[131] And he was criticized by Jewish Christians for doing this.[132] This is exceptionally important because it reveals the early church's mindset. In fact, Acts 11:19 speaks of Christian Jews who fled persecution and went "as far as Phoenicia, Cyprus, and Antioch, preaching the word to no one but the Jews only." Why did the church preach almost exclusively to Jews in the first 12-15 years of its existence? They were still trying to keep the law of Moses. This is the same mistake of our modern tithe preachers.

First-Century Church Legalists Believed One Had to Keep the Law of Moses to Be Saved by Jesus

It is hard to believe that the church founded by Jesus Christ on the foundations of grace and faith in Him alone could fall into the gross error of believing people could not be saved without keeping the law of Moses. Yet despite three years of intense training of the original apostles by the Lord, this was the overwhelming perspective. We can only speculate how such a doctrine was allowed to dominate a church that was governed in person by the original twelve apostles.[133]

Fortunately, however, an incident occurred that forced the apostles to publicly denounce those who were requiring others to obey the law as a requirement of Christian salvation. Acts 15 records how the early church dealt with this issue, and how we ought to deal with it. It is a long passage of Scripture, but bear with me. The length is justified by its priceless value in our battle against legalism.

The Apostles and Legalists Fight It Out in Jerusalem

And certain men came down from Judea and taught the brethren, "Unless you are circumcised according to the custom of Moses, you cannot be saved."

Paul and Barnabas Denounce Mixing Law and Grace
Therefore, when Paul and Barnabas had no small dissension and dispute with them, they determined that Paul and Barnabas and certain others of them should go up to Jerusalem, to the apostles and elders, about this question. So, being sent on their way by the church, they passed through Phonecia and Samaria, describing the conversion of the Gentiles; and they caused great joy to all the brethren. And when they had come to Jerusalem, they were received by the church and the apostles and the elders; and they reported all things that God had done with them.

Christian Pharisees Defend Mixing Law with Grace
But some of the sect of the Pharisee who believed rose up, saying,

"It is necessary to circumcise them, and to command them to keep the law of Moses."

The Jerusalem Council Discusses the Matter of Mixing Law and Grace

Now the apostles and elders came together to consider this matter. And when there had been much dispute, Peter rose up and said to them: "Men and brethren, you know that a good while ago God chose among us, that by my mouth the Gentiles should hear the word of the gospel and believe. "So God, who knows the heart, acknowledged them by giving them the Holy Spirit, just as He did to us, and made no distinction between us and them, purifying their hearts by faith.

Peter Denounces Mixing Law with Grace

Now therefore, why do you test God by putting a yoke on the neck of the disciples which neither our fathers nor we were able to bear? But we believe that through the grace of the Lord Jesus Christ we shall be saved in the same manner as they."

Then all the multitude kept silent and listened to Barnabas and Paul declaring how many miracles and wonders God had worked through them among the Gentiles. And after they had become silent, James answered, saying, "Men and brethren, listen to me: Simon has declared how God at the first visited the Gentiles to take out of them a people for His name. And with this the words of the prophets agree, just as it is written: 'After this I will return and will rebuild the tabernacle of David, which has fallen down; I will rebuild its ruins, and I will set it up; So that the rest of mankind may seek the Lord, even all the Gentiles who are called by My name, says the Lord who does all these things.'

Known to God from eternity are all His works.

James Denounces Mixing Law with Grace

Therefore I judge that we should not trouble those from among the Gentiles who are turning to God, but that we write to them to abstain from things polluted by idols, from sexual immorality, from things strangled, and from blood. For Moses has had throughout many generations those who preach him in every city, being read in the synagogues every Sabbath.

The Apostles, Elders, and Church Formally Denounce in Writing the Mixing of Law and Grace

Then it pleased the apostles and elders, with the whole church, to send chosen men of their own company to Antioch with Paul and Barnabus, namely, Judas who was also named Barsabas, and Silas, leading men among the brethren. They wrote this letter by them:

The Official Letter that Condemned Mixing Law with Grace

The apostles, the elders, and the brethren, to the brethren who are of the Gentiles in Antioch, Syria, and Cilicia:

Greetings.

Since we have heard that some who went out from us have troubled you with words, unsettling your souls, saying, "You must be circumcised and keep the law"—to whom we gave no such commandment—

It seemed good to us, being assembled with one accord, to send chosen men to you with our beloved Barnabas and Paul, men who have risked their lives for the name of our Lord Jesus Christ.

We have therefore sent Judas and Silas, who will also report the same things by word of mouth. For it seemed good to the Holy Spirit, and to us, to lay upon you no greater burden than these necessary things: that you abstain from things offered to idols, from blood, from things strangled, and from sexual immorality. If you keep yourselves from these, you will do well.

Farewell.

How the Letter Affected the Church

So when they were sent off, they came to Antioch; and when they had gathered the multitude together, they delivered the letter. When they had read it, they rejoiced over its encouragement.

An Interesting Observation about the Jerusalem Church

We will examine what this victory means for us and our battle against the modern tithe system. But first we must comment on an observation that was noted earlier. The Jerusalem church had a Dream Team of leaders consisting of apostles, prophets, teachers, healers, and miracle workers. The apostles had been intimate disciples and friends of the Lord Himself. They knew more than anyone how He lived and what He valued. They were there when the Lord regularly battled the Pharisees in public over legalism and hypocrisy. Plus, they had the unique privilege of actually sitting at His feet after the battles and receiving in-depth private explanations and instructions.

Joined with the apostles were other outstanding Christian leaders, miracle workers, prophets, preachers, and teachers. Some of them we know as Stephen, Philip, Silas, and Judas (not Iscariot, the traitor). Others are unknown, such as the seventy preachers, healers, and miracle workers that Jesus sent out to evangelize Jerusalem in Luke 10.

Besides this once-in-a-lifetime group of leaders being in one city church at the same time, there was also the uniqueness of the general church assembly. The Jerusalem Christians witnessed the Lord's ministry. They saw the miracles; they heard the teachings; they witnessed the crucifixion. Some had even seen and spoken to the Lord after His resurrection. And the entire city of Jerusalem had met or heard of someone who had claimed to have seen Him after His resurrection. In fact, on one occasion Jesus appeared to more than five hundred men at once.[134] And not to be overlooked is the outstanding miraculous ministry that was being conducted by Jesus through His followers in Jerusalem.

What does all of this have to do with the battle between legalism, and grace and faith? Here is the point I am laboring to highlight. *A doctrine that is totally foreign and antagonistic to the life and teachings of Christ flourished in a spiritual atmosphere that should have instantly killed it.* If an antichrist doctrine can flourish in a place where Christ's influence was great, how much more can an antichrist doctrine flourish where His influence is weak?

Let's speak more directly. Twenty centuries separate us from the life, death, and resurrection of Christ. Our church is not filled with leaders who have seen the resurrected Christ. Nor is it filled with miracle workers, healers, and prophets. It is instead overwhelmingly an assembly of people who are familiar with a perverted version of the historical Christ, but scarcely acquainted with the risen Christ.[135] Consequently, much of American Christianity is a dead religion: 99% of its activities are initiated, sustained, and culminated by the power of flesh—flesh directly empowered by the false tithe system.[136]

The point is, we are exceedingly weak, and our ignorance of the Truth makes us exceptionally prone to believe a lie. Thus, an antichrist doctrine such as the modern tithe flourishes in our midst.

The Church Formally Confronts the Legalists

Now back to the early Jerusalem church. Legalists in Jerusalem were like stubborn weeds in the beautiful lawn of early Christianity. It was easier for the apostles to celebrate the miracle of the lawn than to deal with the danger of the weeds. The apostles no doubt had tactfully dealt with legalism on a case-by-case basis.[137] But their failure to pull up these weeds by their roots was partly to blame for the growth of this threat. How dangerous is a religious weed left alone!

Legalist Weeds Attack Paul's Lawn

Paul's ministry to the Gentiles in foreign lands was exceptional. Multitudes of Gentiles abandoned their idols and converted to Christ. Soon, however, legalists from Judea arrived and told the new converts, "Unless you are circumcised according to the custom of Moses, you cannot be saved" (Acts 15:1).

The church officially and courageously denounced this as a lie. Their method, logic, and plainness of speech are exactly what we need to pull up the weed of the modern tithe.

Specific Arguments of the Early Church Against Legalism

It is important to note that the legalists of Paul's day did not verbally deny that salvation was found in Christ. No, their error was in teaching that salvation in Christ was only achievable if one also kept the law of Moses. Specifically, one had to be circumcised. This is an example of accepting Christ with words, but denying Him with actions, a favorite tactic of false teachers. The apostles were having none of this.

Paul and Barnabas Vehemently Argued with Legalists about the False Necessity of Circumcision for Salvation

Paul and Barnabas began the debate by having "no small dissension and dispute with them."[138] No small dissension is another way of saying it was a church fight. It was a highly emotional philosophical battle of two apostles who strongly believed salvation was gained solely by grace through faith with legalists who strongly believed faith and grace were not enough. One had to be circumcised!

What do we think of this church fight? What do we think of church leaders energetically arguing over doctrine? Doesn't this violate Christian unity? Isn't the Lord's cause harmed by church fights? That depends on two things: the object and the spirit of the fight. If we argue in the name of the Lord over money, material assets, ego, and fleshly power, then we are rightly condemned for our covetousness and selfishness.[139] Similarly, if we fight for a biblically just cause (in our estimation) with an evil heart, we are still condemned as sinners.[140]

But the apostles' fight with the legalists was not about stuff or ego; it was about the essence of the gospel. Satan, through legalistic teachers, was attempting to undermine the foundation of the gospel by adding man-made requirements for salvation. This doctrinal attack could not be ignored. To protect the new believers, the apostles followed the biblical mandate and tradition of directly and publicly challenging false religious doctrines.

Jude's commentary on this issue should never be forgotten or replaced with another method:

Beloved, while I was very diligent to write to you concerning our common salvation, I found it necessary to write to you exhorting you to contend earnestly for the faith which was once for all delivered to the saints. For certain men have crept in unnoticed....

Jude 3-4

Linking this passage with the modern tithe.

The Old Testament prophets and the New Testament apostles, prophets, and teachers publicly denounced false doctrines that distorted the gospel. It was right to do so then and it is right to do so now.

The modern tithing system distorts the gospel by its man-made requirements for us to pay men ten percent of our income to be blessed by God. It turns the gift and benefits of eternal life into a product to be purchased with money.[141] This man-made door of financial tithes into the blessings of God is no less dangerous and counterfeit than the door of circumcision constructed by the early church legalists. It is worthy of a grand public debate.

Peter Denounced the Legalists on the Basis that God Blessed Gentiles with the Holy Spirit without Circumcision Being Done

The apostle Peter used an irrefutable argument against the legalists. He reminded them of his reluctant trip and ministry to the Gentiles in Caesarea.[142] He reminded them that God had poured out the Holy Spirit upon the uncircumcised Gentiles, "and made no distinction between us and them, purifying their hearts by faith" (Acts 15:8-9).

Peter's argument was obvious: *If circumcision was necessary for salvation, why did Jesus pour out the Holy Spirit on Gentiles who were not circumcised?* He followed this argument with a stunning accusation: "Why do you test [tempt] God by putting a yoke on the neck of the disciples which neither our fathers nor we were able to bear?" (Acts 15:10).

Do not fail to appreciate the significance of this accusation. *To require anything other than genuine faith in Christ for salvation is an offense to God.* Peter called such actions "putting a yoke on the neck of the disciples." In plainer words, bondage.

Linking this passage with the modern tithe.

Christian Pharisees in Jerusalem said Jesus was the Lord, but that salvation could not be received without the additional requirement of circumcision. Today's tithe preachers say Jesus is Lord, but also that salvation can't be received without the additional requirement of strict obedience to the modern financial tithe.

Tithe preachers will object that they do not tell people they can't be saved unless they pay tithes. Yet this is exactly what they do. Only they do it subtly, indirectly, through hints and veiled threats. They will not come right out and tell you that you can't be saved unless you give the institutional church ten percent of your paycheck for life. This sounds too 14th century*ish*, too much like a religious scam. So they say just enough to scare and guilt money from the congregation, while simultaneously saying not enough to be convicted as traditional false prophets.

When a preacher directly or indirectly says, "Give me your money or God will curse you," he threatens your salvation. He takes away its benefits. If a preacher strips away the essential ingredients of salvation (e.g., forgiveness of sin, acceptance by God, fellowship of the Holy Spirit), you no longer have functional salvation. It is like owning a car with no engine or transmission. Technically it's a car, but practically it's useless.

If you consider the argument of Peter, you will never allow preachers to strip your salvation of its benefits. You will never be at the mercy of preachers who try to extort money from you under threat of God's judgment. Peter forced the legalists to publicly acknowledge that God had saved and given the Holy Spirit to people who had not satisfied the religious requirements of circumcision. The requirement obviously there was a commandment of men and not of God.

Apply this same logic to our contention with modern legalists over the false tithe. We are told subtly or otherwise that unless we give professional preachers our money, we can't be blessed. Yet God continues to love and bless us with both spiritual and natural blessings even when we don't submit to their threats.

Three More Arguments of Peter

Peter further pressed his case by citing three things in Acts 15:10 that we must remember as we protect our freedom from the legalists.

One, the legalists were "putting a yoke on the neck of the disciples...." A yoke is an instrument of bondage placed upon an animal to get it to work for the owner. In this case, the owners were the legalists. In our case, the owners are the tithe preachers who would use our labor to finance their dreams and religious bureaucracies.

It is interesting that our relationship with Christ also requires a yoke. But the circumstances are far different:

> Come to Me, all you who labor and are heavy laden, and I will give you rest. Take My yoke upon you and learn from Me, for I am gentle and lowly in heart, and you will find rest for your souls.
>
> For My yoke is easy and My burden is light.
>
> Matthew 11:28-30

Christ doesn't force a yoke upon anyone. He invites those worn out by sin and religion to voluntarily place His yoke upon them. If they do so, He promises, they will find rest for their souls. They find rest because His yoke is not an instrument of bondage to gain control, but an instrument of liberty to grant freedom. This is something that can't honestly be said of tithe preachers.

Two, the legalists rejected genuine believers as counterfeit Christians. Peter, however, discounted their error by recognizing the Gentile believers as disciples: "...on the neck of the disciples." Our tithe preachers commit the same error when they reject the legitimacy of Christians who refuse the bondage of the modern tithe.

Three, the legalists created impossible standards: "...which neither our fathers nor we were able to bear." The fact that every male Jew was circumcised according to the law proves that Peter was not referring to the impossibility of being circumcised. Rather, he referred to the impossibility of pleasing God or attaining righteousness through the law.

It was impossible for the Jews to please God by keeping the law.[143] So isn't it silly to assume that we Gentiles can please God by keeping an illegal modification of an obsolete law?[144] If legitimate animal sacrifices could not earn righteousness under the true law when it was still in effect, how can illegitimate cash sacrifices earn righteousness under a corrupted law two thousand years after it has been declared obsolete? *The tithe preachers have absolutely nothing to stand on except our ignorance of Christ and of the Scriptures.*

James Denounced the Legalists for Troubling Gentile Believers Who Were Turning to God

James added his condemnation in Acts 15:19 of the legalists by stating, "Therefore I judge that we should not trouble those from among the Gentiles who are turning to God...."

Church history and scriptural evidence show that James was one of the most respected apostles and possibly the premier Jerusalem church leader.[145] To not win his approval on a church matter was immensely damaging. To earn his public rebuke was utterly devastating. His spiritual prestige among Jewish believers was such that if he marked you as an enemy of the gospel, you were treated as a spiritual skunk.

This great apostle publicly judged that the legalists were "troubling" the Gentile converts. He did this knowing that his action would cause many legalistic teachers and ministries to be weakened and maybe even destroyed. Yet he did it anyway. He did it because he valued the salvation and well-being of the Gentile converts above the reputations of false teachers.[146]

Linking this passage with the modern tithe.

Church leaders have responsibilities "to take care of the church of God."[147] It is not their responsibility to take care of the reputations of people who destroy the church.

James publicly denounced the legalists because they "troubled" the church. Yet there is a strange silence among church leaders (can we really call them *leaders*?) who know the modern tithe is a farce. They do not require their followers to adhere to this corruption of the law, but they say nothing of other preachers who lay this burden on gullible believers. Why? Is it fear of man? Is it an addiction to praise? Is it indifference? Whatever it is, it isn't a trait of a true leader of God's church.

The Church Issues a Formal Letter Condemning Legalism

This historic meeting ended in a unanimous agreement among Paul and Barnabas and the leaders of the Jerusalem church. They wrote and published an official church letter that clearly denounced the legalists and their false doctrines (Acts 15:23-29). Much of the letter's objections came directly from James.[148]

The letter itself is a surprisingly short response to such a critical and potentially church-derailing situation. But its power far exceeded its mere 138 words.[149]

First, the church stated that the legalists were "troubling" and "unsettling" the souls of the Gentile believers with their words.

Second, the church stated they were doing this in the name of the Jerusalem church, although they had received no such authority from the church.

Third, the church stated that the legalists were teaching their doctrines in defiance of the church and the Holy Spirit.

Linking this passage with the modern tithe.

The Christian church is now too widely dispersed and divided (and corrupt) to authoritatively denounce with one voice our modern legalists as the early church denounced their legalists. But this should not stop true Christian leaders from individually denouncing the modern tithe as a false doctrine.

They can and should specifically follow the example of the early church and denounce our modern tithe preachers for (1) troubling and unsettling the souls of believers (especially the poor), (2) teaching a false doctrine in the name of the Lord, and (3) teaching a doctrine in defiance of the church and the Holy Spirit.

The remnant of Christians who have not sold their souls and ministries to money must courageously speak out against the church's tithing system of extortion and bribery. It is not enough to simply condemn easy-target sins of the world, such as homosexuality and abortion.

What about the church's sins? Did God not say, "For the time has come for judgment to begin at the house of God" (1 Peter 4:17). We have no right to condemn the sins of the world as long as the church sells God's blessings through its illegitimate system of mandatory tithes and offerings. The time to speak out against this modern day superstition is now.

CHAPTER 19

No Christian Tithing in Hebrews 7

Tithe preachers erroneously and irrationally use Hebrews 7 to justify their tithing system. This is surprising, since Hebrews 6–10 condemns as obsolete the need and practice of tithing.

Why would a preacher try to justify present day tithing by using a portion of the Bible that comprehensively destroys its foundation? This comes from desperate rather than ideal circumstances. The tithe preacher is like a drowning man who tries to save himself by reaching for an object that can't possibly support his weight. But he reaches for it anyway because the alternative is certain death.

In this case, it's the death of guaranteed cash flow from illegitimate tithes. With billions of dollars a year at stake, it is no mystery that tithe preachers use desperate and illogical means to preserve their control over this fortune.

How Tithe Preachers Use Hebrews 7 to Support the Modern System of Financial Tithes

Tithe preachers teach that the church must pay them financial tithes and offerings because they are the direct spiritual descendants of the Levites. Of course, the Bible doesn't teach or slightly hint at this. But tithe preachers must claim this connection to bring us under the obligation of Old Testament Jews who had to support the Levitical priesthood.

Hebrews 7 is the only genuine New Testament passage that speaks directly about tithes. It also speaks prominently about the priesthood. Tithes and the priesthood in a single New Testament chapter. A tithe preacher's dream!

The tithing legalists use the first ten verses to construct three defenses of tithes. First, Abraham paid tithes to Melchizedek before the law. *If Abraham had to do it, so do we.* Second, ministers of God are commanded to receive tithes from Christians. *If ministers are commanded to receive tithes, Christians are commanded to pay tithes.* Third, Jesus receives tithes during the New Testament era. *If Jesus receives tithes, someone must pay tithes.* Later in this chapter, we will thoroughly identify and correct this fatal mixture of truth and error.

How the Book of Hebrews Destroys Modern Tithing

Christian tithers are unaware that the book of Hebrews destroys the old and modern tithe systems. It destroys the old tithe system by declaring it obsolete; it destroys the new tithe system by revealing it a fraud. Ignorance of these facts is partially because most Christians have either not read Hebrews, or they have read it, but don't understand it.

From time to time their preacher uses a verse or two in Hebrews 7 in support of tithes, and they accept it as truth. But an honest review of Hebrews proves that attempts to use it to justify the modern tithe are illegitimate and illogical.

An Overview of Hebrews Provides the Proper Context to Discuss Tithes

Hebrews was written to Jewish Christians to prevent them from back-sliding and returning to Judaism—seeking righteousness through keeping the law of Moses.[150] The author's strategy was to show that Christ was infinitely superior to their former religion. To this end, the writer explicitly established critical truths:

- Jesus is superior to the prophets (Hebrews 1:1-3).
- Jesus is superior to the angels (Hebrews 1:4-2:18).
- Jesus is superior to Moses (Hebrews 3:1-19).
- Jesus is superior to Joshua (Hebrews 4:1-13).
- Jesus is superior to Aaron (Hebrews 4:14-5:10).
- Jesus is the new and eternal high priest of a new and better priesthood and covenant (Hebrews 5:5-10; 6:1; 7:1-10:1-23).

Notice the text used to justify Christian tithes (Hebrews 7) is in the middle of the discussion of Christ's superior priesthood and better covenant. It is critical to note the topic of Hebrews 7 is not tithes, but the superiority of Christ. Tithes were mentioned only as part of the argument that established Christ as the best and last tithe and as eternal high priest. The topic is Christ, not tithes or even priesthoods.

The Old Testament Law Represented Christ

It is a mainstream church doctrine that the Old Testament speaks primarily of Christ. In fact, Christ Himself said, "You search the [Old Testament] Scriptures, for in them you think you have eternal life; and these are they which testify of Me" (John 5:39).

Listed below is a small sampling of Old Testament sayings or events that the church agrees testify of Christ:[151]

- Noah built an ark that saved the world (Genesis 6-8).

- The ark represents Christ (1 Peter 3:18-21).

- Israel was saved from the death angel by the blood of a Passover lamb (Exodus 12:1-30).

- The Passover Lamb and its festival, the Feast of Unleavened Bread, represent Christ (1 Corinthians 5:7).

- Israel was supernaturally provided bread from heaven (Exodus 16:1-22).

- The bread from heaven represents Christ (John 6:25-35).

- Israel was supernaturally provided water from a rock (Exodus 17:1-7).

- The rock represents Christ (1 Corinthians 10:4).

- Israel was provided rest through a ceremonial Sabbath (Exodus 16:23-30).

- The Sabbath represents Christ (Hebrews 3:7-19; 4:1-10).

- The Jerusalem temple was the center of religious worship (2 Chronicles 5-7).

- The temple represents Christ (John 2:13-22).

The apostle Paul summed this point conclusively by stating that all of the law represents Christ: "So let no one judge you in food or in drink, or regarding a festival or a new moon or Sabbaths, which are a shadow of things to come, but the substance is of Christ" (Colossians 2:16-17).

Thousands of papers, articles, and books have been written to establish the above points that Christ is represented in the prophets and the law. A comparable volume of work tells us that His birth, life, death, and resurrection fulfilled every demand of the law. Consequently, the law has no power over us.

Christian leaders faithfully complement this written testimony by passionately and consistently telling us that we are free from the law's obligations of special diets, observances of festivals and new moons, strict obedience to Sabbaths, and animal sacrifices. Nonetheless, there is a strange inconsistency concerning the fulfillment of one particular Old Testament religious ordinance: the tithe.

Is the Tithe the Only Old Testament Law to Survive the Cross?

It is strange indeed that preachers who passionately proclaim that Jesus fulfilled and freed us from keeping the law insist that we pay tithes according to the law. Of course, this is illogical. But tithe preachers comfortably sit on this jagged rock because, as they like to proclaim, "tithing existed before the law."

Here is a good place for us to systematically rebut the tithe preachers three main twistings of Scripture in Hebrews.

Tithe Argument #1:
Abraham Paid Tithes to Melchizedek Before the Law

> For this Melchizedek, king of Salem, priest of the Most High God, who met Abraham returning from the slaughter of the kings and blessed him, to whom also Abraham gave a tenth part of all...
>
> Now consider how great this man was, to whom even the patriarch Abraham gave a tenth of the spoils.

> Hebrews 7:1, 2, 4

Tithe preachers rightly teach that Abraham paid tithes to a mysterious Old Testament figure named Melchizedek before the giving of the law (see *Answers to Pre-Law Arguments to Mandatory Tithes*). This is their proof that tithing is a timeless command. The obvious conclusion is if it existed *before* and during the law, it exists *after* the law. So, according to tithe preachers' logic, Christians can't claim exemption from tithing based on the law's end.

Rebuttal to Tithe Argument #1:
Abraham Paid Tithes to Melchizedek Before the Law

1. The Tithes of Abraham and Moses Were Dissimilar
First, it is true that tithes existed prior to the law. However, the tithes

that existed prior to the law are not the tithes that existed during the law. There's virtually no similarity in these two tithes.

As we showed in a previous chapter, *Answers to Pre-Law Arguments for Mandatory Tithes*, pre-law tithes were voluntary. Abraham voluntarily paid tithes once to Melchizedek, and Jacob voluntarily promised to pay tithes to God in exchange for certain benefits. Neither man, however, was obligated by God to pay tithes.

In contrast, once tithes were made part of the law, they were mandatory, highly regulated, and prophetically pointed to Christ. Moses said this concerning the new system of tithes: "You shall not at all do as we are doing here today—every man doing whatever is right in his own eyes...." (Deuteronomy 12:8).

Do not miss these two points: (1) Tithes that existed prior to the law—unregulated, voluntary tithes—were *actions* abolished by the law of Moses; (2) Tithes that existed during the law—regulated, involuntary tithes—were a *system* abolished by the cross of Christ. These two dissimilar tithes existed under different circumstances, for different purposes, in different times. It is as improper to use one tithe in the place of the other as it is to use a football in the place of a baseball.

Tithe preachers, however, are skilled trapeze artists who swing and twirl on the involuntary tithes rung and then fly through the air with the greatest of ease to swing and twirl on the voluntary tithes rung. One moment they tell us we must pay tithes or be cursed. When we tell them we don't pay tithes because we are not under the law, they flip to the other rung and say we must pay tithes because tithes were before the law.

Don't be dazzled by the tithe preacher's dizzying performance on the rungs. Instead ask yourself, how much sense does this twirling make? How can anyone be simultaneously obligated to unregulated, voluntary tithes *and* regulated, involuntary tithes? These two different tithes did not coexist in the Old Testament, and they certainly do not coexist now in the church age. Furthermore, how can anyone be *obligated* to give *voluntary* tithes? Sounds like an offer from Don Corleone of *The Godfather*.

In any event, we are not obligated by the tithe preacher's creative references to Abraham or Moses for the payment of tithes; since

Abraham was replaced by Moses and Moses was replaced by Christ—who provided Himself as the last tithe. (More about this later.)

2. *The Tithe Preacher's Pre-Law Tithe Argument Requires Present-Day Circumcision for Righteousness*

Second, if consistency means anything, the tithe preacher's defense that Christians must pay tithes because Abraham paid tithes indirectly obligates us to perpetually imitate all of Abraham's religious acts. We certainly wouldn't want people to think we are interested only in reviving ancient customs that earn us money. That would be self-serving, manipulative, and dishonest. And that's not us, right? So let's prove this untrue by following Abraham all the way.

In Genesis 17:10-12 (before the law, I remind you) God commands Abraham to enter an everlasting covenant with Him through circumcision:

> This is My covenant which you shall keep, between Me and you and your descendants after you: Every male child among you shall be circumcised; 11and you shall be circumcised in the flesh of your foreskins, and it shall be a sign of the covenant between Me and you. He who is eight days old among you shall be circumcised...And the uncircumcised male child, who is not circumcised in the flesh of his foreskin, that person shall be cut off from his people; he has broken My covenant.

This pre-law command was later made part of the law of Moses, without any modifications.[152] What are we going to do with this command? This is where male tithe preachers stuff hardcover books down the front of their pants as a last line of defense and anxiously explain that religious circumcision is an obsolete Old Testament command that was fulfilled in Christ.

Of course, we could use their pre-law tithe logic (really *illogic*) and argue that since circumcision existed before the law, it exists after the law. But for the moment let's not require tithe preachers to follow their own logic. Who wants to resurrect the blade anyway? Let's simply insist that the logic tithe preachers use to bury circumcision also be used to bury tithes.

3. The Tithe Preacher's Pre-Law Tithe Argument Requires Present-Day Animal Sacrifices for the Forgiveness of Sins

Third, Abraham sacrificed animals as burnt offerings to God prior to the law (Genesis 22). This practice was not only added to the law of Moses, it became its very foundation. Tithe preachers now face the same dilemma they have with circumcision. They can act consistently with their pre-law logic for reviving tithes and revive animal sacrifices. Or they can use their self-serving circumcision strategy. They can explain how the death of Christ made this practice obsolete.

What have they chosen? To revive animal sacrifices the way they have revived tithes? No. They've correctly concluded that Old Testament sacrifices represented the future sacrifice of Christ. Now that Christ has come, there is no longer a need for representative sacrifices.

The entire Christian church, tithers and non-tithers, has effortlessly accepted this as a fundamental, nonnegotiable truth.[153] If any Christian preacher wrote an article or book, or preached a message in support of reviving the sacrifice of animals for the covering of our sins, he would be immediately denounced as a false prophet. This would be the response even if he used the argument that Abraham offered animal sacrifices before the law. Why, oh why, then is it so acceptable to use this faulty logic to revive the obsolete doctrine of tithes?

The answer is shamefully obvious—cash. Money has a way of changing our values and judgments.

Tithe Argument #2:
Ministers Commanded to Receive Tithes from Christians

And indeed those who are of the sons of Levi, who receive the priesthood, have a commandment to receive tithes from the people according to the law, that is from their brethren, though they have come from the loins of Abraham.

Hebrews 7:5

Tithe preachers believe and teach that they are the sons of Levi, who receive the priesthood, and Christians are the people from whom they collect tithes. They also stress they have received "a commandment to receive tithes from the people." This is non-negotiable, they tell us. It's God's idea and they can't alter it.

Rebuttal to Tithe Argument #2:
Ministers Commanded to Receive Tithes from Christians

Christian ministers have naturally gravitated to the belief that they are the spiritual descendants of the Old Testament Levitical priesthood. They are, according to the error, the new Levites. This dangerous elitist belief is built upon several false premises that we have identified or will identify in later chapters. Here we will focus on the abuse of the following Scriptures in Hebrews 7:

> And indeed those who are of the sons of Levi, who receive the priesthood, have a commandment to receive tithes from the people according to the law, that is, from their brethren, though they have come from the loins of Abraham...Here mortal men receive tithes...Even Levi, who receives tithes....

> Hebrews 7:5, 8-9

Slaying the Two-Headed Priesthood Lie that Tithe Preachers Use to Collect Financial Tithes

Tithe preachers use two priesthood lies to justify and collect the illegal tithe. The first one is that the above Scriptures speak literally of Christian ministers. The second is that these Scriptures speak figuratively of Christian ministers. (I know, I know, how does one go up and down or east and west at the same time. All I've been able to come up with is, they've got the gift.) Each lie takes a different path, but both end in our wallets.

1. The Literal Priesthood Lie — One does not have to be a Bible scholar to easily see that Hebrews 7 speaks of literal Jews and not literal

Christians. Verse 5 explicitly tells us these Levites are literal Jews. They (1) are the sons of Levi, (2) receive the priesthood, (3) receive tithes according to the law, and (4) come from the loins of Abraham.

If points one and two are creatively debated and dismissed, we are still left with points three and four. The Levites in Hebrews 7 received tithes *according to the law* and came from *the loins of Abraham.*

When we refuse to pay tithes because we are not under the law, our tithe preachers answer that they are not collecting tithes according to the law of Moses, but according to the example of Abraham. So by their own admission, Hebrews 7 does not speak of them (except when it serves their purposes). Furthermore, our tithe preachers are not Jews from the tribe of Levi, but generally are white guys with European descent and black guys with African descent, both ridiculously claiming to be something they are not to qualify as God's tax collectors.

2. The Figurative Priesthood Lie — Unraveling this lie requires a bit more effort because it is built on more than a few Scriptures taken out of context. The figurative priesthood is built on the psychological needs of people who prefer man more than God and flesh more than Spirit, and the natural tendency of the church to go from the liberty of God to the bondage of man. Therefore, much of our argument must deal with these tendencies.

It is a strange truth that nearly all religious people are more comfortable approaching God through a human being rather than approaching Him directly.[154] A graphic picture of this disturbing tendency is seen in Exodus 19. God told Moses to share with Israel these incredible plans for the nation:

> You have seen what I did to the Egyptians, and how I bore you on eagles' wings and brought you to Myself. Now therefore, if you will indeed obey My voice and keep My covenant, then you shall be a special treasure to Me above all people; for all the earth is Mine. And you shall be to Me a kingdom of priests and a holy nation.

> Exodus 19:4-6

How did Israel respond to the Almighty's invitation to be spiritually intimate? They turned it down (Exodus 20:18-21). An ancient
story with such prophetic overtones.

God desires to speak to His people directly. We desire that He
speak to us through a hierarchy of flesh, a religious bureaucracy.
Do you think I'm reading too much into this one incident? Recall that
this is not the only record we have of Israel rejecting God for a man.
More than 500 years later Israel demanded that God no longer rule
them through the prophet Samuel. They wanted to be ruled by a king
instead. When Samuel prayed to the Lord about this crisis, God
answered, "Heed the voice of the people in all that they say to you; for
they have not rejected you, but they have rejected Me, that I should
not reign over them" (1 Samuel 8:7).

This incident does more than simply reinforces the truth that people have strong tendencies toward religious bureaucracy, thus making
the figurative priesthood lie possible. It undermines this tendency by
powerfully illustrating the cost and danger of such bureaucracy.

Cost and Danger of Choosing Man to Rule You Instead of God

God offered Israel direct access to Himself. They chose instead to
approach Him through the ministry of the prophet, Moses. This
request (and their later actions) made it necessary to create a cumber-
some, though prophetically useful, priesthood and system of
sacrifices, offerings, and ordinances.[155] In terms of bureaucracy,
however, it was extremely expensive. The cost was the addition of
religious rules, and the loss of intimacy with God.

Similarly, there were negative consequences when Israel grew tired
of the prophetic ministry they had demanded and subsequently
demanded a king. God even provided a list of the bad things that
would happen if Israel persisted in their demand. The list is long, but
we need to see it because it describes the present day tithe system (and
its man-made priesthood) with astonishing accuracy:

> Now therefore, heed their voice. However, you shall solemnly fore-
> warn them, and show them the behavior of the king who will reign
> over them.

So Samuel told all the words of the Lord to the people who asked him for a king.

And he said, "This will be the behavior of the king who will reign over you: He will take your sons and appoint them for his own chariots and to be his horsemen, and some will run before his chariots.

He will appoint captains over his thousands and captains over his fifties, will set some to plow his ground and reap his harvest, and some to make his weapons of war and equipment for his chariots.

He will take your daughters to be perfumers, cooks, and bakers. And he will take the best of your fields, your vineyards, and your olive groves, and give them to his servants.

He will take a tenth of your grain and your vintage, and give it to his officers and servants.

And he will take your male servants, your female servants your finest young men, and your donkeys, and put them to his work.

He will take a tenth of your sheep. And you will be his servants.

And you will cry out in that day because of your king whom you have chosen for yourselves, and the Lord will not hear you in that day.

Nevertheless the people refused to obey the voice of Samuel; and they said, "No, but we will have a king over us, that we also may be like all the nations, and that our king may judge us and go out before us and fight our battles."

And Samuel heard all the words of the people, and he repeated them in the hearing of the Lord.

So the Lord said to Samuel, "Heed their voice, and make them a king...."

1 Samuel 8:9-22

Price Israel Paid for Choosing a King to Rule Them Instead of God.

God is merciful; so He warned Israel of the dangers of choosing a king. Yet He is also just; so He allowed them to pay the price for their decision. What was that price? It is summed under four categories.

First, God warned that the nature of kings is to take. Six times in His warning He said, "He will take." Even worse than this, the Lord said the king would "take the best." But how could this be? How could a man simply take from God's people whatever he desired?

His authority came from two things: his army and his calling. His army intimidated God's people through fear; who could resist the king's army? His calling obligated God's people through necessity; how could the king protect the country without access to its goods?

Second, God warned that "you will be his servants." When God ruled Israel through the prophet's ministry, He considered them His own servants. Yet when they transitioned to a nation ruled by a king, He considered them the king's servants—not directly His own. Why?

Prophets had two primary missions in life. They were to hear from God, and to deliver His message to the nation. The only tools prophets had to compel obedience to their message were their own holy lives, moral persuasion, prayer, and supernatural acts of God—if God chose to validate the prophet's message by such means. But this was no guarantee. For this reason, some prophets were obeyed and some were not.

Kings also had two primary missions in life. They were to govern internally, and to protect the nation from external enemies. The king's primary tool to accomplish these missions was his army. This fundamental tool of any successful king was both a blessing and a curse to the nation. It gave him the power to establish internal order and to protect the country from its enemies, but also power to impose his will on God's people.

Third, God warned that "you will cry out in that day because of your king." The path of disobedience often takes one through phases of temporary success. Yet inevitably the final destination is ruin. As is so often the case, the very thing we lust after becomes our greatest trouble. God warned that the system they lusted after would cause them intolerable pain.

Fourth, God warned that "the Lord will not hear you in that day." This was an ominous warning that the consequences of this sin were not of the sort that could be totally erased simply by saying, "I'm sorry." The Christian woman who defies the Lord's command and marries the wrong man may later ask for and receive forgiveness, but she is still married to the wrong man.

Israel would later repent of its sin of desiring a king to rule them instead of God, but that system of government and its inherent weaknesses ruled them for over 400 years. Furthermore, it was only removed when He allowed invading armies to violently overthrow and enslave Israel. Getting rid of the effects of rejecting God is often difficult, costly, and horrifying.

Linking the Tithe Preachers' Figurative Priesthood to Israel's Example

We are those people who rejected direct access to God for indirect access through Moses; we'd rather experience God through the filter of a man. We are those people who later rejected indirect access to God through Samuel for no access to God in exchange for a king; we're willing to allow bureaucracy to kill what remains of our relationship with God if it gets the job done. We've chosen practical efficiency over spiritual intimacy.

The four-part curse that Israel incurred for rejecting God for a human king has similarly fallen upon us for rejecting Him for a human priesthood of pastor-kings. My title of the modern pastor is provocative, but unfortunately accurate. He claims (in one way or another) to have special access to and status with God above every Christian person and ministry, and to function as the mediator between God and the church. This is his claim as prophet and priest. Furthermore, he believes the office of pastor has inherent rights of absolute authority over the church.[156] This is his claim as king.

Curse 1: It is the nature of pastor-kings to take.

Pastor-kings see themselves as the critical element that maintains and furthers the kingdom of God. They are the generals of God's armies, the star quarterbacks, the ace pitchers. Without them, all is doomed.

This delusion of self-importance compels them to make oppressive material demands of God's people—for the good of the kingdom, of course. And like Israel's kings, they not only take, but they take the best: *"Give me ten percent of your gross income for life."*[157] But money is not the worst of their seizures. The worst thing they take from us is our ability to hear God directly and to obey His voice. We'll talk more about this in the next section. Right now, I'll discuss how they're able to take from us.

A king without an army really is no king at all. He has no way to compel obedience. Pastor-kings have no physical armies, but they do have psychological advantages and spiritual tools that give them power over their subjects. These are (1) people's desire for a king, (2) the false authority of their own self-important calling, and (3) their claimed power to invoke curses and blessings on God's people. This is the pastor-king's army of three.

Curse 2: We are the servants of pastor-kings.
Earlier I stated that pastor-kings take our ability to directly hear and obey God. This occurs because we can truly only serve one king at a time. It is inevitable that the interests and demands of our two kings will clash. King Jesus values people above money, and King Pastor values money above people. How do we approach this dilemma? It is then that we must "be loyal to the one and despise the other" (Matthew 6:24). Usually, it is the pastor who gets the loyalty and Jesus who gets the boot.

The reason for this is deep down inside we want to be dominated and told what to do. Recall that Israel's king came to power only because they said, "We will have a king over us, that we also may be like all the nations, and that our king may judge us and go out before us and fight our battles" (1 Samuel 8:19). To this end, we have taken the New Testament title of *pastor,* stripped it of its New Testament character, given it the powers of an Old Testament king, and have created for ourselves a combination pastor-king.

We are servants of the pastor-king because that is the nature of the game. When the king comes to power, his first priority, whether stated or not, is to strengthen himself. He creates a system that sustains and protects his power and kingdom; that is his calling. Dissent is not valued as an inherent right of equals under God, but as treason against the pastor-king—and subsequently against God. Incidentally, in this atmosphere, it is almost impossible to stop the exploitation and cruelty of the modern tithe.

Curse 3: We are crying out because of our pastor-kings.
Obeying the commands of God is hard on the flesh; obeying the commands of man is hard on the spirit. We created and empowered a priesthood of pastor-kings to take the danger and uncertainty out of our spiritual walk. And to a certain degree we have accomplished these goals. Our pastor-kings and their bureaucracies maintain strict order and discipline, and fight our battles, just as we requested of them. Yet this order and safety has come at a ridiculously high price.

Unwittingly, when we removed the danger and uncertainty of obeying the Holy Spirit for the safety and certainty of our priesthood of pastor-kings, we removed God. We removed the discomfort of His ways and of waiting on Him to speak and act. But consequently we also removed the perfection of His ways, the awe of seeing Him act, and the deep satisfaction and results of hearing His voice. All of this has resulted in an embarrassing boredom with church life and a tormenting thirst that can only be satisfied by that which we have rejected: the danger and uncertainty of God.

The church prays for escape from this boredom and thirst. But it does so without understanding that the root of the problem is our love affair with pastor-kings and religious bureaucracy, which produces order, but destroys life.

Curse 4: The Lord does not remove the problems caused by our priesthood of pastor-kings.
The problems caused by our system of pastor-kings and religious bureaucracy are incurable, terminal. They are with us until we take our last breath of minimal religious life. My dismal conclusion admits that individuals and pockets of Christians here and there will mercifully escape this fate. But they are the exceptional minority.

The vast majority of us are terminally afflicted for two reasons. One is that kings love power, and kings have armies to protect their power. Our priesthood of pastor-kings is not going to willingly give up the control they have over us and our money. It can only be taken from them by the wholesale abandonment of their rule by the masses. Prayers for deliverance are never answered of people unwilling to walk away from bondage.

The other reason our condition is terminal is that although multitudes of Christians find their spiritual conditions deplorable, they find much of the pastor-king system attractive. This, too, prevents deliverance.

Tithe Argument #3:
Jesus Receives Tithes During the New Testament Era

Here mortal men receive tithes, but there he receives them, of whom it is witnessed that he lives.

Hebrews 7:8

According to tithe preachers, this is a direct reference to them receiving tithes. They also believe this directly states Jesus receives those tithes. If Jesus receives tithes that are collected from preachers, how can the tithing system be obsolete? And doesn't this collection and acceptance of tithes during the time of the Book of Hebrews validate New Testament tithing? Hhhmmmm....

Rebuttal to Tithe Argument #3:
Jesus Receives Tithes During the New Testament Era

We know logically that Jesus does not receive tithes today, simply because there is no such thing as a New Testament tithe. Christianity is foundationally based on the sacrifice of Christ as our eternal tithe.[158] Since the purpose of the temporary tithes of Moses has been fulfilled, and the price of the eternal tithe of Christ has been paid, there is no need for anyone to continue to pay a debt in cash that could only be, and has already been, satisfied by blood. Nonetheless, there is one Scripture in Hebrews 7 that tithe preachers use to teach otherwise: "Here mortal men receive tithes, but there he receives them, of whom it is witnessed that he lives" (v. 8).

Earlier we saw that the "mortal men" of verse eight who received tithes in Hebrews 7 were "sons of Levi, who receive the priesthood, have a commandment to receive tithes from the people according to the law, that is, from their brethren, though they have come from the loins of Abraham" (v. 5). But who is the implied non-mortal man of verse eight who "receives them, of whom it is witnessed that he lives"? Who else could this be except Christ? The answer is Melchizedek, the guy Abraham paid a tithe to in Genesis 14.

Abraham and Descendants Honored Christ by Tithing to Melchizedek

Hebrews emphasizes with various arguments that Jesus Christ is the only Mediator and Priest between us and God.[159] One of the arguments used is who paid tithes to whom. Obviously, says the writer of Hebrews, the person who blesses the other is greater than the one he blesses (v. 1, 7), and he who receives the tithe is greater than the one who pays it (v. 4).[160] Hebrews 7 explains that Abraham, the father of Israel, was blessed by and paid tithes to Melchizedek (v. 1–3). Therefore, Melchizedek is greater than Abraham. What does this have to do with tithes? Nothing except that the tithe is the tool used to establish the superiority of Melchizedek—really Jesus—over Abraham.

Hebrews further develops this point by showing that when Abraham paid a tithe to Melchizedek, "even Levi, who receives tithes, paid tithes through Abraham, so to speak, for he was still in the loins of his father when Melchizedek met him" (v. 9-10).[161] A truth of critical importance: The Old Testament priesthood that had not yet come from Abraham's lineage figuratively paid tithes to Christ when Abraham paid tithes to Melchizedek. For Melchizedek represents Christ.[162]

So when Hebrews 7:8 says, "Here mortal men receive tithes, *but there he [Melchizedek/Jesus] receives them, of whom it is witnessed that he lives*," it is simply summing up this point: Jesus Christ is greater than Abraham and his descendants because Abraham paid tithes to Melchizedek, who was a type of Christ. Consequently, Jesus is greater than Moses, since Moses is a descendant of Abraham. Naturally, it follows that if Jesus is greater than Moses, He is greater than the law of Moses.

Do you see the gross error of the tithe preachers? They have totally misunderstood Hebrews 7 by focusing on the temporary practice of tithes instead of the eternal priesthood of Christ. This is a proof of my earlier statement that lust for money distorts judgment. Another reason why the Bible says such people are "of corrupt minds and destitute of the truth" (1 Timothy 6:5). The power of money.

Concerning Hebrews 7:8, when we get our eyes off of money, it is easy to see that within the context of the chapter, the verse speaks of Melchizedek. Furthermore, it's nonsense to take a passage of Scripture (Hebrews 7:1-10) that clearly speaks of Melchizedek and how he represents the superiority of Christ, and to creatively interpret one of its Scriptures so that it teaches exactly the opposite of this obvious meaning.

It is apparent that tithe preachers and their followers have not intelligently considered this logical conclusion of their error: The continuation of tithes *in any form* testifies that Christ is a failure and that we are yet in our sins.

The next chapter explains why.

CHAPTER 20

Jesus is the Last Legitimate Tithe: Hebrews 10

The death of Jesus Christ was the last legitimate and acceptable tithe to God. In contrast, any offering designated as a tithe given to God after Christ's death testifies that the death of Christ was an insufficient sacrifice for our sins. Certainly, though, those who participate in the financial tithe do not consciously believe or state this. Preachers do it because of its immense profitability, and regular church people do it because they've been erroneously taught that God requires it. Few participants understand the spiritual significance of their misguided actions.

Spiritual Purpose of the Tithe

The deepest, most fundamental and prophetic purpose of the Old Testament tithe is its representation of the offering of Christ's blood to pay for our sins. This truth is echoed in thousands of Christian books and sermons. It is taught in hundreds of Christian colleges and seminaries. It is a mainstream Christian doctrine that is shared by Christian denominations and organizations that are otherwise deeply divided on doctrinal issues.

We all rally around Scriptures that refer to Christ as "the Lamb of God who takes away the sin of the world" (John 1:29), "Christ, our

Passover, was sacrificed for us" (1 Corinthians 5:17), and "...an offering and a sacrifice to God for a sweet-smelling aroma" (Ephesians 5:2).

We have concluded that these and similar references point back to the sin-sacrifice system of the law of Moses. And we have concluded that the blood of Christ spoken of in the New Testament is a prophetic fulfillment of Old Testament animal sacrifices.

Now I must ask the question, how can we overwhelmingly believe Christ fulfilled the Old Testament sacrifice-tithe system and simultaneously require Christians to pay tithes? Was His blood acceptable to God once and for all, or must we, as tithe preachers contend, supplement Christ's offering of blood with our offering of money?

Acceptable Sacrifice of Christ as Our Tithe Made Old Testament System of Tithes and Offerings Obsolete

The Old Testament system of tithes and offerings was always deficient and temporary. Its deficiency was that it could cover sins, but not permanently remove them: "And every priest stands ministering daily and offering repeatedly the same sacrifices, which can never take away sins" (Hebrews 10:11). Its temporariness was that God's plan was always to permanently remove our sins: "...then He adds, 'Their sins and their lawless deeds I will remember no more" (Hebrews 10:17). God's single answer to this two-fold problem was to offer Christ as a one-time sacrifice-tithe that would eternally remove our sins.

Christ is the Only Tithe that Has Ever Pleased God

Are you aware that the man-made tithes you pay your religious system are based upon a system that never pleased God? That's right; the Old Testament tithe system that God Himself created was something He tolerated not celebrated. It was an imperfect, temporary fix that

He eagerly desired to stop forever, not continue in the New Testament in another form. Speaking of His offering as the final tithe, Christ said of God the Father:

> Therefore, when He [Christ] came into the world, He said: "Sacrifice and offering You did not desire, but a body You have prepared for Me. In burnt offerings and sacrifices for sin You had no pleasure.
>
> Hebrews 10:5-6

The burnt offerings and sacrifices included tithes!

These Scriptures were first spoken prophetically by King David in Psalm 40:6. How is it that a man who lived under and obeyed the law of Moses understood that God received no pleasure from its tithes and offerings, but New Testament preachers do not understand this? And it is apparent they do not understand, or why would they demand we obey their outrageous version of Moses' tithe system?

Furthermore, how is it that they want us to believe God is pleased with their tithe system, which is fictionally based on the law, when even God was not pleased with the law's tithe system? An even more disturbing question is why do so many Christians blindly follow such an illogical lie? One reason we have not discussed is our ignorance of Christ as our tithe.

How Christ is Our Tithe

We are not used to thinking of Christ as our tithe, only as our sacrifice or offering for sin, not realizing this is simply another way of calling Him our tithe. We are not used to this because our preachers can't declare Christ as our tithe and simultaneously require us to pay tithes. If they did so, we may ask why they require us to pay a debt that has been fully paid by Christ. The absurdity of continuing to submit sacrifices and offerings to God that are no longer accepted or required is emphasized in Hebrews. Look at the following verses:

[Christ] who does not need daily, as those high priests, to offer up sacrifices, first for His own sins and then for the people's, for this He did once for all when He offered up Himself (7:27).

But Christ came as High Priest...not with the blood of goats and calves, but with His own blood He entered the Most Holy Place once for all, having obtained eternal redemption (9:11-12).

For the law, having a shadow of the good things to come, and not the very image of the things, can never with these same sacrifices, which they offer continually year by year, make those who approach perfect. For then would they not have ceased to be offered [emphasis mine] (10:1-2).

And every priest stands ministering daily and offering repeatedly the same sacrifices, which can never take away sins. But this Man, after He had offered one sacrifice for sin forever, sat down at the right hand of God (10:11-12).

For by one offering He has perfected forever those who are being sanctified...now where there is remission of these, there is no longer an offering for sin (10:14, 18).

These verses yank the rug from under the feet of tithe preachers. The verses' bottom line is that Christ offered Himself once as our sacrifice-tithe, and not repeatedly, as the Old Testament priests did with their sacrifices, because His offering removes our sins forever. Levites offered their sacrifices "daily," "continually," and "repeatedly" because their sacrifices and offerings were imperfect.

Focus on the last verses I used. Christ's offering "perfected forever those [you] who are being sanctified," and because of this "there is no longer an offering for sin." Now put the pieces of the puzzle together to get a clearer picture of the tithe deception.

God created a temporary and imperfect sacrifice and offering system for Israel in the Old Testament as a way for them to have their sins temporarily covered. The system was facilitated by priests who "daily," "continually," and "repeatedly" offered the people's sacrifices and offerings to God according to strict rules. Yet these sacrifices and offerings never satisfied the eternal claims of justice and, therefore, never brought God pleasure. God revealed within the tithe system itself, and through prophetic Old Testament utterances, that He would provide Himself as the final sacrifice for sin. The New Testament teaches that this occurred through the death of Christ. When Christ died, His sacrifice was accepted by God as perfect. Further sacrifices for sin became unnecessary and unacceptable. Jesus became the last acceptable tithe.

"But," you say, "I don't pay tithes to have my sins covered. I pay tithes because——."

Stop right there. That's' the error; paying tithes, not the reason you pay tithes.

The Levitical tithe system was fundamentally a temporary process to cover sins "until the time of reformation" (Hebrews 9:10), the death of Christ. By what authority do you turn God's temporary, and now obsolete, process of covering the sins of Jews into a modern way to raise money, buy blessings, or demonstrate your love? There is no right way to abuse a doctrine of God—even if it's for money or love.

Again, every time you pay a so-called tithe, you declare the sacrifice of Christ as your tithe unacceptable. It's time to stop insulting God by offering Him man-made offerings that "daily," "continually," and "repeatedly" dishonor the blood of Christ. If you really want to demonstrate love for God, obey Him. Stop giving like a Jew under law and begin to give as a Christian under grace?

CHAPTER 21

Christians Must Give According to the Law of Love

This is not a book against giving. It is a book against religious bondage and preachers raising funds through manipulation, extortion, and bribery. It is an effort to free Christians from the grievous error of tithing so they can hear directly from the Holy Spirit and vigorously participate in the liberating truth of giving.

As stated in this chapter's title, I believe Christians *must* give. That is, I believe Christians are obligated by love to give. "You sound like the legalists," you say. "I thought you were on our side!" Actually I'm on God's side (or so I think). And trust me, my concept of our obligation to give is nothing like the legalists' concept of tithing. You should know this by now.

The Other Side of the Giving Debate

On one hand, the legalists demand systematic payment of ten percent of our income to their bank accounts as a command of God. On the other hand, we non-tithers demand unconditional liberty from any legalistic demands on our money.

We've spent over two hundred pages destroying the illegitimacy of the legalist position. This was the right thing to do. It deserves one thousand pages of destruction. But we would be irresponsible and unbalanced if we didn't address the legitimate concern that non-tithers often use their freedom to justify selfishness and lack of material commitment to the things of God. This is why Paul wrote, "For you, brethren, have been called to liberty; only do not use liberty as an opportunity for the flesh, but through love serve one another" (Galatians 5:13). We shouldn't submit to the false obligation of bondage giving or to the false freedom of selfish keeping. Both are wrong.

The Real Danger of Unconditional Freedom

The real danger of unconditional freedom is that it exists only in the minds of criminals. Theirs is a psychologically twisted world where they are responsible for nothing or no one except their own happiness. Yet this is the kind of freedom that doomed Adam and Eve in the Garden of Eden. Even in Paradise freedom was limited by responsibility. In their case, the responsibility was to leave that doggone tree alone! Similarly, God did not free Israel from slavery in Egypt so they could have unconditional freedom, but freedom conditioned by responsibility. God told Pharoah, "Let My people go, that they may serve Me" (Exodus 8:1). Freedom to serve God, not freedom to serve the flesh.

In our case, we also were not given unconditional freedom, but freedom conditioned by responsibility to serve God. One of the main ways we do this is through good works: "For we are His workmanship, created in Christ Jesus for good works, which God prepared beforehand that we should walk in them" (Ephesians 2:10).

Created in Christ Jesus for Good Works

The world is an incredibly harsh environment for billions of its inhabitants. More than half the world struggles in poverty to live on less than two U.S. dollars a day.[163] War, civil unrest, famine, and natural disasters, as brutal and devastating as they are, hit us so regularly that we are desensitized to their awful effects.

For instance, how much sleep have you lost over the December 26, 2004 tsunami that erupted out of the Indian Ocean and sucked the life out of nearly 250,000 terrified people in only a few minutes?

Or what about the institutional savagery committed against women in the Democratic Republic of Congo (and other African nations)? The civil war has killed over 4,000,000 people in the last ten years; that's bad enough. But the warring factions systematically use rape as a weapon of war. Women, girls, and even young children are routinely raped and sodomized by gangs of disease infested soldiers. Male relatives are ordered to participate in the rapes of their wives, daughters, and even mothers or be murdered. Often this is done as a public show to villages to instill fear. Will this troubling revelation of unimaginable shame and terror be foremost in your mind tomorrow? Probably not.

This is not to shame you, only to acknowledge the truth that we are all desensitized to the horribleness of the world in which we live. We do not think about starvation, institutional rape, natural disasters, and other bad things unless they directly affect us or they are thrust into our faces. But evil and pain do not cease to exist simply because we don't think or know about them.

It may seem that I've gotten off track talking about such large social problems. What does this have to do with giving? It has *everything* to do with giving. Ephesians 2:10 says again, "...we are created in Christ Jesus for good works, which God has before ordained that we should walk in them." God has ordained us to walk in holiness (Hebrews 12:14); holiness is not an option. God has ordained us to walk in faith (Romans 1:17); faith is not an option. God has ordained us to walk in good works (Ephesians 2:10); good works are not an option.

The world is plagued with large social problems and smaller individual problems. These problems mar God's creation, glorify Satan, and afflict humanity with a million miseries that for all practical purposes tell the world there is no God, and if there is a God, He is either cruel, incompetent, or doesn't care about them. We are called by God to prove to the world these are lies. We do this primarily not by our words, but by our actions, what God calls *good works*.[164]

The Importance and Power of Good Works

Hear these incredible words of our Lord:

> You are the light of the world. A city that is set on a hill cannot be hidden. Nor do they light a lamp and put it under a basket, but on a lampstand, and it gives light to all who are in the house. Let your light so shine before men, that they may see your good works and glorify your Father in heaven.

Matthew 5:14-16

Here we are told to deliberately show our good works to a hostile world that persecutes, reviles, and slanders us.[165] This is quite different from the Lord's instructions to "take heed that you do not do your charitable deeds before men, to be seen by them" (Matthew 5:1).[166] The difference in the instructions has to do with our motives.

The latter instructions warn against doing religious works (giving, praying, fasting) to cause people to see and praise us. This behavior is hypocrisy. Conversely, the former instructions encourage publicizing our good works if we do so solely that people may see and praise God: "That they may see your good works *and glorify your Father in heaven*."

Recall that it is a main theme of the Bible that sinners are in gross spiritual darkness and moral deception.[167] What can free them from this condition? The Word of God is exceedingly powerful and able to deliver the worst sinners from the most depraved moral darkness. Yet Jesus said the light of our good works can overcome their darkness and cause them to glorify God.[168] He said this because He expects His Word to be preached within a context of good works. His Word and good works are opposite sides of the same coin.

The Context and Delivery of the Word

The Word is usually not delivered in a vacuum; there's normally a context, a delivery person.[169] The context or delivery person has the ability to weaken the Word of God so that its saving power is ineffective. This sounds heretical, but it is a mainstream Bible truth. Listen to Jesus' words on this issue: "...Thus you have made the commandment of God of no effect by your tradition" (Matthew 15:6).[170]

We must be careful that our behavior doesn't weaken our message. Messages of God's love for sinners that aren't seen in our behavior make us look like (or reveal us as) hypocrites. When we are discredited, so is our message and our God.

Our Tradition of Words without Action Makes the Word of God of No Effect

Material love is the kind that causes us to do something about a problem other than just pray. Unfortunately, though, we tithers and non-tithers alike have developed a tradition of merely praying about situations when we should be doing something materially to change them. This behavior conflicts with the life of Christ, the Spirit of God, and the mission of the church. It also weakens the power of our message. The New Testament is blunt and emphatic in its condemnation of Christians (are they really Christians?) who claim to love God, but fail to materially love people.

For you financial tithers who think your legalistic payments of money to religious organizations satisfy the obligations of grace and the demands of love, you are dead wrong.[171] The New Testament condemns any system that diminishes the authority and ability of the Holy Spirit to personally direct 100% of your material love. Furthermore, your obligation to give is based on your ability to give, not on reaching a certain percentage of income.

For you non-tithers who think you were freed from the bondage of the law to spend the rest of your days serving your flesh and ignoring the needs of the church and problems of the world, you, too, are dead wrong.[172] The New Testament condemns selfish behavior—even if it's done in the name of freedom.

For you givers who reject the bondage and deception of man's false financial tithe system, and the bondage of selfishness disguised as freedom, you serve your Master well and bring great glory to God.

What Jesus and the Apostles Said About Our Obligation to Give

The church has a nasty habit of swinging to bad doctrinal extremes. We believe either this or that. We embrace one truth at the expense of another. This is done to such an extreme that our imbalance turns the truth into a lie. Such is the case with various doctrines relating to tithing and giving (which are not the same).[173] For instance, tithing and giving contain elements of truth. Tithing focuses on obligation: giving focuses on freedom. Obligation and freedom are good when taught properly. But when taught improperly they become false doctrines. An overview of what the New Testament says about obligation and freedom in giving will provide the balance we need.

What Jesus Said About Our Obligation to Give

You may think I have said some things about our obligation to give that are troubling. If so, wait until you hear what the Lord says about giving. It is absolutely terrifying (to my flesh). From the perspective of my carnal mind, He is one hundred percent unreasonable and unrealistic in His expectations of us to live as He lived and to give as He gave.[174] Fortunately, He is fully committed through His Holy Spirit to help us achieve this holy goal. Otherwise I'd throw the towel in now and just quit.

Nonetheless, if I am to be honest, I must admit that even though I know God will help me, and that I desire with all my heart to be like Christ, I am still terrified of the process of becoming like Christ. In times such as this I wish I could just cut a check for ten percent and go about my business.

Losing is Gaining

Below is one of the most troubling statements Jesus made about giving:

> Then Jesus said to His disciples, "If anyone desires to come after Me, let him deny himself, and take up his cross, and follow Me.
>
> For whoever desires to save his life will lose it, but whoever loses his life for My sake will find it."

> Matthew 16:24-25

The Lord's concept of giving is quite different from either the tither's or the nontither's. Tithers give ten percent and feel they've fulfilled the law. Non-tithers give whatever they give (when and *if* they give) and feel they've fulfilled grace. But acceptable giving is infinitely more than any single gift, series of gifts, or acts of service. It begins with an acceptable heart.

An acceptable heart is one governed by a radical mindset of selflessness and commitment to Christ and others that automatically results in a lifestyle of good works, financial or otherwise. So the scrutiny is not on the gift, but the giver.[175]

According to Jesus, we can't follow Him unless we first deny ourselves and take up our cross. This is a clear reference to suffering and even crucifixion. Surely a person who has committed to a life of self-denial, and even to die for Christ, if necessary, should need no prompting to materially love others. There simply is no room in such a life for selfishness.

Furthermore, if we fully embrace the truth that the person who "desires to save his life will lose it" and "whoever loses his life for My [Christ's] sake will find it," we'll see the foolishness and danger of selfishness for what it is. It is a deception that causes us to believe the more we keep, the more we have. The truth is, the more we give, the more we have.[176]

Of course, we're speaking here with an eternal perspective. Life is extremely short, and we are all literally just one moment away from death. Seeing that we are all destined for the grave, what sense does it make to be selfish? What can we keep that we won't lose to death?[177] Only what we give to Christ will benefit us throughout eternity. Keep this in mind the next opportunity you have to give to a Holy Spirit endorsed project or need.

Selfishness Often a Sign of False Conversion to Christ

The Lord gave us a summarized preview of Judgment Day in Matthew 25:31-46. Two groups of people are represented: The first group goes to heaven; the second group goes to hell. What distinguishes one group from the other is its giving.

The first group is welcomed into heaven and commended by God, "Come, you blessed of My Father, inherit the kingdom prepared for you from the foundation of the world" (v. 34). Jesus praises them for giving Him something to eat, drink, and wear; for providing Him lodging, for visiting Him when He was sick and when He was in prison (v. 35-36). Surprised at being lavishly praised by the Lord for good works they did not remember, they asked when they did these things (v. 37-39). Jesus responded that when they did these things to people, they did them to Him (v. 40).

The second group received a far different judgment. They had apparently seen no need for doing such things, or perhaps were too busy or important, or maybe thought it was a waste to spend money and time on such losers. Whatever the reason, they were not lifestyle givers. Here is what happened to them:

> Then He will also say to those on the left hand, 'Depart from Me, you cursed, into the everlasting fire prepared for the devil and his angels'...And these will go away into everlasting punishment, but the righteous into eternal life.

Matthew 25:41, 46

Of course, the moral of the story is not that good works will get you into heaven or that lack of good works will keep you out.[178] The critical truth here is they claimed to have faith in Christ, but possessed no lifestyle proof. They were like the hypocrites spoken of in Titus 1:16, "They profess to know God, but in works they deny Him, being abominable [detestable], disobedient, and disqualified for every good work."

Do you see the glaring contradiction? How can someone claim to follow Christ and be selfish? How can someone embrace the call to self-denial, be willing to die for Christ, if necessary, and be selfish? How can someone truly believe in heaven and simultaneously grasp for the temporary pleasures and material goods of this world in a way that compromises the very foundation of his confession of faith?

This is an unnatural, but fundamental trait of our materialistic version of Christianity that is denounced by God in the strongest terms—terms so strong and inflexible that most preachers refuse to teach them. They are afraid that if they teach the truth about God's expectations for us to be radical lifestyle givers, they will lose their following.[179] This is probably true; since false converts aren't willing to truly live for Christ and His interests.

What John Said About Our Obligation to Give

John strongly preached against Christian selfishness (Christian selfishness—can there be such a thing?) and false conversions. If fact, he directly linked the two. This came from his Christ-like tendency to speak absolute truth without fear of sounding harsh, judgmental, or needlessly confrontational. Like Christ, his concern was not to be politically correct, but morally correct.

If We Love God, We Will Materially Love People
The following passage of Scripture captures a major theme of 1 John: True Christians materially love people; false Christians don't.

> In this the children of God and the children of the devil are manifest: Whoever does not practice righteousness is not of God, nor is

he who does not love his brother...We know that we have passed from death to life, because we love the brethren. He who does not love his brother abides in death...By this we know love, because He laid down His life for us. And we also ought to lay down our lives for the brethren. But whoever has this world's goods, and sees his brother in need, and shuts up his heart from him, how does the love of God abide in him. My little children, let us not love in word or in tongue, but in deed and in truth.

1 John 3:10, 14, 15-18

John was not impressed by confessions of faith. He knew that a confession of faith that wasn't demonstrated as a lifestyle in the confessor was worthless. So he lists the "signs" of true Christians as practicing righteousness and loving people. Those who don't exhibit these signs as a lifestyle are classified as "children of the devil" (v. 10).[180]

Also notice that the apostle questions the salvation of any so-called Christian who sees a person in genuine need, and "shuts up his heart from him."[181] Was he speaking of failing to pray for the person? No. He was talking about doing something material to meet the need: "Let us not love in word or in tongue, but in deed and in truth."[182]

If our professed faith in Christ does not cause us to become "zealous for good works" (Titus 2:14), or to "learn to maintain good works, to meet urgent needs" (Titus 3:14), we should "examine [ourselves] yourselves as to whether [we] you are in the faith" (2 Corinthians 13:5).

The Practical Implications of Our Obligation to Give

So what now? Do we leave the bondage of man's legalistic financial tithe system only to be crushed by guilt under the weight of love's requirements? No, not at all. God does not put on us more than we can bear.[183] Jesus said, "Come to Me, all you who labor and are heavy laden, and I will give you rest" (Matthew 11:28). This rest is found in your relationship with Christ, and not in trying to meet every need you see. Anyway, it is impossible to meet every need you see. So the issue is not meeting every need, but meeting the needs God wants you to meet.

God Gives Responsibilities According to Our Abilities

The Bible is clear that there are varying levels of ability and responsibility within the church. Sure, we all are required to live equally moral lives. Yet when it comes to service, God tasks us differently and judges us accordingly.[184] For instance, teachers of the Word are judged more strictly than non-teachers: "My brethren, let not many of you become teachers, knowing that we shall receive a stricter judgment" (James 3:1). Another statement that conveys this truth is Luke 12:48, "For everyone to whom much is given, from him much will be required; and to whom much has been committed, of him they will ask the more."

It is critical that we understand and embrace this principle in our giving. Otherwise, we will find ourselves trying to give more or less than our ability.

Give According to Your Ability

What exactly is your ability? Tithe preachers will tell you it is at least ten percent of your gross income for life, plus regular generous, and even sacrificial, offerings above the ten percent. I said in an earlier chapter that this is wrong because it violates God's law of fairness and it oppresses the poor.[185]

Another reason it is wrong is it assumes we all are equally tasked and spiritually quipped to obey their financial demands (not that their demands should be obeyed even if we could). It never crosses tithe preachers' minds that God requires us to give and serve according to

His own standard of infinite flexibility. In fact, they can't understand this flexibility for two reasons. One, their version of the tithe is based on the inflexibility of law. And, two, their need for unqualified cash flow is insatiable and inflexible. They have bills to pay and dreams to finance. But our great and merciful God judges us not by their expectations, but by His own.

The Lord's expectations are that we give and serve according to our calling, gifting, and spiritual maturity. These things comprise our ability to give.

Give According to Your Calling

A calling is an identity and station in life. You have a general calling and a unique calling. The general calling is what all Christians are called to, such as: "light of the world" (Matthew 5:14), "children of God" (John 1:12), "imitators of God" (Ephesians 5:1), "a royal priesthood" (1 Peter 2:9), and similar general identity type callings. The unique calling is yours based upon variables.[186] Some examples are: "called to be an apostle" (1 Corinthians 1:1), "called while a slave" (1 Corinthians 7:21), "called while free" (1 Corinthians 7:22), and other unique situations. Our general calling is inflexible, eternal. Our unique calling is flexible, changeable.[187]

Each calling automatically places responsibilities and limitations upon us. Concerning financial giving, certainly our general calling as "imitators of God" requires selfless lifestyles of giving and service. There simply is no such thing as a selfish imitator of God. Similarly, if my unique calling is that of a child or grandchild of a financially destitute widow, I am expected by God to *first* take care of my relative before I give anything to a religious organization. In fact, the Bible says, "But if anyone does not provide for his own, and especially for those of his household, he has denied the faith and is worse than an unbeliever" (1 Timothy 5:8).[188]

Therefore, we see that your general and unique callings will directly affect what you give, the amount you give, to whom you give, and the order in which you give.

Give According to Your Gifting

Your gifting is special ability God gives you to perform tasks He assigns you. These tasks may be the collective responsibilities of all Christians, such as sharing your faith and helping those in need. Or they may be those specially assigned solely to you, such as writing books or being a prophet.

Notice that sharing your faith and helping those in need are general commands to the entire church, but there are also some people specially called to excel in these tasks. Special sharers of the faith are called *evangelists*.[189] And special mercy-givers, although not identified by title, are nonetheless identified.[190] The point here is that God may command the entire church to a task, but hold some people to a higher standard of accountability than others for the completion of the task. This is because for His own purposes, He gives them special ability to perform the task. They receive more for the task, and therefore should produce more and better results.

Similarly, we may all pray for the sick, but we are not all healers.[191] We may all prophesy, but we are not all prophets.[192] We may all cast out demons, but we are not all miracle workers.[193] Get ready. Here it comes: We may all give, but we are not all *givers*.

Obviously, this sounds crazy. Tithe preachers have told us all our lives we are equally responsible to give. What do I mean telling Christians they are not all givers? I mean exactly what I say: *We are not all givers*. But this statement is only true within the context I present. So let's make doubly sure you understand the context.

Every Christian is expected by God to materially love people. We are expected "to lay down our lives for the brethren" (1 John 3:16), to distribute "to the needs of the saints" (Romans 12:13), to "be hospitable to one another without grumbling" (1 Peter 4:9), and to financially support worthy church leaders "who labor in the word and doctrine" (1 Timothy 5:17-18).[194] This, of course, is giving. But we are not expected by God to do so as though we all have the *gift of giving*.

The gift of giving is spoken of in Romans 12:6-8:

⁶Having then gifts differing according to the grace that is given to us, let us use them: if prophecy, let us prophesy in proportion to our faith;

⁷Or ministry, let us use it in our ministering; he who teaches, in teaching;

⁸He who exhorts, in exhortation; he who gives, with liberality; he who leads, with diligence; he who shows mercy, with cheerfulness.

The difference in the gift of giving and the general command to give is the supply of grace provided (see verse six: "*according to the grace that is given*") and the subsequent effort it takes to give. This concept is further developed in 1 Peter 5:10-11:

As each one has received a gift, minister it to one another, as good stewards of the manifold grace of God...If anyone ministers, let him do it with the ability which God supplies [emphasis mine], that in all things God may be glorified through Jesus Christ....

The person with the gift of giving gives first because she is a grateful child of God, and it would be unnatural to not give. But this grateful child of God with the general responsibility and privilege to give also has a gift of giving; so another dynamic is present. This dynamic is her spiritual gift that manifests itself through her personality, intellect, worldview, priorities, giving, and probably her ability to generate (whether spiritually or naturally) things to give.

Let me try to explain this by using the example of a person with a gift of writing. Literally any literate person with a functioning mind and body can write, and is expected to do so. But this does not mean he has the gift of writing.

A person without the gift will write, but it will require considerably more effort than the person with the writing gift. Plus, without the gift, the task will probably be seen as a chore, a burden. So why does the non-gifted writer write? He does so out of necessity.

Someone with the writing gift has not only advanced skills in writing, but a natural love of writing. She gets excited thinking about putting words on paper. Her gift is so much a part of her that it naturally and indiscernibly affects her personality, intellect, worldview, and priorities. She finds it difficult to understand why everyone isn't excited about writing.

When we give "according to the grace that is given" and "do it with the ability which God supplies," Christ is glorified. He is glorified because we do not give less or more than we should. Obviously, giving less than we should brings shame on His name and causes many people with genuine needs to needlessly suffer. But what is rarely discussed is that the same thing happens when we give too much.

Tithe preachers have created an atmosphere where many people are convinced to give beyond healthy spiritual and financial limits. Each Sunday multitudes of people who do not have the spiritual or financial support system to give as much as they give, do so anyway. They are coached to exuberantly praise God during the offering as they donate money they can't afford to give. Then something sad happens once they go home: They have to live with the immediate consequences of their unwise giving.

This is an example of giving beyond one's gifting. When this occurs, Christ is shamed and needs go unmet. Christ is shamed because the purity of the gospel is corrupted. Needs go unmet because money that should have been used to take care of *people* needs has been diverted to the bottomless pit of religious bureaucracy.

No matter how stern the threats or how appetizing the bribes, you would be wise to consider this truth about giving before you give:

> [12]For if there is first a willing mind, it is accepted according to what one has, and not according to what he does not have [emphasis mine].
>
> [13]For I do not mean that others should be eased and you be burdened;
>
> [14]But by an equality, that now at this time your abundance may supply their lack [emphasis mine], that their abundance also may supply your lack—that there may be equality.

2 Corinthians 8:12-14

Notice that God expects you to give what you have, not what you don't have. This automatically rules out using credit cards to give, as well as making inflexible pledges.[195] It also rules out paying a so-called tithe on our gross income. It's just plain foolish to allow someone to guilt us into paying a tithe on money that isn't even ours. At some point we just have to use common sense!

Finally, notice that these givers in Corinth gave abundantly out of their abundance, not out of their lack. If you are giving abundantly out of your lack, you may be tempting God. Tempting God is never a good idea. Satan tried to get Jesus to tempt God by asking Christ to prove His deity by jumping off a cliff so God would send angels to protect Him. Basically, Satan was asking Jesus to create a crisis on the premise that the Scriptures obligated God to protect Him.[196] Jesus knew, however, that this was an abuse of Scripture. Almighty God cannot be manipulated, even by the Bible.

My questions to you are: Are you tempting God by jumping off a financial cliff and trying to use a few scriptures to force Him to save you? Do you think that if you create a crisis through your unwise giving that Almighty God is obligated to fix your emergency? I guarantee that if you continue to give unwisely God will prove to you He cannot be manipulated by man-made emergencies. Do yourself a favor and stop giving beyond your gifting...and spiritual maturity. Speaking of spiritual maturity....

Give According to Your Spiritual Maturity

Christians are also expected by God to give according to their spiritual maturity. This is different than giving according to calling and gifting. Our general call is created and imposed by God. Our unique call can be imposed by God or by natural forces outside of ourselves. Our spiritual maturity, however, is totally the result of our spiritual action or inaction. We own our spiritual maturity. It begins and ends with us, and directly reflects our relationship with God. It is always unwise and often dangerous to give beyond our level of spiritual maturity.

Spiritual maturity is defined here as love, faith, and wisdom. It is absolutely impossible to please God without love (1 John 4:8), or faith

(Romans 1:17; Hebrews 11:6), or wisdom (the *entire* book of Proverbs!). Ideal giving is the product of spiritual maturity, not threats or bribes.

1. Give According to Your Level of Love

God commands us all to love, but we all grow in love at varying speeds.[197] I believe this has more to do with our quality of conversion (Mark 4:1-20),[198] our understanding of God,[199] and our sense of gratitude for salvation,[200] than simply obedience or deliberate disobedience.[201] It is more a natural, unconscious response within the context of what we are, our spiritual condition, than it is conscious rebellion.

For instance, we effortlessly breathe air because our lungs are designed to do so. Yet despite our best intentions and efforts, we cannot breathe in much water without dying unless our lungs are changed. When we try to love beyond our capacity, we breathe in water. If we courageously, but foolishly, ignore the difficulty of breathing water, we and our good intentions will die. Obviously then, the answer is not to give until it hurts, but to give until we reach our limit of love.

So am I suggesting we should never give if it will cause us discomfort? No, that is the extreme of what I recommend. If Jesus stopped giving because it caused Him discomfort, we would all still be in our sins and condemned to hell.

What I do strongly recommend is that we stop giving according to the law of man (which is merciless and brings death) and start giving according to our present spiritual capacity to love. Nonetheless, when we determine that we have reached our love limit, we must cry out to God for strength to do more if the situation legitimately requires it. This is what Jesus did just prior to going to the cross.[202]

This process allows us (like Jesus) to do what we can presently do and yet acknowledges that more should and must be done—by us. The result is a Christian community that presently does all it can to meet needs, while simultaneously crying out to God for grace to do more. The difference in this process and the tithe preacher's across-the-board command of ten percent is God's way actually meets the need, and in a way that doesn't destroy the giver. Conversely, man's way often only transfers the need from one person to another. How do you know when this has happened? If giving a gift causes your bills to go unpaid, the need has not truly been met. It has simply been transferred to you.

2. Give According to Your Level of Faith

Faith is another spiritual quality that is measurable and varies in size from person to person. Some people have strong faith (Romans 4:20), weak faith (Romans 14:1), no faith (2 Thessalonians 3:2), and when the Holy Spirit sovereignly distributes for a task, the special gift of faith (1 Corinthians 12:9). Then there is saving faith.

Saving faith is that quality of heart that responds to the gospel in repentance. In fact, in the context of salvation, this faith is not qualified by size, but repentance. If you hear the gospel and repent, you have saving faith. If you hear the gospel and do not repent, you do not have saving faith. You have it or you don't.

The kind of faith that should govern your giving is threefold. First, it is the faith that exists and grows as a natural result of your interactions with God, and as a result of deliberately adding to your faith.[203] This is character faith. Second, it is the faith that God distributes to you based on your unique, God-appointed function in the church and world.[204] This is ministry faith. And, third, it is the faith that God gives to certain Christians for certain tasks for (apparently) limited periods of time. This is miracle faith.

The point is not to split so many faith hairs that we go spiritually bald, but rather that we may understand giving in the context of faith. We give according to the level of our faith by first understanding that there are differing levels of faith, and that giving should flow from our character growth, our ministry function, and our supernatural giftings. The key word is *our*.

One of the gravest and most cruel errors of the modern tithe system is it requires everyone to give the same without considering our uniqueness. It demands our money without regard to the size and kind of our faith, the depth of our character faith, the uniqueness of our ministry faith, or the probability that we don't have miracle faith.

For the tithe system's priority is not the spiritual development and well-being of the tither. Rather, it is the achievement of organizational financial goals. If people are destroyed in the process, *Oh well.*[205]

But when God asks you to give, He asks within the context of the size and uniqueness of your faith. He looks at your gift and weighs it against who and what you are. This is a personal matter between you and God. How could it be otherwise? Who is qualified to accurately judge your faith and the amount of giving it should produce at this stage in your life? A tithe preacher? I don't think so.

Now what about the issue of retarded faith growth? There are some people who through negligence, fear, laziness, or other reasons are spiritually underdeveloped, and therefore unable to give as they should. They've been saved for years and still give like they are hungry, abused orphans. They can't give to anyone else because the sharp hunger pains of their own material lust and lack of care for others will not allow them.

If this is you, hear what God says about your self-inflicted condition:

> [11]...Of whom we have much to say, and hard to explain, since you have become dull of hearing.
>
> [12]For though by this time you ought to be teachers, you need someone to teach you again the first principles of the oracles of God; and you have come to need milk and not solid food.
>
> [13]For everyone who partakes only of milk is unskilled in the word of righteousness, for he is a babe.
>
> [14]But solid food belongs to those who are of full age, that is, those who by reason of use have their senses exercised to discern both good and evil.
>
> Hebrews 5:11-14

It is understandable that a new convert to Christ may exhibit some selfish tendencies. But it is totally bizarre, unacceptable, and even shameful for a seasoned Christian to exhibit a lifestyle of selfishness. How can a person who has experienced Christ and has grown in the things of God behave as a person who has done neither? *"Examine yourselves as to whether you are in the faith. Test yourselves"* (2 Corinthians 13:5).

3. Give According to Your Level of Wisdom

Finally, take what I have said about your level of love and faith and apply it to your level of wisdom. Every request for your money must be filtered through godly wisdom.

The preacher says you ought to give a particular amount of money. But what does wisdom say?

The preacher says the starving widow gave Elijah the prophet her last morsel of food and was blessed for it, and therefore you ought to give him your last little bit. But what does wisdom say?

The preacher says if you bless him, God will bless you. But what does wisdom say?

The preacher says....

But what does wisdom say?

About the Author

Eric keeps himself busy with his writing, teaching, and deliverance ministries. He is also the author of Deliverance from Demons and Diseases: Freedom from Incurable Diseases and Persistent Problems. As the Lord directs, he and his wonderful wife conduct small teaching and deliverance sessions to individuals and groups. He may be contacted at www.PowerEvangelism.org or www.SunHillPublishers.com.

Afterword

There I was, sitting on my upper level deck, living the life of a blessed non-tither, drinking a cup of coffee and reading the paper. It was a weekday morning, but I had this kind of time on my hands because I am a United States Air Force retiree. I taught undergraduate classes one day a week for a university. The rest of my time was spent writing this book, praying, teaching the Bible, ministering deliverance and healing, and enjoying the company of my wonderful wife. Aahhh, life was good.

Then it happened. I made a terrible mistake. I prayed a dangerous prayer that took me from my upper level deck and placed me in someone else's lower level cubicle. Well, that's an exaggeration. It's not a cubicle. It's an actual office. But still, what a demotion. One moment I'm living a life of relative ease, and the next moment I'm slaving away in an office. Oh, how the mighty have fallen!

Let me explain to you how I got suckered into this deal.

One of the main themes of this book is that there is no need for clergy to bribe or extort money from Christians because we can go directly to God for whatever we need. If He agrees with the project, and if we agree and cooperate with God's method and timing of enabling the project, it'll be done. But if we aren't in agreement with God, He won't enable the project (though we may do it anyway without His help).

A certain Scripture (which I am sorely tempted to erase from my Bible) says, "The hardworking farmer must be first to partake of the crops" (2 Timothy 2:6). In context, this means that preachers must be the first to practice what they preach. At the time, I had no problem with this. I had already planned to follow the example of George Muller, who had created and sustained his multi-million dollar work of taking care of thousands of orphans solely through private and persistent prayer. I was quite familiar with the art and benefits of persistent prayer and knew that I could and would validate my book through my own real life example of getting funding for the book solely by crying out mightily to my faithful God.

I began crying out to God on June 25, 2009 for the full production cost of this book, which I felt was around $15,000. I did not speak to anyone about this need except God. No hints were dropped. No letters were written. No Malachi threats or bribes were issued or offered. By early September, I had more than half of the money. What an exhilarating feeling! I was proving the major premise of my book: We can go directly to God for whatever we need. I was on a roll. It was all downhill now. I'd probably spend several more weeks in private prayer, God would supply the rest of the money, and at the appropriate time, I'd declare to the Christian world how I had funded the book's production solely through prayer. Well, here's where I got sucker punched by the Holy Spirit. At least, I believe He was behind this whole thing.

It was some time in September (I'm trying to forget), and I was deep in travailing prayer before the Lord. As usual, I was pleading my case and listing before the Lord the many reasons why I felt He should continue to answer my prayer. I explained how I would need this fresh prayer victory to counter the rebuttals of those who would say I was being impractical, and for those who would imply that such a fundraising method would bankrupt the church. It was somewhere in mid travail that I—oh, Eric, how could you?—said something to this effect, "Lord, I'm not telling you how to answer this prayer. You are the potter; I am the clay. I do what you say, and not the other way around. Lord, you've been supplying this money solely through my prayers. But just for the record, I want you to know that I am willing to get a job if that's the method you have chosen."

Now I'm not totally naïve. I knew that I had to make this thing tough for God. So I added what I thought would be an impenetrable qualification, especially since we were in the middle of what's been called The Great Recession. "Lord, all I ask is that if you want me to get a job, make someone walk up to me and offer a job without any action on my part. This way I'll know that it's you."

Now, Holy Spirit, let's see you get past that one. Over ten million people out of work. People with degrees are lined up hundreds deep and waiting in the cold for hours in downtown Atlanta just to get into a job fair. Another successful session of prayer. I'm going to make me some coffee and relax on the deck and read the paper.

The next day someone asked me if I wanted a job.

I was stunned, shocked. Yet even though I knew that God was snatching away my newspaper (I still have my coffee mug), I was elated that I was witnessing another incredible answer to prayer. Furthermore, I knew that I was being asked to participate in a process that would show others how to put into practice the things that I've written about in this book.

First, if you believe God has given you a task that requires funds that you don't have, spend considerable time in private, persistent prayer to determine whether you are actually hearing from Him and not your own flesh. Just because a thing is a good idea doesn't mean that it's God.

Second, learn how to pray until you get unmistakable answers from God. This most often will require great perseverance in prayer, and consequently great patience while you wait on God. This means you must make no irreversible commitments toward the attainment of your goal until you know that this is also God's goal. Don't underestimate the temptation to minimize this process. It's much easier to do something in the flesh than to wait on God.

Third, be willing to do something that you'd rather not do. I absolutely did not have a desire to get a traditional job to fund this book. And I had already proven that I could pray the money in. So why get a job? Why leave my deck?

Fourth, don't despise traditional, so-called secular jobs. There is no such thing as a secular job if you are a servant of Jesus Christ. "And whatever you do in word or deed, do all in the name of the Lord Jesus, giving thanks to God the Father through him" (Colossians 3:17). Also, "The just shall live by faith" (Romans 1:17). All of our jobs are to be done as unto the Lord, and in faith, whether we are preachers or painters, apostles or accountants. Don't make the error of declaring pulpit ministry spiritual and traditional jobs carnal. Are so-called full-time ministers walking by faith more than the person who has a traditional job and knows where his next check is coming from? Does knowing in advance where my next check is coming from make me less spiritual than when I was praying the money in? Didn't I get this job through prayer? And don't tithe preachers know where their next check is coming from? Didn't Elijah know where his meal was coming from when God told him, "Arise, go to Zarephath, which belongs to Sidon, and dwell there. See, I have commanded a widow there to provide for you" (1 Kings 17:9). Faith or lack of faith is not determined by whether or not you know where your provision is coming from. It's determined by whether you obey God.

Fifth, believe God in the most dire circumstances. The Lord is not limited to the economy. A job was offered to me during one of the most economically trying times in our nation's history. I did absolutely nothing—nothing!—to orchestrate this event except live close to God and pray. You can build your ministry the same way. Instead of trusting in man-made fundraising methods, why not trust in God? Just live close to the Lord, cry out mightily to Him in prayer, and obey what He tells you. It'll turn out all right in the end.

Endnotes

[1] Matthew 13:24-30.

[2] I strongly encourage you to read, *The Autobiography of George Muller* mass market edition, Whitaker House. His 60-year example of trusting God is exactly opposite of what we see in modern preachers. He never used the tithe to raise funds because his trust was in God and not in man-made financial fundraising schemes. He says on page 195: "How much should you give of your income? God lays down no rule concerning this point."

[3] "For you put up with it if one brings you into bondage, if one devours you, if one takes from you, if one exalts himself, if one strikes you on the face" (2 Corinthians 11:20).

[4] 2 Corinthians 11:20.

[5] Matthew 25:41-46 tells the rest of the story.

[6] Brown, M.S., Harris, J.C., & Rooney, P.M. (2004). *Reconciling Estimates of Religious Giving*. Indianapolis: Center for Philanthropy at Indiana University. These researchers put the figures at $82.83 to $86.28 billion.

[7] John L. Ronsvalle and Sylvia Ronsvalle. *The State of Church Giving through 2000*. Champaign, IL: Empty Tomb®. (2002, p. 51). Visit their website at www.emptytomb.org.

[8] This web site cited the quote as taken from "World Christian Trends AD 30-AD 2000: Interpreting the Annual Christian Megacensus," page 661, by David B. Barrett and Todd M. Johnson.

[9] 1887 quote taken from a letter written by Lord Acton, a British historian.

[10] If we're going to spend so much money on facilities, we should at least aggressively use them for community service during the week. This probably would still not justify the expense, but perhaps it would minimize the level of waste.

[11] Some even put the building in their personal name. This means that for all practical purposes, the building is theirs.

[12] The object here is not whether or not we should financially support worthy ministers of the gospel who are called to devote all of their time to taking care of the church—we should. The issue is the dysfunctional system we've created that paralyzes the masses of God's would-be workers in favor of paying a few people to do what many people would gladly do for free if they were only trained and allowed to do so.

[13] Ezra and Nehemiah prohibited the Samaritans from assisting them or sharing in the inheritance of Israel (Ezra 4:1-3; Nehemiah 2:1-20).

[14] Josephus, Book 12, Chapter 5.

[15] Obviously they had no radio, television, or automated printing technology. I use this hyperbole to make a point of what we would have done.

[16] It must not be overlooked, however, that the Samaritan model worked in large part because (1) Jesus relied upon supernatural knowledge from the Holy Spirit, (2) Jesus offered the woman a relationship with God instead of more bondage to religious institutions, (3) Jesus dramatically demonstrated His interest in the Samaritans by risking His reputation and safety to visit them, and (4) Jesus stayed with them for two full days sharing His life with them. Our evangelistic efforts must include these ingredients.

[17] "For what is highly esteemed among men is an abomination to God" (Luke 16:15).

[18] He then gave them instructions to take all of those things which He had prohibited (Luke 22:35-38). A preacher can be trusted with "things" only after being trained by God to "distrust" them. This often takes many years and devastating trials. An unbroken preacher with a pocketful of money is a dangerous combination!

[19] Matthew 15:32-38; Mark 8:1-9

[20] 1 Thessalonians 5:21

[21] Matthew 21:21

[22] Acts 6:8; 9:10-18, 32-42; 10:1-48; 13:1-2; 16:13-18; 19:1-7; 21:8-11; 1 Corinthians 12:1-11, 28-31; 14:1-40; 1 Thessalonians 5:19-20; James 5:14-15. These scriptures show the supernatural culture of the early church.

[23] Acts 4:4

[24] James 1:22-25; 2:14-26

[25] Mark 9:38-39; Acts 6:8; 8:5-8; 1 Corinthians 12:28-29

[26] Also see Acts 6:14.

[27] This is not theory; the church of Acts is not a fable. Plus we don't have to look back to Acts. We can look at the church in China for modern proof of my conclusions. It is considered an enemy of the state by the government, and is treated as such. Its members suffer discrimination, beatings, imprisonment, and even death. Yet the church grows because of its culture of purpose, prayer, and power.

[28] I apologize if my use of this word offends you. It is a word that connotes shame and illegitimacy, but in my opinion is not a "curse" word in the traditional sense. I use it in the same v av it is used in Hebrews 12:8 of the King James Version of the Bible.

[29] Galatians 1:8-9; 2 Timothy 3:16.

[30] "Protestant" is the name given to Christians who formally broke away from the Roman Catholic Church in the 16th century Reformation for its abuses and superstitions, and those who later joined churches that identify with this movement. Unfortunately, our tendency to believe our own decrees and traditions above the Bible shows that we have more in common with Roman Catholicism than we admit.

[31] Various loosely connected doctrines of mysticism that conflicted with the foundational beliefs of Christianity.

[32] Epistle 65.1 of *Cyprian*; Christian Classics Ethereal Library; http://www.ccel.org/ccel/schaff/anf05.iv.iv.lxv.html; Retrieved December 30, 2008.

[33] The word "clergy" has well deserved negative connotations: fleshly control, greed, pride, self-gain, elitism, etc. Nonetheless, I use it here to identify those among the universal priesthood of believers who are called by God in a leadership role to "take care of the church of God" (1 Timothy 3:5), to "watch out" for our souls (Hebrews 13:17), and to "shepherd the flock of God" (1 Peter 5:2).

[34] It is important to know the correct timeline of the creation and evolution of the modern tithe. Otherwise, we may miss the connection between clergy salaries and buildings, and the modern financial tithe.

[35] The New Merriam-Webster Dictionary.

[36] Cyprian hated covetousness and was famous for his detachment from worldliness and materialism. These were primary considerations when he was uncharacteristically chosen as bishop of Carthage, an eminent and large city in the Roman Empire, after only three years of serving Christ (*The Life and Passion of Cyprian, Bishop, and Martyr* – by Pontius the Deacon; Section 1).

[37] Are we more fervent and focused than Bishop Cyprian, who sold his estate and gave the proceeds to the poor, and who sealed his testimony with his own blood? If such a man could trust God to take care of him through the generosity of His saints, why can't our modern leaders do the same?

[38] Why were bishops arguing for the creation of a financial tithe? Two reasons: (1) Historically, the church did not have a financial tithe; (2) Their ambitions and bureaucracy now exceeded the limitations of freewill offerings.

[39] Henry Bettenson, *Documents of the Christian Church*, Oxford University Press, 1967, 2ⁿᵈ ed., p. 22. A part of the actual decree, extracted from the *Codex Theodosianus* XVI 1.2., says, "We authorize the followers of this law to assume the title of Catholic Christians; but as for the others, since, in our judgment they are foolish madmen, we decree that they shall be branded with the ignominious name of heretics...They will suffer in the first place the chastisement of the divine condemnation and in the second the punishment of our authority which in accordance with the will of Heaven shall decide to inflict." This wasn't a good time to not be a Christian!

[40] Organization by itself is not bad, and it is a mistake to celebrate failure to plan and chaos under the guise of being led of the Spirit. This is a fault of many foolish, lazy, and undisciplined Christians.

[41] This is not to say that every ancient bishop and priest was greedy. That generalization would be unfair and inaccurate. But it is historically accurate to refer to the much documented material excesses and unprecedented greed of the Catholic Church during this period.

[42] I challenge you tithers to look in the mirror and ask yourselves the same question. They believed the benefits of their salvation were directly limited by their participation or nonparticipation in the revived and modified tithe system. Isn't this what you believe? Aren't you "cursed with a curse" for not giving ten percent of your income to the church bureaucracy? There's not a lot of difference in your 21st century superstition and theirs. Actually, yours

is a lot worse because you have access to the Bible. You have no excuse for your bondage. Preachers may have placed the chains of superstition on your soul, but you refuse to use the key of the Bible to free yourself.

[43] The Gutenberg press was invented in 1450. Other earlier printing technologies existed in Asia, but were impractical for mass production.

[44] Recall Dr. David Croteau's research on the writings of the early church fathers: Hilary of Poitiers (366), Basil of Caesarea (370), Ambrose (374), John Chrysostom (375), and Augustine (400).

[45] A capitulary is a document "recording the legislative acts of certain Carolingian kings:" *Medieval France: An Encyclopedia;* p. 169; William W. Kibler. Grover A. Zinn, John Jr. Bell Henneman and Lawrence Earp; published 1995 by Routledge. A translation of this capitulary may be read in *Readings in Medieval History*, 3rd edition; p. 297; number 7; Patrick J. Geary.

[46] This period of time and its conflicts are known as the *Wars of Religion*.

[47] The most famous religious divorce between a country and the Catholic Church was that of France. The general uprising of the French people against the Church, coupled with corresponding actions by the government, exploded into what is commonly known as *The French Revolution*.

[48] The parliament of England passed the first Act of Supremacy which made the king the head of the Church of England.

[49] From page 9, *In Pursuit of the Almighty's Dollar: A History of Money and American Protestantism* by James Hudnut-Beumler. Copyright (c) 2007 by the University of North Carolina Press. Used by permission of the publisher. www.uncpress.unc.edu .

[50] Ibid.

[51] Ibid; (pp. 3-75).

[52] James 2:1-4, 9 says, "My brethren, do not hold the faith of our Lord Jesus Christ, the Lord of glory, with partiality. For if there should come into your assembly a man with gold rings, in fine apparel, and there should also come in a poor man in filthy clothes, and you pay attention to the one wearing the fine clothes and say to him, "You sit here in a good place," and say to the poor man, "You stand there," or, "Sit here at my footstool," have you not shown partiality among yourselves, and become judges with evil thoughts... but if you show partiality, you commit sin, and are convicted by the law as

transgressors." Yet not surprisingly, under pressure to raise money, the Church disregarded this basic command of love and shamefully rented pew seats the same way stadiums rent seats today. The more money you pay, the better the location of your seat. Unfortunately, this was a mainstream practice of the Church.

[53] Michael L. Webb and Mitchell T. Webb thoroughly debunk this error in *Beyond Tithes & Offerings*, (pp. 117-130), copyright 1998.

[54] Leviticus 2:14, 23:17; Numbers 18:12; Deuteronomy 18:4.

[55] Here is one example of many where tithes and firstfruits are clearly not the same thing: "And at the same time some were appointed over the rooms of the storehouse for the offerings, the firstfruits, and the tithes...." (Nehemiah 12:44.

[56] Here's a sample of the word *firstfruits* being used figuratively: Romans 8:22-23, 16:5; 1 Corinthians 15:20-23; James 1:18; and Revelation 14:4. This is the same way you should interpret Scriptures similar to this one: "Honor the Lord with your possessions, and with the firstfruits of all your increase" (Proverbs 3:9). If God uses the word figuratively, why would you allow some preacher to put you into legalistic bondage by convincing you that firstfruits mean ten percent of your income, or some other figure he pulls out of the air?

[57] Malachi 1:6-14. It is ironic how Malachi is routinely used to intimidate God's people into giving to preachers. Yet the book was written to sternly rebuke preachers for giving bad offerings. Preachers who use fear to raise money cause bad offerings. Therefore, the professional clergy is as guilty today of accepting bad offerings as they were in the book of Malachi! Bad offerings satisfy preachers as much as good offerings, but bad offerings do not please God: Matthew 5:23-24, 6:1; 1 Corinthians 13:3; 2 Corinthians 9:7

[58]This is a reference to Malachi 3:10, the scripture that is routinely used to convince us that if we give ten percent of our money to the preacher, God will bless us.

[59] Genesis 13:1-2.

[60] Although it is clear in Genesis 18 that Abraham did not give tithes to the Lord when He appeared to him.

[61] *Encyclopedia of Religion, Mircea Elliad, editor;* 1987, s.v. "tithe."

[62] John D. Davis, ed., *Westminster Dictionary of the Bible* (Philadelphia: Westminster Press, 1964), s.v. "tithe."

[63] *Should the Church Teach Tithing: A Theologian's Conclusions about a Taboo Doctrine,* Russell Earl Kelly, PhD; (Lincoln, Nebraska: Writers Club Press, 2000). Reprinted by permission of the author.

[64] We are not, however, to honor sinful customs (Leviticus 18:30; Jeremiah 10:3). Nor are we to honor customs that make the word of God of no effect (Matthew 15:1-9). I believe the modern obligatory tithe, depending on how it's presented, falls in one or both of these categories.

[65] The shekel was a measure of money. Look up the word "shekel" and "shekels" in *Strong's Exhaustive Concordance* and you will see over 100 references to the uses of money in every manner of Jewish life from Genesis to Amos.

[66] Numbers 18:25-26

[67] They do, however, benefit indirectly by paying for the church building and the church's programs. Nonetheless, offering an edible tithe to God that is eaten by the tither in the presence of God can only be compared to today's modern illegitimate money-tithe system by twisting, overlooking, or adding to the Scriptures.

[68] "Having wiped out the handwriting of requirements that was against us, which was contrary to us. And He has taken it out of the way, having nailed it to the cross" (Colossians 2:14).

[69] 1 Peter 4:17

[70] Tithing was linked with increases in livestock or produce. The command to not gather produce in the sixth year automatically meant those people who made their living in produce had no occasion to pay tithes. A modern example would be if you had no income for a year, you would not be required to pay taxes.

[71] It is also interesting to note that Israel wasn't required to tithe until they entered the promised land of Canaan. This means that all of the blessings they received on their 40-year journey in the wilderness with Moses were given and received without paying tithes. This included supernatural health, protection, provision, and guidance!

[72] 1 Samuel 17.

[73] Data extracted on November 21, 2007 from
http://www.census.gov/hhes/www/income/earnings/call1usboth.html; 2000
U.S. census.

[74] For an excellent read on this topic, check out Annette Lareau's book:
"Unequal Childhoods: Class, Race, and Family Life" (Berkeley: University of
California Press, 2003). And don't overlook this absolutely fabulous book
by the original thinking Malcolm Gladwell: *"Outliers: The Story of Success"*
(New York: Little, Brown and Company, 2008).

[75] For every person who receives a blessing that can be arguably linked to
the payment of tithes and offerings, there are many more who can testify to
suffering financial hardship as a direct result of giving money that should
have gone to paying bills, taking care of family needs, or getting out of
poverty. These "testimonies" are rarely highlighted by preachers. If they are,
they are done in a way that blames the tither for not doing enough of "this"
or doing too much of "that." Keep this in mind the next time a preacher
tries to get your money by telling how God blessed someone for giving.

[76] Russell Earl Kelly, Ph.D., author of the outstanding book, *"Should the
Church Teach Tithing?: A Theologian's Conclusions About A Taboo Doctrine,"*
suggests emphatically that you read Nehemiah before you read Malachi;
I agree. Nehemiah and Malachi are like Matthew and Luke. They are com-
plementary texts that speak of the same events. What you don't get from
one, you may get from the other. Thanks, Russ!

[77] Deuteronomy 18:1-7. All priests and Levites are descendants of Levi, one
of the 12 sons of Jacob; therefore, they are all Levites. The distinction in the
two, however, is that priests were descendents of Aaron. In one sense,
priests were the highest order of ministers under the Law. They had the
closest religious ceremonial access to God, with direct access to and ministry of the holy altar. Levites had special religious, political, and practical
duties, but could not approach the altar. Yet they also had privileges that
were not given to the priests. In essence, the priesthood can be seen as the
special priesthood of Aaron and the general priesthood of the Levites. One
priesthood; two functions.

[78] Leviticus 22:17-25.

[79] Further proof that priests had already been given the tithes and offerings
is seen in Malachi 1:14: "But cursed be the deceiver who has in his flock a

male, and takes a vow, but sacrifices to the Lord what is blemished." This could not be talking about the average Jew because their sacrifices were examined by Levites and then by priests before acceptance. Only the priests had opportunity for this kind of deception. If there were a shortage of healthy animals in the storehouse, it was because they had switched their bad animals for God's good animals. They had actually stolen God's sacrifices!

[80] Further proof can be found in Nehemiah 13. The Levites were so fed up with the priests stealing their tithes that they left the service of the temple and went home. Russell Earl Kelly, Ph.D., comprehensively deals with this topic in his outstanding book, "*Should the Church Teach Tithing?: A Theologian's Conclusions About A Taboo Doctrine.*"

[81] Even if this scripture referred to common Jews (which it does not), it still would have nothing to do with obligating New Testament Christians to obey the wholly man-made, money tithe system of the institutional church.

[82] Numbers 18:20-23.

[83] Fortunately, this arbitrary pastoral rule is often limited by various forms of church government. But these limits are too often nonexistent in charismatic, nondenominational, and so-called independent churches. Conversely, in churches where these limits exist, they are often wrongly used to weaken good pastoral leadership. Lord, help us!

[84] Nehemiah 10:35-38.

[85] 1 Timothy 4:1-2; 1 John 4:6.

[86] But if it's not worthy of your financial support, you shouldn't be there. Why would you expose yourself to a ministry that's unworthy of support?

[87] 1 Kings 5-6; 2 Chronicles 36:15-21.

[88] Ezra 1:6; 2:68-69; 6:7-10; 7:12-26.

[89] The first thing a tithe church does when it is asked for financial assistance from a member is to check the financial database. If the person is not a tither, no help is given. If it is given, it is minimal and it has several strings attached.

[90] It is significant that God declared the seventh day special immediately upon finishing creation, but He didn't require any special observation of it until after Israel was delivered from Egyptian bondage. That's a period of

approximately 1,400 years without a Sabbath requirement. This proves that God reserves the right to create and abolish religious rituals at His own discretion. It is rebellion to disobey a present ritual requirement; it is also rebellion to require obedience to an obsolete ritual requirement.

[91] For instance, the Old Testament is filled with prohibitions and restrictions on diet, and special requirements to observe religious laws. Yet the New Testament teaches us that these dietary and non-moral religious laws strategically represented the coming Christ. When the Christ came, the signs had served their purpose and were no longer needed. God, therefore, rescinded these temporary requirements. See Acts 10:1-16; Romans 14:1-23; 1 Corinthians 10:23-33; Galatians 5:6; Colossians 2:8-23; Hebrews 8-10:1-18.

[92] Genesis 3:22.

[93] Exodus 11-12.

[94] This is similar to preachers who tell us we must believe in Christ AND obey their modern version of tithes to be saved. It was a lie in Paul's day and it is a lie today.

[95] See Matthew 19:3-8; Mark 10:2-9. These passages clearly show that Jesus used the Creation narrative to correct Israel's bad beliefs and practices. It is wise for us to go back to God's original blueprint to build our doctrines.

[96] Romans 5:12-21; 1 Corinthians 15:1-49; 1 Timothy 2.

[97] Ancient Israel had a tendency to live in gross sin and simultaneously offer God tithes, offerings, and elaborate but empty worship. They equated form with substance. God showed the foolishness of trusting in tithes and offerings to please Him by reminding them that there was no such system in their 40-year wanderings: "Did you offer Me sacrifices and offerings in the wilderness forty years, O house of Israel?" (Amos 5:25).

[98] It is also significant that keeping the Sabbath was included in the Ten Commandments. In contrast, tithing was not included in the Ten Commandments.

[99] This is not to say that Christianity is false; only that there is a false version of serving Christ. This false version places more importance on fulfilling external rules than on leading people to freedom in Christ. In fact, religion absolutely hates Christian liberty, the liberty that is founded upon obedience to and love of Christ and love of people.

[100] I know of one church that has received new members from a pastor who has begun a campaign of cleansing his church of non-tithers. This pastor told a pastor friend of mine that since he has begun this campaign, his ministry has elevated to a new level. This evil minister of darkness believes he has a right to excommunicate Christians from the church body if they do not give him a certain amount of money. Of course, he wraps his extortion in scriptures. He is right, however, in one thing. Those who have remained in this church assembly under his reign are compliant, docile, and easily controlled. Certainly it would be easier for him to control people who behave as slaves instead of people led by the Holy Spirit. So his ministry has for the time being reached a new level of earthly success. But it is short-lived. At the appropriate time God will judge this imposter.

[101] Leviticus 24:5-9.

[102] The rent on this building was extremely low and affordable to the congregation. To this day I don't know for certain where all of the extra money went. Although I do recall that the pastor was infatuated by a certain national prosperity preacher and believed that our little church should tithe to the national prosperity preacher's ministry.

[103] The Old Testament is filled with examples of the priests working on the Sabbath. Actually, Sabbaths were their busiest work days! For instance, look at the annual day of Atonement (Leviticus 16).

[104] The presentation of the tithe message comes in many packages. The presenter may come across as harmless as a dove and as humble as a lamb. But the bottom line is you better pay ten percent or more of your income or be cursed.

[105] Jesus came from the tribe of Judah (Revelation 5:5).

[106] Ten percent from the poor is much more in "real" terms than ten percent from the middle-class and rich. A person who grosses $2,000 a month ($24,000 annually) will have approximately $1,500 left after taxes. The person must then pay for health insurance, dental insurance, rent, utilities, food, perhaps a car note, car repairs, definitely car insurance, perhaps child care, and other expenses. Note that none of these are expenses that can be trimmed. What is left over to build wealth? If the person gives the church $200, he or she now has $1,300 to pay all of these bills. To this person, his or her $200 a month church tax bill is much more than the $500 a month church tax bill that a person must pay if he or she earns $5,000 a month

($60,000 annually). It's what's left over after the ten percent that counts. That's why Jesus said that the poverty stricken lady who gave less than half a penny had given more than the rich (Mark 12:41-44; Luke 21:1-4). Therefore, in the eyes of God, ten percent from the poor is more than ten percent from the middle class and rich. What kind of heartless organization would place such a disproportionate burden on its poor? This is a shame and a disgrace! I wish to God that every preacher would find enough backbone or conscience to stop such a cruel practice of unrestrained religious evil.

[107] Read Galatians. It was written to prevent Christians from trying to keep any part of the Old Testament law. The main item discussed was circumcision, but it could have been any part of the law. Circumcision was discussed because false teachers taught the Gentile Galatians that they had to be circumcised to be saved. Today false teachers tell Christians that they must pay monetary tithes to the church to please God. This lie must be resisted with the same energy with which Paul resisted the lie of circumcision.

[108] The healing of the crippled woman, (Luke 13:1-17). The healing of the paralyzed man, (John 5:1-16). The healing of the blind man, (John 9:1-16).

[109] The incident, of course, happened in a synagogue. I use the word "church" because the synagogue and the church are comparable institutions.

[110] Matthew 9:32-34; Luke 11:14-15.

[111] Combustible means to catch fire easily.

[112] Preemptive means to strike first. It is usually done by someone who believes such an action will provide an advantage.

[113] Similarly, there is no place for common sense in the modern tithe.

[114] Apply this same question in the context of the modern tithe: "Of how much more value then is a person than a tithe?"

[115] This is not to say that everyone who pays the modern tithe or demands such payment is not a Christian. I am merely referring to the depth of our knowledge and understanding of the tithe and of Christ. It is possible to be a Christian and yet be extremely deficient in knowledge and understanding in certain areas.

[116] "Jesus Christ is the same yesterday, today, and forever" (Hebrews 13:8).

[117] "But if anyone does not provide for his own, and especially for those of his household, he has denied the faith and is worse than an unbeliever" (1 Timothy 5:8).

[118] I emphasize "immediate" because preachers routinely tell us that if we give now, God will reward us later. We must be wise enough to see that they are saying their needs being met now are more important than our needs being met now. Is that the Spirit of Christ? If this practice of giving out of our need is appropriate, why don't they do it?

[119] See Matthew 12:1-14; John 5:1-16; 9:1-34.

[120] See 1 Samuel 16:7; Luke 18:9-14. The Pharisees paid tithes and gave offerings; yet Jesus regularly denounced them in the strongest terms.

[121] This assumes the need presented to you isn't an emergency request to help an individual with the necessities of life (e.g., utility bills, shelter, clothes, transportation, etc.), and it assumes your own bills are paid

[122] Naaman the leper almost forfeited his healing because he expected God to do something spectacular to affect the healing. But God chose a very mundane and ordinary thing. He told the man to dip in the river seven times and he would be healed. Not very dramatic, but it got the job done. Don't miss the Spirit by focusing on the spectacular (2 Kings 5:1-14).

[123] Telling Old Testament Jews to keep the law was routine for Jesus. He also told a leper who was healed to "go your way, show yourself to the priest, and offer the gift that Moses commanded, as a testimony to them" (Matthew 8:4). This was a requirement of the law.

[124] It is not what percent you give, but how much money you have left over after you give that determines the "true" amount of your giving to God. "And He looked up and saw the rich putting their gifts into the treasury, and He saw also a certain poor widow putting in two mites. So He said, 'Truly I say to you that this poor widow has put in more than all; for all these out of their abundance have put in offerings for God, but she out of her poverty put in all the livelihood that she had" (Luke 21:1-4).

[125] If you cared, you'd immediately stop this extortion. How will you defend this behavior on Judgment Day?

[126] "Take heed that you do not do your charitable deeds before men, to be seen by them. Otherwise you have no reward from your Father in heaven. Therefore, when you do a charitable deed, do not sound a trumpet before

you as the hypocrites do in the synagogues and in the streets, that they may have glory from men. Assuredly, I say to you, they have their reward. But when you do a charitable deed, do not let your left hand know what your right hand is doing, that your charitable deed may be in secret; and your Father who sees in secret will reward you openly" (Matthew 6:1-4).

[127] At the other extreme, permissive preachers were another grave threat to the church. These preachers were as fanatically dedicated to abolishing legitimate laws of morality as legalistic preachers were fanatically dedicated to creating illegitimate rules of religion. Read 2 Peter 2-4; 1 John 2-3; 2 John 6-11; Jude.

[128] 1 Corinthians 1:30-31.

[129] They do this because they consider non-tithing Christians weak, ignorant, defiant, greedy, fearful, uncommitted, false, or all of the above. Obviously a person in such a condition can't receive God's blessing, so they think and teach. But if this is true, how and why are so many "evil" people blessed of God? He "is kind to the unthankful and evil" (Luke 6:35) and "He makes His sun rise on the evil and on the good, and sends rain on the just and on the unjust" (Matthew 5:45). Ask yourself this common sense question: Did God send His Son to die for your sins before or after you became a child of God? Now if He would sacrifice Himself for you when you were a servant of sin and Satan, why would He now withhold any good thing from you just because some preacher is twisting the Bible to try to blackmail you for money? Sometimes we just need to use common sense! Read Romans 5:6-10.

[130] Roman 8:15-17; Colossians 1:12-14.

[131] Acts 10:1-48. This was approximately ten years or so after the resurrection of Jesus! But had not Jesus commanded the church to "go into all the world and preach the gospel to every creature" (Mark 16:15). And had not the Lord said, "You shall be witnesses to Me in Jerusalem, and in all Judea and Samaria, and to the end of the earth" (Acts 1:8). Somehow the apostles interpreted this as meaning they were to only go to the Jews in those places!

[132] Acts 11:1-18.

[133] I am equally baffled as to how the church has made such an oppressive and antichrist doctrine as the modern day tithe a foundational part of Christianity. But this should be no surprise. This is what happens when we follow man instead of Christ.

[134] 1 Corinthians 15:6.

[135] A Christ who no longer heals the sick, casts out demons, and otherwise manifests Himself through gifts of the Spirit is a false Christ, a Christ of our own anemic making.

[136] This is a direct reference to that portion of the church that teaches the modern tithe.

[137] The evidence for this is strong. Stephen was stoned because he challenged the roots and practices of legalism (Acts 6:7-15; 7:1-60). When persecution erupted against the Jerusalem church, Christians were scattered throughout the regions of other cities. The apostles, however, didn't leave Jerusalem. Was this because they weren't targeted? If so, why weren't they targeted? Or were they targeted and bravely refused to run away? Whatever the answer is, we know that the apostles at that time were not seen as enemies of legalism, as Christ had been. For many years later we see that legalists in Jerusalem (including James!) had considerable influence (Acts 15; Galatians 2:11-14).

[138] Acts 15:2.

[139] "Then one from the crowd said to Him [Jesus], "Teacher, tell my brother to divide the inheritance with me." But He said to him, "Man, who made Me a judge or an arbitrator over you? And He said to them, "Take heed and beware of covetousness, for one's life does not consist in the abundance of the things he possesses" (Luke 12:13-15).

[140] "For the wrath of man does not produce the righteousness of God" (James 1:20).

[141] The apostle Peter strongly and publicly denounced a man for thinking he could purchase God's blessings with money (Acts 8:14-23). Isn't it strange that something so strongly denounced by Peter has become a foundational teaching of the modern Church?

[142] Acts 10:1-48.

[143] Hebrews 10:1-4.

[144] Hebrews 8:7-13.

[145] (1) James was the natural brother of the Lord (Mark 6:3); (2) When Peter was miraculously released from prison by an angel, James was the only apostle specifically named by Peter to be informed of the details (Acts

12:17); (3) James appears to be the main apostolic figure in Jerusalem (Acts 21:18); (4) Paul refers to James as an apostle and one of the pillars of the Jerusalem church (Galatians 1:19; 2:9); and (5) James was so influential that Peter, as well as members of Paul's own apostolic team, were afraid to offend him (Galatians 2:11-13).

[146] I use the term "false teacher" without regard to whether a teacher is saved or not. The issue is not whether the teacher is saved, but whether he or she teaches a doctrine that contradicts and significantly undermines the Christian faith. One may do this with a good or evil heart, in full knowledge of what one is doing, or be in gross darkness. The issue is not the condition of the teacher, but the content and effect of the doctrine.

[147] 1 Timothy 3:5.

[148] Notice the striking similarity of James' personal comments in Acts 15:19-21 and the Church's official letter in Acts 15:24, 28-29.

[149] This excludes the 22 words in the greeting and salutation. Also, the number of words may differ modestly based upon Bible translators' use of different words in their translations.

[150] Hebrews is filled with encouragement and moderate to extremely stern warnings for these Jewish Christians to remain faithful to Christ: 2:1-3; 3:7-19; 4:1-3, 11-16; 6:1-12; 10:23-39; 12:25.

[151] Go to www.ChristianBooks.com and search under "Christ Old Testament." You'll see possibly a hundred books written and published by a wide variety of Christian authors and publishers that prove my point that it is a mainstream church belief that the Old Testament in general, and the Law in particular, represent Christ.

[152] Exodus 4:24-26; 12:44, 48; Leviticus 12:1-3; John 7:22-23.

[153] The Christian Church historically has been and presently is deeply divided on many issues: water baptism, gifts of the Spirit, women in ministry, politics, unconditional eternal security, irresistible grace, etc. Yet all Christian bodies agree that the death of Jesus Christ made animal sacrifices obsolete.

[154] I believe this is based on people's natural intuition that they are not good enough or knowledgeable enough to directly approach God. Their hope is that their religious representative can represent them before God in much the same way attorneys represent clients before a court.

[155] The Ten Commandments that were delivered by Moses to the people appear to have been the plan all along. But the hundreds of reinforcing lesser laws, along with the priesthood, were given because of Israel's behavior: "What purpose then does the law serve? It was added because of transgressions...." (Galatians 3:19).

[156] This authority is apparently given by God in widely disconnected ways. In most denominational churches, this kingly authority comes from God only after a person graduates from seminary and is either assigned or starts a church. In most independent churches, however, all that is needed to get this divine authority is two or more people to call you their pastor. This can be done even before the arrival of business cards with the pastor's title—or in some cases, the bishop's title.

[157] Even the federal government is not so wicked and heartless that it demands taxes on our gross income without allowing us innumerable exemptions. An American can legally shield some or all income used for interest paid on mortgages, contributions to retirement accounts, donations to charities, medical expenses, college expenses, childcare, etc. Do tithe preachers allow exemptions on the money they demand from Christians? No! This is because their primary concern is the protection of their kingdom: salaries, benefits, buildings, administration, etc. If their tithe taxes prevent us from ever purchasing a home, securing adequate health care, going to college, or paying for child care, so be it. Is it not shameful that the government has more concern and mercy for its subjects than the Church has for its own?

[158] Hebrews 10:5-10.

[159] "For there is one God and one Mediator between God and men, the Man Christ Jesus" (1 Timothy 2:5); Hebrews 8:6; 9:15; 12:24.

[160] There is no legitimate New Testament tithe; so power hungry men can't use this statement to justify their self-importance. Even the Levitical priesthood was not built on a supposed superiority of Levi over the rest of Israel. God went out of His way to emphasize this point: (1) He killed Moses, the greatest Old Testament Levitical priest, for sinning against Him (Numbers 20:1-12; Deuteronomy 32:48-52); and (2) He built ceremonial rules within the Levitical priesthood that identified them as fellow sinners and servants of Israel (Numbers 8:5-19). Even the high priest had to give a burnt offering for himself before representing others (Leviticus 16:1-11).

[161] The Levi spoken of here is not modern day tithe preachers, as they would have us believe. It was the actual Levitical priesthood that was still following the law of Moses. Hebrews makes this abundantly clear.

[162] Psalm 110:4 prophetically speaks of Christ when it says, "The Lord has sworn and will not relent, 'You are a priest forever according to the order of Melchizedek.'" This Scripture is also used twice in Hebrews 7:17, 21 to speak of Christ.

[163] According to the United Nations' *Report on the World Social Situation, 2005.*

[164] This does not mean I consider the Word of God less important than good works. The point I am trying to make is that the spoken Word of God has no perceived credibility spoken through a person who does not demonstrate the truth of the words spoken. It is foolish to expect the world to believe our message that an invisible God loves them if we do not demonstrate this truth through visible actions.

[165] Blessed are you when they revile and persecute you, and say all kinds of evil against you falsely for My sake. Rejoice and be exceedingly glad, for great is your reward in heaven, for so they persecuted the prophets who were before you" (Matthew 5:11-12).

[166] Read Matthew 6:1-18. This passage deals with giving, praying, and fasting with impure motives. The issue is not that it's wrong to let it be known that we're giving, praying, or fasting, but why we're letting these things be known. Motive is always the qualifier.

[167] Psalm 107:10; Proverbs 2:13; 4:19; Isaiah 60:2; John 3:19; Acts 26:18; Romans 1:21; 2 Corinthians 4:3-4; 6:14; Ephesians 4:18; 5:8, 11; Colossians 1:13.

[168] It is assumed by Christ that we are also faithfully preaching His Word (Matthew 28:18-20; Mark 16:15).

[169] "How then shall they call on Him in whom they have not believed? And how shall they believe in Him of whom they have not heard? And how shall they hear without a preacher?" (Romans 10:14).

[170] 1 Corinthians 1:17 cautions not to mix man's wisdom with God's wisdom "lest the cross of Christ should be made of no effect."

[171] I acknowledge that not every person who systematically gives ten percent of income to the institutional Church does so out of legalism. Some do it with no compulsion other than their love of God and personal discipline. It is my belief and experience, however, that the vast majority of financial tithers do so either out of fear or as an attempt to purchase blessings from God.

[172] I acknowledge that not every non-tither is negligent in giving and materially serving others. It is my belief and experience, however, that many non-tithers are more consumed with their freedom from legalistic giving than their obligation of love to give.

[173] New Testament tithing is a man-made legalistic debt determined by man; New Testament giving is a love-initiated voluntary offering provided according to one's ability.

[174] Of course, from the perspective of spiritual truth it is altogether reasonable.

[175] This is why Paul said in 1 Corinthians 13:3, "And though I bestow all my goods to feed the poor, and though I give my body to be burned, but have not love, it profits me nothing."

[176] Matthew 6:19-21; 10:40-42; 16:26-27; Luke 14:12-14; Acts 10:1-4; 1 Corinthians 3:11-15.

[177] Luke 12:15-21.

[178] The thief on the cross made it into heaven without being able to offer God anything to show for his life except a last minute appeal for mercy, which He received (Luke 23:39-43).

[179] Many tithe preachers do teach a counterfeit version of radical giving. Their version almost always is based on getting people to give to them. Radical lifestyle giving is selfless giving that is totally directed by the Holy Spirit, is free of manipulation, and is done foremost because of gratitude to God and because of an eternal perspective. This kind of giving comes from within and is not the result of man's pressure.

[180] Practicing denotes behavioral commitment. It is something done repeatedly because of a person's nature. This is different from committing a single or intermittent act in violation of one's nature, conscience, or truest desire to serve God (see Romans 7:14-25 and Galatians 5:16-17). Do not worry: God knows the difference between a hypocrite and a struggling Christian.

[181] If you read 1 John (it's only five chapters), you'll see that John treated absence of the love of God, and absence of love for people, as absence of salvation. I know this is hard, but it was Jesus who said, "Narrow is the gate and difficult is the way which leads to life, and there are few who find it" (Matthew 7:14).

[182] James says basically the same thing in 2:14-18.

[183] 1 Corinthians 10:13. Also, "I still have many things to say to you, but you cannot bear them now" (John 16:12). I believe this reveals a timeless principle of how God deals with us. He wisely reveals His plans and expectations to us as we are able to receive them. This way we aren't overwhelmed.

[184] See Matthew 25:14-30. Notice that the Lord's goods are distributed "to each according to his own ability" (v. 15). This concept is also in 1 Corinthians 12:11, 18, 28.

[185] 2 Corinthians 8:12-15.

[186] Variables are things that can change.

[187] If a Christian is paralyzed and confined to a wheelchair, his general, eternal call is that of a priest—this never changes. But his unique, flexible call is that of someone confined to a wheelchair—this may change by a miracle of God or by advances in medical science.

[188] The heartless Pharisees concocted a religious scam to get around the responsibility to financially take care of their parents. They did this by "dedicating" to God and the temple money that should have been given for their parents' support. So they could now say, "Mother, I would help you, but I can't; my money has already been given to God. This is a popular error of many tithers. Jesus declared it hypocrisy (Mark 7:5-13). You tithers better start taking care of your family obligations before sending money to your preachers!

[189] Acts 21:8; Ephesians 4:11; 2 Timothy 4:5.

[190] Romans 12:6-8.

[191] Mark 16:17-18; John 14:12; 1 Corinthians 12:18, 28, 30.

[192] 1 Corinthians 12:29; 14:31; 39.

[193] Mark 16:17; 1 Corinthians 12:29.

[194] Covetousness automatically disqualifies one from financial support. The preacher's lifestyle, humility, and track record should be stringently examined for signs of greed, fleshly ambition, and results. If your preacher passes the test, support him or her to the best of your ability. Of course, this should be done after you have taken care of your family and distributed to the necessity of the saints.

[195] I don't see anything wrong with giving an offering with a credit card "if"—and only if—you pay the credit card offering in full before you charge it. This means you must write and mail the check before the transaction. This will prevent you from foolishly charging offerings you can't afford.

[196] Luke 4:9-12.

[197] Paul prayed for the Ephesian church to grow in love. If we can grow in love, there must be varying levels of love.

[198] Notice that of the four kinds of soil, or people, identified by Christ, only the first group, the wayside group, is "immediately" identified as people who do not receive Christ (v. 15). The stony ground, thorn, and good groups all received the word. However, over the passage of time only the good ground group survived the pressures of time. Yet this does not necessarily mean that the stony ground and thorn groups were hypocrites It appears to me that they believed the gospel and simply lost the battle with the world. We know this is possible because Adam sinned, even though he was not deceived (1 Timothy 2:14), and Demas, a trusted and respected co-laborer of Paul, fell away from Christ "having loved this present world" (2 Timothy 4:10). The point is these kinds of Christians have an exceptionally hard time growing in the love of God.

[199] Paul prayed for the Ephesian church to receive the spirit of wisdom and revelation in the knowledge of God (Ephesians 1:15-23). This answered prayer would result in knowing (1) the hope of His calling, (2) the riches of the glory of His inheritance in the saints, and (3) the exceeding greatness of His power toward us who believe. Obviously, Christians who excel in these areas are theoretically able to give more because they see reality more clearly than worldly-minded Christians.

[200] Luke 7:36-50 tells a story that links our sense of gratitude for salvation to our revelation of personal sin. The greater our understanding of how much God has forgiven us, the greater our level of love of God.

[201] I am speaking of Christians who have a genuine desire to love.

[202] Luke 22:39-43. Remember that Jesus performed His ministry as a man anointed by the Holy Spirit and not by using His divine power as God (Philippians 2:5-11).

[203] 2 Peter 1:5-8.

[204] Romans 12:3-8.

[205] Of course, there are some tithe preachers who are wrestling with their consciences on this issue. They see the damage and are greatly troubled by it. My prayer is that they will fully acknowledge the truth and totally abandon this cruel system of fundraising.

Index